PENGUIN BOOKS

The Money Machine

After being educated at Sidney Sussex College, Cambridge, Philip Coggan became Assistant Editor of *Euromoney Currency Report* and *Euromoney Corporate Finance*. He was a journalist for the *Financial Times* from 1986 to 2006, including spells as personal finance editor, economics correspondent, Lex columnist and investment editor. He now works for the *Economist* where he writes the Buttonwood column in addition to being Capital Markets Editor. In 2009, he was awarded the title of Senior Financial Journalist of the Year by The Wincott Foundation.

The Money Machine
How the City Works

SEVENTH EDITION

Philip Coggan

PENGUIN BOOKS

PENGUIN BOOKS

UK | USA | Canada | Ireland | Australia
India | New Zealand | South Africa

Penguin Books is part of the Penguin Random House group of companies
whose addresses can be found at global.penguinrandomhouse.com.

First published in Penguin Books 1986
Second edition 1989
Third edition 1995
Fourth edition 1999
Fifth edition 2002
Sixth edition 2009
Seventh edition 2015
004

Set in 9.47/12 pt Minion
Typeset by Jouve (UK), Milton Keynes
Printed in Great Britain by Clays Ltd, St Ives plc

A CIP catalogue record for this book is available from the British Library

ISBN: 978–0–141–98073–7

www.greenpenguin.co.uk

Contents

Acknowledgements

A book covering such a wide field could not be produced without the help and advice of many people. First and foremost, I would like to thank Nick Shepherd and Diane Pengelly for reading through all the chapters and pointing out the numerous grammatical errors and nonsensical statements. Many others read through individual chapters: my father, Ken Ferris, John Presland, David Bowen, Clifford German, Paul and Vanessa Gilbert, Lynton Jones, David Morrison and Nigel Falls, and I thank them for their helpful comments. Jeremy Stone made many useful points about the structure and the contents of the book. All mistakes are, of course, mine and not theirs. A distinguished mention should be given to Mr Alan Michael Sugar for bringing out his Amstrad word processor at just the right time and price to allow me to benefit. Last but not least, I thank Churchy for all the help in typing and for putting up with the sight of my back as I slaved away on the manuscript.

P. C.
March 1986

ACKNOWLEDGEMENTS TO FOURTH, FIFTH AND SIXTH EDITIONS

The City changes so fast these days that it is hard work keeping up. I would like to thank my former colleagues at the *Financial Times* and my current colleagues at the *Economist* for their immense knowledge and expertise. And most of all, my wife Sandie, whose love and support have changed my life.

P. C.
December 2008

Introduction

Finance has moved onto the front page. The collapse of some of Britain's leading banks in 2007 and 2008 has cost the taxpayer billions. It has brought the City, once seen as Britain's most successful industry, into disrepute. Many people think the financial sector has been too powerful, imposing free-market dogma on unwilling populations. They resent the way that financiers make millions in bonuses when times go well but expect the taxpayer to bail them out when things go badly, as they did in 2008.

This ambivalent attitude towards financiers dates back over centuries. Roman emperors and medieval monarchs had to flatter financiers when they needed to borrow money; the attitude quickly turned to revulsion when the time came to pay it back. Whole populations have been caught up in frenzies of speculation dating back from Dutch tulip mania through the South Sea Bubble to the Florida land boom of the 1920s. Individual financiers have found it laughably easy to buy popularity when their schemes were prospering (think of Robert Maxwell). But there have been no shortages of commentators saying 'I told you so' when their empires subsequently collapsed.

Perhaps the public has tended to treat the subject of finance as a soap opera (complete with heroes and villains) because too few people attempt to understand the workings of the financial system. Although the details of individual financial deals can be very complex, there are basic principles in finance which everyone can understand and which apply as much to the finances of Mr Smith, the grocer, as to Barclays Bank. The more fully people understand these principles, the more they will be able and willing to criticize, and perhaps even participate in, the workings of the financial system. Like all areas of public life, it needs criticism to ensure its efficiency.

Even those who do not own shares should care about how the City performs. It is one of the UK's biggest industries and a vital overseas earner in areas such as insurance and fund management.

THE CITY

First of all, what is the role of the UK financial system, and in particular of the City of London, which is at its heart?

Its primary function is to put people who want to lend (invest) in touch with people who want to borrow. A simple example of this role is that of the building societies. They collect the small savings of individuals and lend them to house buyers who want mortgages.

Why do the savers not just lend directly to borrowers, without the intervention of financial institutions? The main reason is that their needs are not compatible with those of the end borrowers. People with mortgages, for example, want to borrow for twenty-five years. Savers may want to withdraw their money next week. In addition, the amounts needed are dissimilar. Companies and governments need to borrow amounts far beyond the resources of most individuals. Only by bundling together all the savings of many individuals can the financial institutions provide funds on an appropriate scale.

Who are the borrowers? Businesses are one group. Companies will always need money to pay for raw materials, buildings, machinery and wages before they can generate their own revenues by selling their goods or services. To cover the period before the cash flows in, companies either borrow from the banks or raise capital in the form of shares or bonds. Without this capital it would be impossible for companies to invest and for the economy to expand.

The second major set of borrowers is governments. No matter what their claims to fiscal rectitude, few governments have ever managed to avoid spending more than they receive. The UK government and other nations' governments come to the City to cover the difference.

Who wants to lend? In general, the only part of the economy which is a net saver (i.e. its savings are greater than its borrowings) is the personal sector – individuals like you and me. Rarely do we lend directly to the government or industry or other individuals: instead we save, either through the medium of banks and building societies or, in a more planned way, through pension and life assurance schemes. Lending, saving and investing are thus different ways of looking at the same activity.

So financial institutions are there to channel the funds of those who want to lend into the hands of those who want to borrow. They take their cut as middlemen. That cut can come in three forms: banks can charge a higher interest rate to the people to whom they lend than they pay to the people from whom they borrow, or they can simply charge a fee for bringing lender and borrower, or issuer and investor, together. Over the last twenty years, they have increasingly added a third activity: trading assets. This contributed to the credit crunch that started in 2007.

There is no doubt that financial institutions perform an immensely valuable service: imagine life without cashpoint cards, credit cards, mortgages and car loans. Even those Britons who do not have a bank account would never be paid if the companies for which they work did not have one. Indeed, the companies might not have been founded without loans from banks.

It is important, when considering some of the practices discussed in this book, to remember that the business of financial institutions is the handling of money. Some of their more esoteric activities, like financial futures, can appear to the observer to be mere speculation. But speculation is an unavoidable part of the world of financial institutions. They must speculate, when they borrow at one rate, that they will be able to lend at a higher rate. They must speculate that the companies to whom they lend will not go bust. To criticize the mechanisms by which they do speculate is to ignore the basic facts of financial life.

Financial institutions are a vital part of the British economy. Whether the rewards they receive are in keeping with the importance of the part they play is another question, which we will examine in the final chapter.

THE INSTITUTIONS

The most prominent financial institutions are the banks, which can be divided roughly into two groups, commercial (retail) and investment, formerly known as merchant, banks. The former rely on the deposits drawn from ordinary individuals, on which they pay little or no interest and which they re-lend at a profit. Commercial banks must ensure that they have enough money to repay their customers, so they need to own some safe assets they can sell quickly. The latter group traditionally relied more on fees earned from arranging deals such as takeovers; nowadays, these banks also get heavily involved in market trading. However, the division between the two groups is not clear-cut since many commercial banks have investment banking arms.

The second group of financial institutions, known as the investment institutions, include the pension funds and life insurance companies. They bundle together the monthly savings of individuals and invest them in a range of assets, including the shares of British and foreign companies and commercial property. This is a vital function, since industry needs long-term funds to expand. Banks lend money to industry, but by tradition they have been less ready to invest for long periods. Pension funds can count on regular contributions and can normally calculate in advance when and how much they will have to pay out to claimants. Life insurance companies have the laws of actuarial probabilities to help them calculate their likely outgoings.

But pension funds and insurance companies are less significant, in stock market terms, than they used to be. Nowadays, the investors who dominate the market tend to be more aggressive and short-term in outlook. Two prominent groups, hedge funds and private equity firms, will be discussed at length.

The third main group is the exchanges, which provide a market for trading in the capital that companies and governments have raised. People and institutions are more willing to invest money in tradeable instruments, since they can easily reclaim their money if the need arises. The best-known exchange in the UK is the Stock Exchange.

Within and outside these groups is a host of institutions which perform specialized functions. The building societies have already been mentioned, but we will also need to look at the Bank of England, insurance brokers and underwriters, to name but a few.

THE INSTRUMENTS

Chapter 2 examines in detail questions about the definition of money and the determination of interest rates. But for the moment the best way to understand the workings of the financial system is to stop thinking of money as a homogeneous commodity and instead to think of notes and coins as constituting one of a range of financial assets. It is the *liquidity* of those assets that distinguishes them from each other. The liquidity of an asset is judged by the speed with which it can be exchanged for goods without financial loss.

Notes and coins are easily the most liquid because they can be traded immediately for goods. At the opposite extreme is a long-term loan, which may not be repaid for twenty-five years. Between the two extremes are various financial assets which have grown up in response to the needs of the individuals and institutions that take part in the financial markets.

Essentially, financial assets can be divided into four types: *loans, bonds, equities* and *derivatives.*

Loans are the simplest to understand. One party agrees to lend another money in return for a payment called *interest,* normally quoted as an annual rate. It is possible, as in the case of many mortgages or hire-purchase agreements, for the principal sum (that is, the original amount borrowed) to be paid back in instalments with the interest. Alternatively, the principal sum can be paid back in one lump at the end of the agreed term.

Bonds are pieces of paper like IOUs, which borrowers issue in return for a loan and which are bought by investors, who can sell them to other parties as and when they choose. Bonds are normally medium-to-long-term (between five and twenty-five years) in duration. The period for which a loan or bond lasts is normally known as its *maturity,* and the interest rate a bond pays is called the *coupon.* Shorter-term bonds (lasting three months or so) are generally known as *bills.*

Equities are issued only by companies and offer a share in the assets and profits of the firm, which has led to their being given the more common name of *shares.* They differ from other financial instruments in that they confer ownership of something more than just a piece of paper. In the financial sense, shareholders *are* the company, whereas bondholders are merely outside creditors.

The initial capital invested in shares will rarely be repaid unless the company folds. (But shares, like bonds, can be sold to other investors.) The company will generally announce a semi-annual or quarterly dividend (a sum payable to each shareholder as a proportion of the profit), depending on the size of its profits. All ordinary shareholders will receive that dividend. However, it is not compulsory for companies to pay dividends. Some companies choose not to do so because they wish to reinvest all their profits with the aim of expanding the business. Others may omit paying a dividend because they are in financial difficulties.

Equity investors only get paid after the demands of lenders and bond-holders are satisfied. If a company gets into trouble, equity investors may well lose the bulk of their money whereas bondholders have a chance of getting a chunk of their capital back. The good news for equity investors is they get all the upside. Whereas the claims of lenders and bondholders are fixed, equity owners benefit from a company's growth.

That brings us to one of the most important principles in finance. *Greater risk demands greater reward.* If a lender is dubious about whether a borrower will be able to repay the loan, he or she will charge a higher rate on that loan. Why lend money at 10 per cent to a bad risk when you can lend money at 10 per cent to a good risk and be sure that your money will be returned with interest? To compensate for the extra risk, you will demand a rate of, say, 12 per cent, for the borrower with a doubtful reputation.

Derivatives are financial assets that are based on other products; their value is *derived* from elsewhere. Among the best-known derivative instruments are *futures*, *options* and *swaps*.

They perform a number of functions, allowing some people to insure themselves against price moves in other assets and others to speculate on price changes. These functions allow derivative users to get involved in *hedging* and *leverage*. *Hedging* is the process whereby an institution buys or sells a financial instrument in order to offset the risk that the price of another financial instrument or commodity may rise or fall. For example, coffee importers buy coffee futures to lock in the cost of their raw materials and reduce the risk that a rise in commodity prices will cut their profits.

Leverage gives the investor an opportunity for a large profit with a small stake. Options, futures and warrants all provide the chance of lever-age because their prices vary more sharply than those of the underlying commodities to which they are linked. These concepts are more fully explained in Chapters 12 and 13.

ALCHEMY

Financial institutions must perform a feat of alchemy. They must trans-
form the cash savings of ordinary depositors, who may want to withdraw
their money at any moment, into funds which industry can borrow for
twenty-five years or more. This process involves risk – the risk that the
funds will be withdrawn before the institutions' investments mature.
They must therefore demand a higher return for tying up their money for
long periods, so that they can offset that risk. This brings us to a second
important principle of finance. *Lesser liquidity demands greater reward.*
The longer an investor must hold an asset before being sure of achieving
a return, the larger he will expect that return to be. However, this is not an
iron rule. In Chapter 2 we shall see how, for a variety of reasons, long-term
interest rates can be below short-term rates.

The range of financial assets extends from cash to long-term loans.
Cash, the most liquid of assets, gives no return at all. A building society
account that can be withdrawn without notice might give a return of, say,
5 per cent. In the circumstances, why should lenders make a twenty-five-
year loan at less than 5 per cent? They would be incurring an unnecessary
risk for no reward. So lenders generally demand a greater return to compensate them for locking up their money for a long period. In the same
way some banks and building societies offer higher-interest accounts to
those who agree to give ninety days' notice before withdrawal. The borrowers (in this case, the banks and building societies) are willing to pay
more for the certainty of retaining the funds.

Bonds and shares are usually liquid in the sense that they can be sold,
but the seller has no guarantee of the price that he or she will receive for
them. This differentiates them from savings accounts, which guarantee
the return of the capital invested. Thus bond- and shareholders will generally demand a higher return. For both, that extra return may come
through an increase in the price of the investment rather than through a
high interest rate or dividend. This applies especially to shares. As a consequence, the dividend paid on shares is often, in percentage terms, well
below the interest paid on bonds such as gilts (highly reliable investments
because they are issued by the UK government).

THE CITY'S INTERNATIONAL ROLE

The City, of course, plays a role that far exceeds the dimensions of the national economy. It is this role that the supporters of the City invoke when they defend its actions and its privileges. And it is to preserve this role that the City has undergone so many changes in recent years.

In the nineteenth century the City's importance in the world financial markets reflected the way in which Britannia ruled the waves. Britain financed the development of Argentinian and North American railways, for example. By 1914 Britain owned an enormous range of foreign assets, which brought it a steady overseas income. Much of the world's trade was conducted in sterling because it was a respected and valued currency.

The two world wars ended Britain's financial predominance. Foreign assets were repatriated to pay for the fighting. As the Empire disintegrated, so too did the world's use of sterling as a trading instrument. Just as the US emerged as the world's biggest economic power, so New York challenged London for the market in financial services and the dollar took over from sterling as the major trading currency. It seemed that Britain and the City would become backwaters on the edge of Europe.

One thing saved the City. The US, which had regarded banks with suspicion since the Great Crash of 1929, did not welcome the growth of New York as a financial centre. The US authorities began to place restrictions on the activities of its banks and investors. International business began to flow back to London, where there were fewer restrictions. The Euromarket grew into the most important capital market in the world and made London its base.

The revival of the City in the 1960s brought many foreign banks to London and they have stayed as Britain's capital has become one of the world's three great trading centres, together with New York and Tokyo. But the challenge is never-ending. The development of the European single currency caused some to fear that London could lose its place to Paris or Frankfurt; so far, the challenge has been seen off fairly easily.

However, London does face what has been called the 'Wimbledon' problem; Britain may be the venue for a great tennis tournament but the best players come from elsewhere. The London Stock Exchange has narrowly fought off takeover bids from the Frankfurt exchange and from the

US electronic market, NASDAQ; the ultimate owner of the London futures market is now the Intercontinental Exchange. The banks that dominate activity in the London markets are overwhelmingly foreign, particularly the Americans, Swiss, Germans, French and Japanese.

It is best that we look at these changes before we examine in detail the workings of the UK financial system. Discussion of these changes requires an assumption of some knowledge on the part of the reader as to how the system works. However, this book is also designed to be read by those who know little of finance. They may well want to start at Chapter 2 and return to the first chapter after they have read the rest.

1 The International Financial Revolution

In the past thirty years, London's financial centre, known as the City, has changed beyond recognition. Those who work in the financial sector have always been better paid than average; they have always had the power to influence economic policy. But that wealth and power seems to have grown exponentially. Anyone who looks across the skyline of London can see a visible representation of the City's power in the massed skyscrapers of Canary Wharf as well as modern temples of Mammon in the form of the Gherkin or the Cheesegrater.

The great towers contain workers from all parts of the world in the service of (mainly) foreign banks: Citigroup, J. P. Morgan, Goldman Sachs and Morgan Stanley of America, UBS and Credit Suisse of Switzerland, Deutsche Bank of Germany, Nomura of Japan and so on. Britain's representatives have shrunk, especially after the 2008 crisis pushed the Royal Bank of Scotland into the government's hands; Barclays is still a global bank, as is HSBC, although the latter owes a significant allegiance to China.

These big banks make a huge contribution to the British government's coffers. A report by PricewaterhouseCoopers in 2010 found that the financial sector made a total contribution of £53.4 billion that year, or more than 11 per cent of all taxes paid. Within that total, the sector's one million workers paid the equivalent of £24.5 billion in employment taxes (including national insurance). Nevertheless, given the scale of the banking bailouts needed in 2008, many people are dubious about the benefits that the City brings. Under Tony Blair, the Labour government kept a top tax rate of 40 per cent in order to encourage high-earners to stay in Britain; Gordon Brown pushed it up to 50 per cent. Even David Cameron's

Conservative-led government only felt able to reduce the rate to 45 per cent, fearful of the notion that they were giving handouts to millionaires.

Controversy over the role of the City is not unusual. Many blame a 'bankers' ramp' for forcing out the Labour government in 1931, and subsequent Labour governments ran into problems over sterling in 1948, 1967 and 1976. But now the financial markets' influence seems all-pervasive. Governments round the world find themselves constrained in their economic policies for fear of offending the markets. James Carville, one of President Clinton's key advisers, remarked that he would like to be reincarnated as the bond market so he could 'intimidate everybody'. When the financial system wobbles as it did in 2007 and 2008, the whole economy is threatened.

In addition, a combination of lower tax rates and liberalized financial markets has widened income differentials. Many City employees earn as much in a year as normal people might hope to earn in a lifetime, helping to force the prices of properties in London beyond the reach of teachers and nurses. Years of economic austerity, which have squeezed real wages and prompted the government to cut welfare benefits, are seen as the consequence of a crisis caused by the financial sector. All this has created a lot of resentment against 'greedy' bankers.

Interest in the City is not just political. News bulletins regularly include reports from the business sector; newspapers have substantial sections of company news and personal finance. Wider share ownership, encouraged by the government through privatizations and tax breaks, has created much greater interest in financial markets, reflected in greater coverage in newspapers and on TV. And, with governments round the world quailing in the face of the cost of state pension schemes, citizens are realizing that they may depend on the financial markets for their security in old age.

Why has the financial sector become so important? In part, it is because of the breakdown of the financial system that prevailed from the end of the Second World War until the early 1970s. That system, generally known as Bretton Woods, combined fixed exchange rates with strict controls on capital flows, so restricting the scope for financial market activity. Under fixed exchange rates, currency speculation was only profitable at occasional times, such as when Britain was forced to devalue sterling in 1967.

Foreign-exchange controls also made it difficult for investors to buy equities outside their home markets. That reduced the scope for share trading and ensured that the UK equity market was a protected haven, dominated by small firms operating in a climate which author Philip Augar has described as 'gentlemanly capitalism'.

But the system broke down in the early 1970s (for a full description see Chapter 14). The first domino to fall was fixed exchange rates. The system had depended on the US dollar but that currency buckled in the face of the costs of the Vietnam War.

Once exchange rates began to float, two things started to happen. First, companies faced foreign-exchange risk when selling goods. For example, Mercedes' costs were in Deutschmarks; when it sold a car in the US, it received dollars. If the dollar fell against the Deutschmark, that would be bad news. So companies looked for ways to protect themselves from these risks.

Secondly, floating exchange rates created the potential for continuous speculation. The 1970s saw the creation of the financial futures market in Chicago, which allowed traders to bet on the likely movement of exchange rates.

Both developments were opportunities for financial companies. They could make money speculating on the markets and they could make money helping companies protect themselves from foreign-exchange risk. Both opportunities were taken.

Floating exchange rates also had significant implications for governments. Think of three key elements of monetary policy: exchange rates, interest rates and capital controls. Under the Bretton Woods system, countries controlled their exchange rates and capital flows. However, if countries ran a substantial trade deficit, capital would still flow out of the country.

Take the UK, a country which habitually runs a trade deficit. When a foreign company sells goods to the UK, it receives sterling in return. (Even if it asks for dollars, the UK buyer of the goods must sell sterling and buy dollars in order to make the payment. Sterling will still flow out of the country.) Eventually, those companies will become less and less willing to hold sterling at the prevailing exchange rate. The Bank of England may be willing to buy that sterling off the overseas companies but it needs foreign-exchange reserves to do so. After a while the money will run out.

To avoid this problem, governments tried to cut the trade deficit. The easiest way of doing so was to raise interest rates; this had the effect of cutting consumer demand for foreign goods. But the result was a stop–go kind of economy, in which periods of rapid expansion were suddenly cut short as governments raised interest rates to protect sterling.

In a world of floating exchange rates, there is no requirement for governments to ratchet up interest rates every time the currency falls. Voters naturally don't like high interest rates. Furthermore, governments were very keen to keep unemployment low; at the slightest sign of economic weakness, they acted to boost the economy.

So in the 1970s, governments let their currencies sag, and kept interest rates lower than they might have been. The result (higher import prices, too much money chasing too few goods) was inflation. By the end of the 1970s, there was a general feeling that the old system of economic policy had failed. Governments had tried to micromanage the economy but in their attempts to keep down unemployment, they had merely achieved stagflation: high inflation and unemployment. Right-wing politicians such as Ronald Reagan and Margaret Thatcher argued that state intervention in industry had stifled the economy, concentrating resources in sunset industries such as coal and steel, and starving the growth sectors of the economy such as technology.

Inflation was eventually brought to heel with the help of very high interest rates, which also prompted massive job losses in those sunset industries. This process caused much distress and protest at the time and would have been politically impossible without the economic chaos of the 1970s.

At the same time (and to rather less fanfare), governments in the US and the UK relaxed the regulations on the financial sector and abolished capital controls. The idea was that the economy would function best when the markets, rather than bureaucrats, decided where to allocate capital.

Suddenly, investors were free to invest anywhere in the globe. Instead of concentrating on old UK stalwarts such as Imperial Chemical Industries or Marks & Spencer, they were free to invest in the likes of Bayer of Germany or Wal-Mart of the US.

These changes had enormous consequences for those who traded shares in the City. The old system had been like a gentlemen's club. A group of people called jobbers did all the trading in shares. They were not allowed to deal directly with investors. Instead, a group of intermediaries called brokers linked investors and jobbers, finding the best prices for the former in return for a fixed commission.

In theory, this system protected the interests of investors. Because brokers did not trade in shares, they could give independent advice to investors. And because brokers could shop around, jobbers had to offer competitive prices.

But there were two problems with this system. The first was that it was clearly not a free market: jobbers and brokers were restricted in the roles they could play and commissions were fixed. Brokers could not compete on price.

The second was that the broking and jobbing firms were all small. This was fine in a world where equity trading was limited to the home market. But when investment became international, the domestic firms were just too small to cope; they did not have the capital to deal with the risks involved.

BIG BANG

The City's solution was the Big Bang: a set of sweeping changes that were implemented in 1986. The old distinction between brokers and jobbers was abolished – firms could both act for investors and trade in shares. Outside capital was brought in, with UK, European and US banks buying up existing broking and jobbing firms.

A whole generation of senior brokers and jobbers retired on the proceeds of the sales and famous names such as de Zoete & Bevan, or Akroyd & Smithers, either disappeared or were subsumed within larger groups. (The process is well described in *The Death of Gentlemanly Capitalism* by Philip Augar, published by Penguin.) The old Stock Exchange floor, where brokers and jobbers met face to face, became a museum piece. Now the bulk of the trading was done by telephone, with investors kept constantly updated on share prices by brightly coloured Topic computer screens – with red signalling a falling price and blue, a rising one.

The whole process brought benefits to institutional investors, since the abolition of fixed commissions substantially cut their trading costs. But it had its downsides as well. One substantial problem was that the integration of broking and trading created an automatic conflict of interest within the financial sector. When a broker recommended a stock, was that because of a genuine opinion or because the trading arm of his firm had a large position in the shares? In recent years, a more significant conflict of interest has arisen. The abolition of fixed commissions has gradually ensured that commissions are only a small part of any bank's revenues. But, in theory, institutional investors are supposed to reward analysts for their advice by placing trades with the firms concerned. The sums do not add up.

Instead, banks have concentrated on increasing their revenues from transaction fees – acting for corporations in issuing new shares or bonds and making takeovers. This has led to analysts becoming 'cheerleaders' for such companies, talking up their prospects so that the deals will be successful. The idea of thoughtful, unbiased research has been severely compromised.

The second problem that followed the Big Bang was that control of equity trading moved out of the hands of UK institutions. It was inevitable that control of part of the City would move overseas: the US, European and Japanese banks all had a lot of capital. But it seemed for a while as if the UK could develop domestic champions. One such was S. G. Warburg, a successful merchant bank that bought brokers Rowe & Pitman, Mullens, and the jobber Akroyd & Smithers. The bank was eventually bought by Morgan Stanley.

For those who worked in the City, ownership did not matter much. The financial markets had become truly global, thanks to the economic and political developments of the late 1980s and early 1990s.

THE END OF THE COLD WAR

Free-market philosophy may have swept the board in the US and the UK during the 1980s but it was not so successful elsewhere. Many observers believed that this so-called Anglo-Saxon model was inferior to those developed elsewhere, particularly in Germany and Japan.

Both countries decided against giving the markets free rein. In Germany, hostile corporate takeovers were virtually unknown: companies had close relationships with their banks, which had seats on the boards. Maximizing returns to shareholders was not the priority it was in the Anglo-Saxon system; instead the interests of customers, suppliers and employees were taken into account.

In Japan, takeovers were also unheard of. Companies were protected against them by elaborate cross-shareholding with friendly groups. Maximizing profits was seen as less important to Japanese managers than maximizing sales and market share.

To their admirers, the German and Japanese systems seemed to offer many advantages. The absence of takeovers allowed companies to plan for the future, regardless of short-term profit performance. The result was higher investment. And the focus on employees seemed far less socially divisive than the Anglo-Saxon model.

Under the German–Japanese models, the freedom of financial markets played second fiddle to other factors. That did not stop the Japanese stock market soaring to unprecedented heights in the late 1980s.

Of course, until the end of the Cold War, a large part of the world followed a communist or socialist-style model, in which the financial markets played virtually no role at all.

All this changed during the course of the 1990s. The collapse of communism was clearly an epochal event and appeared to underline the fact that there was no alternative to capitalism as an economic model. Suddenly a whole raft of countries moved into the Western economic system, adopting stock markets and allowing US companies like McDonald's to open for business.

The collapse of communism also led to the reunification of Germany. The immense costs involved in taking on the old East Germany led to the imposition of high interest rates by the Bundesbank, the German central bank, in an attempt to control inflationary pressures. (This also eventually led to the breakup of the Exchange Rate Mechanism.) By the mid-1990s, the German model no longer looked so attractive. German unemployment was far higher than that prevailing in the US. German social costs were also far higher, prompting some German companies to site facilities overseas. German politicians began to feel that high taxes were deterring entrepreneurship and causing sluggish economic growth. An ageing German population suggested that, in the long run, pension costs could become a massive burden on the German state.

So, slowly but surely, Germany and the rest of Europe started to edge towards the Anglo-Saxon model. Businesses began to talk of 'shareholder value'; they divested themselves of non-core operations, simplified their shareholding structures and focused on improving profits. Perhaps the ultimate signal of the change in culture came in early 2000 when Mannesmann of Germany was taken over by Vodafone of the UK; this in a culture where hostile takeovers were extremely rare, let alone a hostile takeover by a foreign company.

As Germany moved in an Anglo-Saxon direction, the attractions of the Japanese model also faded. In the late 1980s, Japan's economy developed all the symptoms of a speculative bubble: share prices rose to record levels in terms of profits or dividends while land prices also soared.

The bubble popped in 1990 and some of Japan's apparent virtues began to be revealed as vices. Companies did not worry about short-term profits, but this led them to invest in unsuitable projects. The absence of takeovers meant there was no market discipline on poor companies to perform well. The soaring stock market also led companies to indulge in speculation which proved ill-timed once the market turned. The friendly relationship between banks and the corporate sector meant that the banks were saddled with bad loans, a problem that took more than a decade to sort.

Japan spent much of the 1990s stuck in a deflationary trap. Despite a host of government spending packages and interest rates that eventually fell to zero, the Japanese authorities found no way of reviving their economy.

The problems of Japan caused an almost 180-degree turn in the commentaries of those writing about economics and management. In the late 1980s, bestselling books were written about how the US should copy the Japanese; by the late 1990s, there was almost unanimous agreement on the need for all countries to copy the US.

THE US ECONOMIC MIRACLE

The retreat from the German and Japanese models was not just about their perceived failures; it was also about the perceived success of the US.

By the late 1990s, the US seemed by far the most dynamic of the world's economies. Growth averaged more than 4 per cent a year, and that growth was achieved with barely a trace of inflation. At the same time, European economies struggled to grow at 2–3 per cent a year; the Japanese economy struggled to grow at all. Unemployment fell to 4–5 per cent, around half the level prevailing in Europe. There was, apparently, a productivity miracle (the figures were subsequently revised down but still showed a substantial improvement over the 1980s).

In almost every growth industry – software, hardware, the internet, biotechnology, media – the US appeared to lead the world. The US accordingly attracted floods of capital from overseas; both the dollar and the US stock market rose substantially.

Economists attributed the US success to the openness of its economy, the lack of regulations, the use of share options to motivate executives and employees, and a host of other 'free-market' factors. Understandably, countries trying to emulate the US example tended to adopt some of those measures.

Free-market enthusiasts also pointed to the success of those Asian countries that had followed a broadly free-market view, such as Singapore, Hong Kong and Taiwan, and the failure of those countries, notably in Africa, that had followed a statist or socialist model.

A so-called 'Washington consensus' argued that any economy which wanted to prosper should follow the free-market model: lower taxes, reduced government deficits and open capital markets. These policies were often made a condition for countries requiring aid from the International Monetary Fund, the Washington-based organization that underpins the global financial system.

The period since 2000 has seen the Washington consensus come under attack. First, the US model looks not quite as attractive as it did in the late 1990s. The dotcom bubble burst in 2000 and then a housing boom ended in a credit crunch in 2007 and 2008. Critics argue that the American financial free-for-all leads to recurrent crises. Meanwhile, emerging countries like China and Russia showed it was possible to achieve rapid economic growth while still retaining a fair degree of government control. Having seen what the IMF could do to debtor countries, many developing nations focused on building up trade surpluses, so they would not be dependent on foreign money. Now it is the US which is dependent on the Asians and the oil producers to finance its deficit. Some argue that this imbalance created the conditions for the credit crunch. Americans used cheap money from abroad to speculate on their property market.

GLOBALIZATION

What is globalization? It is one of those terms that is often used, but more rarely defined. Broadly speaking, it is a trend whereby trade, investment and culture have become ever more international. The phenomenal change came with the collapse of communism in eastern Europe and the opening up of China to the international economy. Suddenly, it was possible for Western investors to buy shares in Russia and for Russian billionaires to buy property (and football teams) in London. The developing countries (or as investors like to call them, the emerging markets) turned from basket cases that were forever defaulting on their debts into high-growth economies with young populations and low labour costs. China's success in growing its economy at 9–10 per cent a year stimulated demand for the commodities that many of these emerging markets produced.

After a nasty crisis in the late 1990s, many Asian countries started to build up trade surpluses and thus to accumulate substantial foreign-exchange reserves. In turn, this led to the creation of sovereign wealth funds, which invested all over the world. China, like Japan before it, became one of the biggest investors in US government debt. Singapore and Hong Kong in Asia, and Dubai in the Middle East, became international financial centres.

Emerging markets are now around half of the global economy, on some measures, and have regularly been driving global growth. They have been blamed for driving down wages in the Western world (via competition) and driving up commodity prices (via high demand).

Is globalization new? Not in terms of trade. In the UK, exports formed 29.8 per cent of GDP back in 1913: in 2000, they were just 20.7 per cent. Other countries are more open to trade than they were before the First World War but arguably, in this respect, the modern economy is not that much different from the one familiar to the Edwardians. It was the opening up of the US prairie states, and the consequent arrival of cheap wheat, that devastated British agriculture in the late nineteenth century.

In terms of trade and population movements, the world was pretty 'globalized' before the First World War; the subsequent battles with fascism and communism sent that process into reverse for sixty years.

In two respects, however, globalization has surpassed the pre-First World War system. In terms of investment, ownership of foreign assets peaked as a proportion of world GDP in 1900, at 18.6 per cent. By 1945, the proportion had dropped to 4.9 per cent. Pre-First World War levels were finally reached by 1980, at 17.7 per cent. But since then there has been a massive acceleration; around a third of the UK stock market is owned by foreign investors, for example.

In cultural terms, also, globalization is more powerful than ever before. Clearly, before 1914, educated people in Europe and the US had a common culture based on the classics, orchestral music, opera and so on. Most people would have known little about events in the rest of the world. But the power of TV, radio and the internet has made many people more aware of conflicts in the Middle East and North Africa as well as aware of the cultural influence of American films and music. This is one factor that can cause great resentment, with some people feeling their culture is being swamped by American imports.

THE UK'S ROLE IN THE FINANCIAL SYSTEM

What is the effect of globalization in the UK? The UK economy may have had its problems but the UK's financial system has traditionally punched above its weight in global terms. The leading operators may well be US or European but they still choose London as their base. Even though the UK is not part of the Eurozone, European banks have not left en masse for Frankfurt, the financial centre of the Eurozone and home of the European Central Bank.

Some of this success as a financial centre is due to luck: the UK speaks the same language as the US, the world's leading economy and financial powerhouse. US bankers feel more comfortable in an English-speaking country; in addition, London seems a more attractive place to live than Frankfurt.

Some of the success is due to the UK regulatory regime, which has consistently been fairly welcoming to financial institutions. The financial reforms of the Conservative administrations of 1979–97, and the higher-rate tax cuts it introduced, have played their part. The Labour governments of 1997–2010 did little to reverse this trend. Arguably, the system became too lax in allowing banks to expand. Some economists feel that the UK economy has become over-dependent on the finance sector.

Globalization is not going away. It is now generally accepted that the UK needs to offer an economy that is appealing to foreign investors and foreign companies. The UK has been quite successful in attracting what is known as 'direct investment' from overseas companies: the building of factories, often in areas of high unemployment in Wales, Scotland or the North East. Politicians have argued that the UK has been successful in this quest because the government has cut taxes on corporate profits and because of more flexible labour markets (a euphemism for saying that companies face fewer problems in firing workers). Wider share ownership has also served the UK government's purpose. The cost of providing state pensions is a great burden on European countries, with their ageing populations. The Conservative governments of 1979–97 cut this cost substantially, by linking future pension payments to prices rather than earnings. But the effect after twenty years is that the state pension now provides a pretty measly income.

UK citizens have therefore come to realize that they will depend on their own savings for a decent retirement income. Since shares have historically provided better returns than other assets, investors have welcomed government schemes such as personal equity plans and individual savings accounts which give tax breaks to savers. They have also opted for personal pension schemes, which offer tax advantages for long-term savers.

But we have got ahead of ourselves. Before we discuss these issues in more detail, it is time to go back to first principles.

2

Money and Interest Rates

MONEY

Primitive societies did not have money, since they traded rarely. When trade began it was under a barter system. Goats might be exchanged for corn, or sheep for axes. As society became more complex, barter grew inadequate as a trading system. Goats might be acceptable as payment to one man but not to another, who might prefer sheep or cattle. Even then it was easy to dispute the question of how many sheep were worth a sack of corn.

Gradually precious metals and, most notably, gold and silver were used as payment and became the first money. Precious metals had several advantages. Money had to be scarce. It was no good basing a monetary system on the leaf. Everyone would soon grab all the leaves around and the smallest payment would require a wheelbarrowful. Money also had to be easy to carry and in divisible units – making the goat a poor monetary unit. Gold and silver were sufficiently scarce and sufficiently portable to meet society's requirements.

Of course, it soon became inconvenient to carry gold and silver ingots. Coins were created by the kings of Lydia in the eighth century BC. From the days of Alexander the Great the custom began of depicting the head of the sovereign on coins.

There are a variety of functions which money serves. It is a *measure of value*. Sheep can be compared with goats and chalk with cheese by referring to the amount of money one would pay for each product. Money is also a *store of value*. It can be saved until it is needed, unlike the goods it buys, which are often perishable. Creditors will accept money as a future payment, confident that its value will remain stable in the meantime. Crucially, money is a *means of exchange*. It is the way we pay for goods and the way we get paid for our labour.

Of course, today's money is made from neither gold nor silver. Coins are made from copper or nickel, notes are made from paper, and from 2016 will start being made of plastic (to make them more durable). But most money is electronic, in the sense of information stored on a computer. We pay with credit cards, smart cards, mobile phones or simply direct transfers from one bank account to another. When the Bank of England used 'quantitative easing' in 2009, it did not have to print banknotes to create money, it simply bought assets in the market, and credited the seller's bank account; a benign version of computer hacking.

There are three main reasons why money has moved away from its metallic roots. The first is sheer convenience; we do not want to lug precious metals around. Indeed, given the value of gold (around $1,300 an ounce at the time of writing), we would need microscopic amounts to pay for our purchases. Even if our paper or electronic money were linked to gold in some way, we would face a second problem: the supply of gold and silver changes very slowly over time, whereas our need for money constantly expands. Fixing the supply of money can cause severe economic problems, as occurred in the 1930s, when most countries abandoned the formal gold standard; they have never returned. The third problem is known as Gresham's Law: bad money drives out good. If people have the choice between handing out gold or paper money for their morning coffee, they will choose the paper and keep the gold. Gold will thus cease to circulate.

The modern monetary system depends on the confidence of all those concerned. Shopkeepers accept credit cards because banks will honour them; utility companies accept direct debits as payment for gas and electricity bills. Bank accounts are therefore money in the same sense as notes and coins are, since they can be used instantly to purchase goods.

Banks can thus create money. This is because only a small proportion of the deposits they hold is needed to meet the claims of those who want to withdraw cash. Much of the need is met by those who deposit cash. A simple way for a bank to lend money is to create a deposit (or account) in someone's favour.

Suppose that a country has only one bank, which finds that it needs to keep 20 per cent of its deposits in the form of cash. It receives an extra

£200 worth of cash deposits. The bank then buys £160 of BT shares, leaving £40 cash free to meet any claims from depositors. The person from whom it bought the shares now has £160 in cash, which is deposited with the bank. So the bank has £360 in deposits (the original £200 plus the new deposit of £160), of which it needs to keep only £72 (20 per cent) in the form of cash. The bank is therefore able to increase its total investments to £288 (£360 – £72) and can buy a further £128 of BT shares. Once again the person from whom it buys the shares will receive cash, depositing this with the bank. This process will continue until the bank has deposits of £1,000, of which £200 is held in the form of cash. The bank's balance sheet will then look like this:

ASSETS		LIABILITIES	
Cash	£200	Customer deposits	£1,000
BT shares	£800		
TOTAL	£1,000		£1,000

(Note that customer deposits are a liability, since they might at any time have to be repaid.)

To find out the total amount of deposits that can be created from the original cash base, divide 100 by the percentage which the bank needs to hold as cash (known as the *cash ratio*). Then multiply the result by the amount of the original deposit. Thus, in this example, dividing 100 by the cash ratio of 20 per cent gives 5, and multiplying that by the original deposit equals £1,000.

The cash ratio is therefore very important. If, in the example, the ratio had been only 10 per cent, the amount of deposits created from the original deposit would have been £2,000 and not £1,000. In practice, banks find that they need to keep around 8 per cent of their deposits in the form of liquid assets.

This relation between the money which banks need to hold in liquid form and the amount which they can lend has, in the past, been used by the Bank of England to control the level of credit in the economy (see Chapter 5). Nowadays, central banks are less concerned about the cash that banks hold and more about the capital that banks have put aside in case their loans go bad.

DEFINING THE MONEY SUPPLY

As money has become increasingly sophisticated, so it has become more and more difficult to define exactly what it is. This issue assumed particular importance with the prominence of the monetarist school of economics, which believed that the level of inflation is closely related to the rate of increase of the money supply. Clearly this is true at the extremes, as in Weimar Germany or Zimbabwe where so much money was printed that prices were rising almost constantly. In the late 1970s and early 1980s many Western governments, including the UK's, were strong adherents of the monetarist school and attempted to base economic polices on its theories. Accordingly, they needed to define the money supply before they could control it.

This proved to be difficult; Professor Charles Goodhart of the London School of Economics remarked that any measure of money supply would misbehave as soon as it became used as a policy guideline. The financial sector is constantly finding new instruments and ways of lending money. As a result, the Bank of England has published several definitions of money over the years. But with the money supply data less crucial to the formation of economic policy, it now focuses on just two – narrow money, broadly defined as notes and coins in circulation with the public, and broad money, known as M4. The latter largely consists of lending by UK banks and building societies to the private sector. Lending to small and medium-sized businesses is seen as particularly important in driving economic growth; those businesses will use the money to invest in new equipment and take on more workers. A lack of this kind of lending after the 2008 crisis made central banks worry that the money supply was growing too slowly, not too rapidly. That explains why they attempted to boost money creation via quantitative easing (QE); the creation of money to buy assets.

INTEREST RATES

Money on its own is a very useful but, in the long run, unprofitable possession. That £200 stashed under the mattress will in ten years' time still be only £200. In the meantime inflation will have eroded its purchasing power, so that it may be able to purchase only half as many goods as it could ten years before. Had the money been deposited with a building society, however, interest would have been added periodically. At 5 per cent a year the original cash deposit would have increased to £310.27 at the end of the ten-year period. This interest rate is essentially the *price* of money. The price is paid by the borrower in return for the use of the lender's money. The lender is compensated for *not* having the use of his money.

There are two alternative methods of calculating interest: *simple* and *compound*.

Simple interest can be easily explained. If a deposit of £100 is placed in a building society and simple interest of 10 per cent per annum is paid, then after one year the deposit will be £110, after two years £120 and so on. Nearly all interest is paid, however, on a compound basis.

Compound interest involves the payment of interest on previous interest. In the above example the depositor would still receive £10 interest in the first year. In the second year, however, interest would be calculated on £110, rather than on £100. The depositor would thus earn £11 interest in the second year, bringing his deposit to £121. In the third year he would earn £12.10 interest and so on. The cumulative effect is impressive. The same £100 deposit would become £350 after twenty-five years of simple interest but £1,083.50 with compound interest. Most savings accounts operate on the principle of compound interest, but most securities pay only simple interest. A bond may pay 5 per cent a year but only on the principal amount borrowed. That amount does not increase over the bond's lifetime.

When dealing with a bond or with a share, it is more important to talk of the *yield* than merely of the interest rate or dividend.

YIELD

A deposit account in a building society carries an annual interest rate. The money deposited will be returned in full with the accumulated interest, but the lump sum (capital) will not grow. Other investments, like shares, bonds and houses, are not as safe as a building society account but offer the potential for capital growth. Shares, bonds and property can all increase in price as well as provide income in the form of dividends, interest or rent. Since the price of these securities can alter, the interest rate or dividend will be more or less significant as the price falls or rises. The interest rate or dividend, expressed as a percentage of the price of the asset, is the *yield*. A security with a price of £80 that pays interest of £8 a year has a yield of 10 per cent. If the value of the security rises to £100, the yield will fall to 8 per cent. In assessing the profitability of various assets, calculating their yield is very important; articles in the financial press will talk about equity yields and bond yields as much as about dividends and interest rates.

Until the 1950s, the yield on shares was higher than that on most bonds, since shares were perceived as a riskier form of investment. Since then, shares have offered lower yields than bonds or savings accounts because the prospects of capital growth are much greater. That changed in the case of the credit crunch as share prices plummeted. It is too early to tell whether it is the start of a new era.

Probably the best way of showing the importance of yields is to cite the bond market. Suppose that in a year of low interest rates the Jupiter Corporation issues a bond with a face value of £100 and an interest rate (normally called the coupon) of 5 per cent. In the following year interest rates rise and bond investors demand a return of 10 per cent from newly issued bonds. Those investors who bought Jupiter bonds are now stuck with bonds which give them only half the market rate. Many of them will therefore sell their Jupiter bonds and buy newly issued bonds.

Who will they sell the bonds to? Potential buyers of Jupiter bonds will be no more willing to accept a yield of only 5 per cent than the sellers. Bond sellers will therefore have to accept a reduced price for the Jupiter bonds. The price will have to fall until the returns from Jupiter and other bonds are roughly equal. If the bond price fell from £100 to £50, then each year bondholders would still receive £5 on a bond which cost them £50 – a return, or yield, of 10 per cent. The Jupiter bond would be as attractive as a bond priced at £100 with a 10 per cent coupon, which would also yield 10 per cent.

Calculating the yield on a bond is not quite that easy, however. The bond will be repaid at some future point. Say, for example, it has a nominal value of £100, sells for £96, pays £5 interest a year and has one year to go before it is repaid. Over the next year the bondholder will receive £5 interest and £4 capital – the difference between the £96 it sells for and the £100 which will be repaid. So the bond yields £9 on a price of £96, just under 10 per cent. A yield which is calculated to allow for capital repayment is called the *gross yield to redemption*. Going back to the Jupiter issue, the bonds would not have to fall in price as low as £50 to keep their yields in line. If they had a five-year maturity, they would have to fall only to around £83 to have a gross yield to redemption of about 10 per cent. Bond trading depends on quick and sophisticated calculation of yields and exploitation of anomalies in the market.

This process of adjusting prices to bring yields in line gives bond investors the prospect of capital gain (or loss) on their holdings. An investor who buys Jupiter bonds at £100 would lose £25 if the price fell to £75 because of the yield adjustment. That would more than wipe out any interest earned on the bond. However, if the interest rate offered on other bonds fell back to 5 per cent again, then Jupiter's bonds would climb back to their face value of £100. An investor who bought at the low of £75 would have made a capital gain of 33 per cent and still earned interest in the process.

Because of the yield factor, bond prices have an inverse relationship with interest rates: bond markets are generally euphoric when interest rates are falling, depressed when they are rising.

INTEREST-RATE DETERMINANTS

Having understood the difference between simple and compound interest and the importance of yields, we can now look at the factors that determine an interest rate. In fact, it is more correct to talk of interest *rates*. At any one time a host of different rates are charged throughout the economy. So it is important to distinguish the determinants of specific interest rates as well as those which affect the general level of rates in the economy.

One of the principal elements is risk. There is always the chance, whomever money is lent to, that it will not be repaid. That risk will be reflected in a higher interest rate. This is one of the general principles of finance. The riskier the investment, the higher the return demanded by the investor. It is a principle which sometimes is ignored, mainly because investors do not always assess risk adequately. Nevertheless, it is a useful principle to bear in mind, especially when it is stood on its head. Those investors who seek extremely high returns would be wise to remember that such investments normally involve extremely high risk.

Governments are usually presumed to be the least risky debtors of all, at least by lenders in their own country. (Other countries' governments are a different matter, as many banks who lent to Brazil and Argentina in the 1970s discovered.) But the government of a lender's country can always print more money to repay the debt if necessary. In any case, if the government does not repay debt, it is reasonable for investors to presume that no one else in the country will.

Banks were traditionally rated next on the credit ladder. Nowadays, however, many large corporations are considered better credit risks than even the biggest banks. For the benefit of potential investors, some agencies have devised elaborate rating systems to assess the creditworthiness of banks and corporations (see Chapter 11).

At the bottom of the ratings come individuals like you and me. Individuals have a sad tendency to lose jobs, get sick, overcommit themselves and default on their loans. Unless they are exceptionally wealthy, individuals thus pay the highest interest rates of all.

One of the other main elements involved is liquidity. The house buyer with a mortgage has to pay a higher rate than is received by the building society depositor because the society needs to be compensated for the loss of liquidity involved in tying up its money for twenty-five years. The society faces the risk that it will at some point need the funds that it has lent to the house buyer but will be unable to gain access to them. As I mentioned in the Introduction, this is another of the basic principles of finance. The more liquid the asset, the lower the return. The most liquid asset of all, cash, bears no interest at all.

Logical though the above arguments are, it often happens that long-term interest rates are below short-term rates. To understand why, we must look at the yield curve.

THE YIELD CURVE

We have already proposed a general principle of finance – that lesser liquidity demands greater reward. That being the case, longer-term instruments should always bear a higher interest rate than short-term ones. This is not always true. Long-term rates can be the same as, or lower than, those of short-term instruments.

A curve can be drawn which links the different levels of rates with the different maturities of debt. If long-term rates are above short-term ones, this is described as a *positive* or upward-sloping yield curve. If short-term rates are higher, the curve is described as *negative* or *inverted*.

What determines the shape of the yield curve? The three main theories used to explain its structure are the liquidity theory, the expectations theory and the market-segmentation theory.

The *liquidity* theory, which has already been outlined, states simply that investors will demand an extra reward (in the form of a higher interest rate) for investing their money for a long period. They may do so because they fear that they will need the funds suddenly but will be unable to obtain them, or they may be worried about the possibility of default. Borrowers (in particular, businesses) will be prepared to pay higher interest rates in order to secure long-term funds for investment. Thus, other things being equal, the yield curve will be upward-sloping.

The *expectations* theory holds that the yield curve represents investors' views on the likely future movement of short-term interest rates. If one-year interest rates are 10 per cent and an investor expects them to rise to 12 per cent in a year's time, he will be unwilling to accept 10 per cent on a two-year loan. It would be more profitable for him to lend for one year and then re-lend his money at the higher rate. A two-year loan will therefore have to offer at least 11 per cent a year before the investor will be attracted. Thus if interest rates are expected to *rise*, the yield curve will be *upward-sloping*. If investors expect short-term interest rates to *fall*, however, they will seek to lend long-term. That will increase the supply of long-term funds and bring down their price (i.e. long-term interest rates). Thus the yield curve will be *downward-sloping*.

What determines investors' expectations of future interest-rate movements? Much may depend on future inflation rates. If inflation is set to rise, then price rises will absorb much of an investor's interest income. So investors will demand higher rates when they think inflation is set to increase.

The economist John Maynard Keynes constructed a more elaborate theory which depended on the yield of securities. If people expect interest rates to rise, Keynes argued, they will hold on to their money in the form of cash, in order to avoid capital loss. But if they expect rates to fall, they will invest their money to profit from capital gains. Of course, this principle applies to bonds rather than to interest-bearing accounts. As we have seen, if interest rates rise, the price of previously issued bonds falls until investors earn a similar yield from equivalent bonds. Thus a bond investor who expects rates to rise will sell his bonds before the rise in rates and the resultant fall in the bond price occurs. The investor will hold the funds in the most liquid form available so that he can reinvest them as soon as rates rise. If the same investor expects interest rates to fall, he will hold on to the bonds because their price will rise as rates fall.

The third theory of the yield curve is the *market-segmentation* theory. This assumes that the markets for the different maturities of debt instruments are entirely separate. Within each segment interest rates are set by supply and demand. The shape of the yield curve will be determined by the different results of supply/demand trade-offs. If a lot of borrowers have long-term financing needs and few investors want to lend for such periods, the curve will be upward-sloping. If borrowers demand short-term funds and investors prefer to lend for longer periods, the curve will be downward-sloping.

ECONOMIC THEORIES ON THE GENERAL LEVEL OF INTEREST RATES

We have already looked at the factors which affect the level of interest rates for different maturities, instruments and borrowers. It is also worth considering theories which concern the general level of rates in the economy.

As already mentioned, the rate of inflation is generally accepted to be a substantial ingredient of interest rates. Lenders normally expect interest rates at least to compensate them for the effect of rising prices. They therefore watch closely the *real* interest rate – that is, the interest received after inflation has been taken into account. Historically, real interest rates have averaged around 2–3 per cent; that is, if inflation were 7 per cent, interest rates would be 9–10 per cent. However, this relationship is far from permanent: real interest rates have often been negative in the wake of the 2008 crisis, partly because central banks have pushed rates down, and partly because there have been more willing savers than willing borrowers.

The most important inflation rate is the rate which a lender *expects* to occur during the lifetime of his or her investment. The inflation rate which is published by the government, the consumer price index, gives only the *previous year*'s price rises, but it is *next year*'s price rises which will affect the value of the lender's investment. So lenders must undertake a difficult piece of economic forecasting.

It is very important to remember that financial markets are now international. Rates of return in Britain cannot be separated from those in other countries. UK investors can invest abroad if there is the chance for higher rates overseas, and foreign investors can invest here if UK rates are above their own. Both decisions are linked with the level of exchange rates. An investment in the US might yield a high dollar rate of return, but if the dollar fell against sterling, investors would find themselves worse off.

Central banks concerned about the level of interest rates will often intervene to try to influence their movement. They may be concerned about the exchange rate and may push interest rates up to defend the pound. Alternatively, they may be concerned about the amount of credit in the economy. People may be borrowing too much because interest rates are low, with the result that excessive demand is leading to inflationary pressures. After 2008, many central banks were worried that people were saving too much and borrowing too little; in response, they pushed rates down to historic lows.

Central banks can influence interest rates because they are the lender of last resort to the banking system, and also because banks keep some of their reserves on deposit with the central bank. If the central bank increases the rate it charges (or pays), banks are likely to pass that higher rate on to their depositors and borrowers. The influence of the central bank used to be restricted to just short-term borrowing. But the quantitative easing (QE) policy involves the bank buying bonds; by doing so, they push the price of the bonds up and their yield down. The aim is to reduce the cost of longer-term borrowing for businesses and consumers, in the form of mortgages.

The classical explanation of the level of interest rates is associated with the theory of supply and demand. Thus the interest rate is the balancing point between the flow of funds from savers and the need for investment funds from business. If more funds become available from savers, or if industry has less need to borrow, interest rates will fall. If the funds available from savers are reduced, or if industry has a greater need to borrow, interest rates will rise. The demand for funds is likely to be affected by business people's expectations of future profits. If they believe that they will achieve a high rate of return on investment, they will be willing to borrow.

The supply of funds for borrowers depends largely on the willingness of the personal sector to save. Why do people save? One of the main reasons is to provide for old age or for children and spouses in the event of early death. This form of saving normally takes the form of investment in pension funds and life assurance and is helped by tax advantages. There has been a substantial growth in this form of saving since the 1960s. Another reason is to guard against rainy days caused by illness or unemployment: by its nature, such saving needs to be very liquid and is normally placed in building societies or interest-bearing bank accounts. A third reason for saving is to allow for major purchases or for holidays: again, such savings need a liquid home like a building society account.

Just as important as the reasons why people save are the reasons why the proportion of their income that they save changes over time. A certain amount of wealth is necessary before people can save – if all of someone's income is needed just to pay for food and rent, there will be no money left to save. However, it is not correct to assume the reverse: that the larger a person's income, the more he or she saves. The highest income-earners are often among the biggest *borrowers*, since banks will extend credit only to those who they think will be able to repay. The greater a person's income, therefore, the greater the possibility for incurring debt. Debt is negative saving. In fact, the cautious middle classes have traditionally been the biggest savers.

However, academic explanations of movements in the savings ratio (the proportion of income which is saved) have focused on income levels. If income rises, according to theory, there will be a larger increase in the level of savings; if income falls, savings will drop disproportionately as people run down their incomes to pay for their expenditure.

During the inflationary 1970s the savings ratio increased sharply, much to most economists' surprise. Since inflation erodes the purchasing power of savings, it was assumed that consumers would run down their cash balances and deposits, which bear a negative real interest rate, and would prefer to hold physical assets such as property, the value of which tends to increase in line with inflation.

What seems to have happened instead is that savers, perhaps for the rainy-day reasons outlined above, were concerned to maintain the purchasing power of their savings. Because of the rate of inflation, they needed to save a greater proportion of their income merely to keep the value of their savings constant. The rise in the savings ratio in the 1970s was followed by an equally sharp decline in the 1980s as inflation fell and it became easier to maintain the value of savings.

Saving seems to have a clear correlation to the state of the economy. In times of boom, people tend to save less. They are more confident about their job prospects and are happy to borrow money to make expensive purchases, such as cars and durable goods. In times of economic slowdown, they cut back their expenditure because they are less confident about their job prospects.

In analysing savings patterns an important distinction to recognize is that between committed and discretionary savings. Committed savings are made up of contributions to life assurance and pensions schemes and, as such, are relatively inflexible to changes in income. Discretionary savings represent payments into building society accounts or perhaps unit trusts. Such savings adjust much more quickly to income movements. Repayment of a mortgage represents committed savings in that it is an investment in the value of a real asset (i.e. a house).

Indeed, many believe that the housing market has distorted UK savings patterns. Years of inflation, and the favourable tax treatment of home ownership, has taught British investors that property is the safest store of wealth.

However, in recent years, a lot of theories have gone by the wayside. Central banks have been by far the most important actor in the markets. The Bank of England has kept its short-term rate at 0.5 per cent, a level never before reached in its 300-year history. That has allowed the British government and some companies to borrow at very low rates as well. It is far from clear when rates can return to what would once have been considered normal levels; the economy might not stand the strain.

3

The Retail Banks and Building Societies

Banks are at the heart of the financial system. They are the one type of financial institution with which all of us are bound to come into contact at some point in our lives. When they falter, as they did in 2007 and 2008, governments feel obliged to come to their rescue since, without them, the economy could not function.

Like banks, building societies take deposits from individuals and lend them to others. Over the last twenty years or so, many societies have either turned into, or been acquired by, banks. So whereas in previous editions they merited a separate chapter, they now need to be treated as part of the banking industry.

THE FIRST BANKERS

Gold and silver have traditionally been the two predominant monetary metals for the reasons outlined in Chapter 2. As a result, goldsmiths and silversmiths became the earliest bankers. Nervous citizens, who were well aware of the dangers of keeping their gold under the mattress, began to use the smiths, who had safes to store their wares, as a place to keep their wealth. In return, the smiths would give the depositor a handwritten receipt. It soon became easier for the depositors to pay their creditors with the smiths' receipts, rather than go through the time-consuming process of recovering the gold or silver and giving it to the creditor, who might only re-deposit it with the smith. Creditors were willing to accept the receipts as payment, provided that they were sure that they could always redeem the receipts for gold or silver when necessary.

The receipts were the first banknotes. The legacy of those early receipts is visible today in the form of the confident statement on banknotes: 'I promise to pay the bearer on demand the sum of . . .'

Despite having the image of the Queen to back it up, that statement is of no value today and anyone attempting to redeem a five pound note for gold at his local bank will be disappointed.

Smart goldsmiths were able to take the development of banking one stage further. They noticed that, of the gold stored in their safes, only a small quantity was ever required for withdrawal and that amount was roughly matched by fresh deposits. There was therefore a substantial quantity of money sitting idle. The money could be lent (and interest earned) in the knowledge that the day-to-day requirements of depositors could still easily be covered (see Chapter 2).

THE ITALIAN INFLUENCE

Among the earliest bankers were goldsmiths and silversmiths from the Lombardy region of Italy who were granted land in London by King Edward I. One of the sites they received – Lombard Street – is at the heart of the modern City of London. Back in Italy, the money lenders had conducted their business from wooden benches in marketplaces. The Italian word for bench, *banco,* was corrupted by the English into 'bank'. The Italians were also responsible for introducing the symbols that were synonymous with British money until 1971 – £, s. and d., or *lire, solidi* and *denarii.* It is a nice irony that those who wear the £ symbol as a signal of opposition to Europe are in fact displaying an Italian figure.

Many of the early bankers misjudged their ability to absorb 'runs' – times of financial panic when investors rushed to claim back their gold. In such cases, bankers had insufficient funds to meet the claims of depositors upon them and thus became 'bankrupt' (literally 'broken bench'). Such runs could easily become self-fulfilling. As soon as depositors feared that a bank might become bankrupt, they would flock to the banks in order to demand their money back, thus accelerating the bank's deterioration into ruin. Because of the nature of banking, no bank could stand a determined run. Some tried ingenious methods to do so. One bank arranged for a few

wealthy depositors to arrive by carriage at the front of the bank and withdraw their gold ostentatiously. The queuing small depositors were
impressed. Meanwhile, the wealthy depositors sent their footmen round
the back to re-deposit the gold, so it could be used to meet the claims of
the other depositors.

Bankruptcies did not reduce the total number of banks. The seeming
ease with which it was possible to make money from banking soon
attracted others to take the places of the institutions that had failed. Gradually, depositors regained confidence in the trustworthiness of the banks.
Thus began a regular banking cycle of boom and bust. Professor Galbraith explained that the length of these cycles 'came to accord roughly
with the time it took people to forget the last disaster – for the financial
geniuses of one generation to die in disrepute and be replaced by new
craftsmen who the gullible and the gulled could believe had, this time but
truly, the Midas touch'.

In the UK Charles I, that unlikely saint, gave banking an unwitting
boost in 1640 by seizing £130,000, which merchants had unwisely committed to his safe-keeping by placing it in the Royal Mint. Merchants
decided that in future it would be rather safer to deposit their funds with
the bankers in the City. It was not until 1694 that the government's financial reputation could be restored and the Bank of England established: by
that time, the crown was on the head of the sober and respectable Dutch-
man, William of Orange.

MODERN BANKING

The history of the Bank of England is considered in Chapter 5. This
section considers the modern banks which have grown out of the early
activities of the goldsmiths.

There are many varieties of banks, but the two types that are best
known in Britain are the retail and the investment banks. Investment
banks are considered in the next chapter and are best known for arranging
complex financial deals and for financing trade. Retail banks take deposits
from customers and lend them out to companies and individuals.

The banks which most people know, and which are indeed at the heart
of the UK financial system, are the clearing banks, so called because

individual transactions between them are cleared through the London Clearing House system. This saves the banks, and therefore their customers, a lot of time. Rather than have Lloyds pay over £20 to Barclays for Mr Brown's gas bill and Barclays pay £15 to HSBC for Mrs Smith's shopping, the clearing house tots up all the individual transactions and arrives with a net position for each bank at the end of the day. Lloyds might owe Royal Bank of Scotland £20,000 and HSBC owe Barclays £15,000 – the important fact is that on a daily basis, each bank is involved in only one clearing house transaction with any other.

In 1984, the clearing process was much improved by the introduction of the Clearing House Automated Payment System (CHAPS), which replaced the old manual system for processing cheques and bankers' payments. Rather than laboriously adding up the total of each bank's payments and receipts by hand, a CHAPS payment results in an adjustment to a running total held on the system. At the end of the day, each bank has logged up a deficit or surplus *vis-à-vis* the other banks in the system. Payments are cleared in a few minutes rather than the hour and a half of the old system.

The work that the clearing banks handle is huge. In 2010, CHAPS handled 32 million transactions worth £61 trillion. And CHAPS is part of the Target 2 system that settles deals across the European Union.

Twenty years ago, there were four big banks – Barclays, Lloyds, Midland and National Westminster. That pattern has changed significantly thanks to takeovers and the conversion of building societies into banks. Some banks are still recognizable. For example, Lloyds still uses the black horse logo and is largely a retail bank. But in the last twenty years, the bank has gone through a whole host of changes. First, it acquired the Trustee Savings Bank and became Lloyds TSB; then it bought the Cheltenham & Gloucester building society and Scottish Widows, an insurer. At the height of the 2008 crisis, it agreed the takeover of HBOS (Halifax Bank of Scotland, itself the product of a merger), a disastrous move which led to a government rescue. It has since spun off TSB and is back to being Lloyds again.

Barclays is another bank that has gone through enormous changes; periodically building up and then reducing its investment banking business in the form first of BZW and then Barclays Capital. A highly successful investment management business, Barclays Global Investment, was sold to BlackRock of the US. A series of scandals led to the appointment of a new chief executive: Antony Jenkins in August 2012 and he seems to be focusing the bank on its retail business once more.

Midland Bank has long since lost its independence, agreeing to a take-over by the Hong Kong and Shanghai Banking Corporation (HSBC) in 1992. The Midland brand name was duly phased out. HSBC has its head-quarters in London and is a genuinely global bank, although like the others it has had its problems with acquisitions, buying Household International in 2002, a deal that brought billions in losses on bad loans. It also paid $1.9 billion to US regulators because its Mexican arm was implicated in money laundering.

NatWest was acquired by the Royal Bank of Scotland in 2000, after a fierce bidding battle, but still trades under its original name on the high street. RBS went on to buy ABN Amro of the Netherlands, a terrible deal that ended up forcing the government to rescue the bank. Again, the result has been a shrinking of the bank in response to cost-cutting and a focus on retail, rather than investment, banking.

Another big British banking presence is the Spanish Grupo Santander, which acquired the former building societies Abbey National in 2004 and Alliance & Leicester (along with the savings accounts of Bradford & Bingley) in 2008.

The reduction of the investment banking operations of Barclays and RBS means that, once again, the British banks seem like quite minor players in the field. But the problem with the all-singing, all-dancing banks is that every few years they tend to hit a flat note or trip over their own feet. The solid commercial bankers start to resent the flashy, highly paid investment bankers who tend to lurch from one disaster to another. The concept is thus highly expensive and very risky. Mind you, the commercial banks have managed to have plenty of disasters in the theoretically safer area of domestic personal and corporate banking.

THE IMPORTANCE OF RETAIL DEPOSITS

The retail banks long had a built-in advantage – the current accounts of ordinary depositors like you and me. Such accounts traditionally paid no interest whereas the banks could charge as much as 20 per cent on overdrafts – a fairly hefty profit margin. Banks without retail deposits have to borrow at market rates in the money markets in order to obtain funds. It can be said in justification of the retail banks that the costs of such a large network of branches, in terms of buildings, staff and paperwork, take a substantial slice of that margin.

This so-called endowment effect started to disappear in the 1980s when competition from building societies forced the banks to offer interest-bearing accounts. In the late 1990s, retail deposits started to look as much of a burden as a boon. The problem was that servicing those depositors required the maintenance of a vast and expensive branch network.

Rivals emerged with the ability to 'cherry pick' the best retail customers. One group was the supermarkets, which offered interest-bearing accounts to their customers. Another was internet banks, such as Egg, which were able to offer interest-bearing accounts without the need for branch networks. The big banks reacted by cutting costs, laying off staff and closing banks in rural areas and small towns. They also encouraged investors to switch to banking over the telephone or the internet, and focused on other, higher-margin products such as life insurance and fund management.

But internet banking has created a new class of 'rate tarts', investors who will take the highest rate on offer but will switch as soon as another more attactive deal comes along. This allowed overseas banks, such as ING of the Netherlands and Landesbanki of Iceland, to win market share (when the latter went bust in 2008, 300,000 British savers were affected). As a result, deposits are less 'sticky' than they used to be – in other words, banks cannot be sure of hanging on to them. This caused some banks to depend more on the wholesale, or money, markets for funding, with important consequences.

BANKS AND THE SUBPRIME CRISIS

Over the last decade or so, there has been a global move away from depending on retail deposits and towards what is known as an 'originate and distribute' model. Banks raise money from other institutions in the wholesale markets. They still make loans – to individuals, companies and so on – but they do not hang on to them. They bundle them up into pools of assets and sell them to outside investors, a process known as securitization.

Why does this occur? From a bank's point of view, the approach is attractive because of regulations. Under the Basel regulations, banks need to hold a certain amount of capital on their balance sheet to protect depositors in the event that loans go bad (a bank's assets are the loans it makes, the deposits it takes are its liabilities). The capital is in the form of equity or certain types of long-term bonds. Since banks are often judged by their return on equity, they had an incentive to sell loans and free their capital for other purposes. Indeed, before the 2008 crisis, banks had an incentive to sell off their safer loans and use the proceeds to lend money to riskier borrowers, who paid higher rates.

Why would anyone want to buy such securitized loans? Low inflation in the 1990s and 2000s drove the yields on government bonds down to very low levels. This made investors desperate for assets offering higher returns. Asset-backed securities, as they became known, offered such returns. They might be pools of mortgages, car loans or credit cards. In theory, because the pools were diversified, the losses would be predictable. This process of securitization has been going on for thirty years or so but it took off amazingly quickly in the early part of this century. Regulators were keen on securitization because it seemed to spread risk; if the loans turned bad, the hit would not be taken by the banks.

Credit booms tend to be self-reinforcing. Say the average house price is £100,000 and banks are willing to lend 80 per cent of the home value. The average homeowner puts down a deposit of £20,000, borrows £80,000 and buys the house. Prices rise by 20 per cent, so the average home is now worth £120,000. Homeowners are better off and banks are now feeling better about lending to them; after all, the value of their collateral has gone up. So they now figure they can lend against 90 per cent of a house's value. Now potential homeowners only need £12,000 for a deposit. So there will be more potential buyers, which will push house prices up further, making banks more confident about lending and so on.

This is what happened in the early years of this century in America and to a lesser extent in Britain. As house prices rose, lending standards were relaxed. Securitization speeded this process. After all, if you were going to sell the loan within a few months, why worry about whether the borrower would be able to repay in a few years' time? And why would borrowers worry about repaying if they expected to sell the house for a quick profit?

In the US, the extreme part of the process was so-called 'liar loans' which were made to borrowers who had to provide no proof of their income. Of course, such loans carried higher rates of interest, but they were not high enough. Some of these borrowers were 'Ninjas', a term indicating they had no job, no income and no assets.

All was well while house prices were going up. But as soon as they started to falter, it became clear that many borrowers could not afford to keep up the interest payments. Indeed, once it became clear that house prices were falling, some walked away without making any payments at all. The bonds backed by these mortgages, known as subprime in the jargon because of the low credit ratings of the borrowers, started to default.

But what made the crisis worse was that the mortgage-backed bonds themselves had been bundled up and repackaged. Securities known as collateralized debt obligations or CDOs had been created. These were made up of bundles of asset-backed bonds.

The CDOs were sliced and diced into different elements, known as tranches. The riskiest slice, known as equity, paid the highest yield. But in return, they suffered the first loss when any of the underlying assets defaulted. The higher tiers in the pyramid carried less risk but paid a lower yield. The top tier of all, often known as supersenior, was in theory extremely safe.

There were lots of problems, however, with this structure. One was the tiering of risk. Portfolios were assembled that comprised the riskiest parts of mortgage-backed securities. As a result, when they were pooled together in CDOs, risks were concentrated, not diversified; if one part of the portfolio was likely to default, so was the rest. This meant the more senior parts of the portfolio were more risky than the owners had thought.

This problem was compounded by the use of borrowed money, or leverage. As already explained, supersenior tranches offered fairly low yields. This made them unexciting investments. But if you could borrow money for less than the yield on the supersenior, this made them potentially a lot more enticing. And the regulations that governed the level of bank capital did indeed make this an attractive option, on the assumption that the bonds would never default.

Alas, when the scale of the subprime crisis became apparent, the prices of these securities fell and banks were forced to reveal their losses. The problem was made worse by the existence of specialist vehicles such as conduits and structured investment vehicles (SIVs). These, like the banks, had used borrowed money to invest in mortgage-backed securities and CDOs. In fact, they had borrowed the money from the banks. In some cases, they were unable to repay their loans; in others, the vehicles were clearly creatures of individual banks, and the banks were forced to rescue them. Rather than diversifying risk, as regulators had hoped, securitization had focused it. Worse still, because the process was so opaque, no one knew the extent of the banks' exposure. So they played it safe and refused to lend money to banks that they thought might be in trouble. The collapse in lending was self-fulfilling; banks did get in trouble as a result.

Britain was not immune to this problem, even though it originated in the US. In part, this was because some of the banks had invested in the complex CDOs that proved so difficult to value when the housing market turned down. But it was also because British banks had moved to the originate and distribute model. When the credit crunch hit, some of those banks were particularly vulnerable.

THE NORTHERN ROCK COLLAPSE

Building up a base of retail deposits takes time and resources. Either you need a big base of branches (with lots of costly property and staff), or a call centre to handle consumer enquiries, or you need to offer a high return to attract the rate tarts who surf the internet.

The originate and distribute model seemed to offer a quicker and easier route to gain market share. Instead of waiting for deposits to build up, a bank could go out and make the mortgage loans it desired and then sell those loans in the financial markets. Provided it received a higher rate from homeowners than it paid in the market, such a strategy would be profitable.

Northern Rock, a Newcastle building society turned bank, was the British institution that proved most aggressive in pursuing this strategy. By 2007, it was Britain's fifth biggest mortgage provider even though it had just 76 branches. At the moment it ran into trouble, only a quarter of its funds came from retail customers.

The strategy had enabled Northern Rock to expand very quickly; in the first half of 2007, its lending was 31 per cent higher than the year before. This approach looked highly profitable. Ironically enough, the last annual results that it produced before its collapse showed record pre-tax profits of £627 million, 27 per cent higher than the previous year. Indeed, anyone who looked at the raw data might have been surprised by Northern Rock's implosion; the repayment arrears on its mortgages were less than half the industry average.

But these headline numbers belied some fundamental weaknesses. It takes time for mortgages to go wrong and when it got into trouble, a third of Northern Rock's loans were less than two years old. As it expanded, it was increasing the proportion of loans to homebuyers with a small deposit (and to those who wanted to borrow more than the value of the house itself). It was also heavily involved in the buy-to-let market. Investors were well aware that it might be vulnerable if house prices fell; its share price was declining steadily from the spring of 2007.

The bank had also made one fatal assumption: that the money markets would always be open to it. But in August 2007, alarmed by losses on subprime loans, investors suddenly wanted nothing to do with mortgage-backed securities. Northern Rock had raised money from the markets in January and May, and was scheduled to do so in September. In August, it was thus low in cash. It had not thought to put emergency funding plans in place.

So the bank had to turn to others for help. An attempt was made to sell the bank to Lloyds TSB but Lloyds wanted a £30 billion loan from the Bank of England before it would sign the deal. The central bank was unwilling to agree; ironically, its eventual exposure to Northern Rock proved much larger. The only option left was direct help from the Bank of England, and when news of that deal leaked, retail customers started to demand their money back. What emerged was a classic 'run on the bank' such has been seen many times in history.

Even without the run, Northern Rock was probably finished as an independent entity. But the run ruined Northern Rock's brand name, making it more difficult to sell the bank to a private company. Eventually, it had to be nationalized. And the run on the bank caused the authorities to worry that other banks might be threatened; Alistair Darling, the Chancellor, was forced into making the extraordinary pledge of guaranteeing not just Northern Rock's deposits, but those of any other bank that got into trouble.

Order was eventually restored with the help of a change to the deposit insurance scheme, that guaranteed the first £35,000 of all deposits (in 2008, this had to be increased to £50,000 and in 2011, £85,000). But the whole affair dented confidence in Britain's financial system. When the credit crunch bit again in 2008, worries about the dependence of HBOS on the wholesale markets forced it into the arms of Lloyds TSB, and Bradford & Bingley was closed by the government.

These measures only seemed to exacerbate the crisis, by decreasing investor confidence in the banking system. It became either impossible or very expensive for banks to get finance from the wholesale markets. In turn, that made them more cautious about lending to companies and consumers. The crisis reached such a peak that, in October 2008, the government was forced to unveil a massive £400 billion rescue scheme that involved buying bank shares, guaranteeing their loans and lending them money to tide them over until the markets resumed normal trading.

The effective nationalization of parts of the banking industry raised some difficult questions which have plagued the government and the banks ever since. Should the government control the pay of individual bankers? And should it direct where banks make their loans? Many small businesses complained that it was hard to get credit, even from state-controlled banks.

ASSETS AND LIABILITIES

The demise of Northern Rock illustrated one of the perennial weaknesses of banks; they borrow short and lend long. In other words, if people lose confidence in the banks, they can get in trouble very quickly.

Understanding bank finances requires a good grip on the terminology and this can be a little counter-intuitive. The monies we hold in our current accounts are not the assets of the banks; they are their liabilities since we can ask for them back at any moment.

Banks' assets are the loans and investments which they make with the deposits provided and which earn them interest. Those assets are held in a variety of forms. A substantial proportion is lent out short term – either at call (effectively overnight) or in the form of short-term deposits in the money markets (see Chapter 6). The bulk of banks' assets is held in the form of loans – to individuals and to businesses.

The banks also lend longer term, both domestically and internationally. In the UK, the loans are vital to the development of industry. Most companies start with the help of a bank loan, usually secured on the assets of a company. That means that if the firm folds, the bank has a claim on the firm's fixed capital such as machinery or buildings.

The proportion of the banks' assets which they need to hold in the form of cash is known as the cash ratio. The ratio has from time to time been set by the Bank of England to ensure that banks remain sound. It determines to some extent the total amount banks can lend. However, there are other factors involved.

One of the most important is the supply of creditworthy customers. Banks are normally cautious about the people to whom they grant loans. If we assume that the number of people who are good credit risks (i.e. they have a steady job, good references, a good financial record) remains fairly constant, that puts a limit on banks' expansion.

The general state of the economy will also affect the growth of bank lending. If the economy is healthy, more businesses will be seeking to borrow funds to finance their investment plans. If the economy is in recession, however, few industries will be prepared to invest and therefore to borrow. Banks might seek to attract more borrowers by lowering their interest rates, but there is an obvious limit to such a process. The banks cannot afford the return from their lending to fall below the cost of their borrowing. The return from lending must always be significantly higher, because of the substantial costs involved in running a branch network.

Banks tend to follow a feast-and-famine process. Lots of loans will be made in times of economic boom, and when asset prices are rising. But when the economy starts to contract, and asset prices fall, some of those loans will fail to be repaid. That will prompt banks to suffer losses in the form of write-downs of their loan portfolios. The whole process is self-reinforcing. If consumers and businesses have greater access to credit, they will spend more and the economy will boom; this will make it more likely that the banks will be paid back. But if the banks restrict credit access, consumers and companies will have less money to spend, economic activity will contract and bad debts will rise.

Regulators from around the world have attempted to tackle these problems in the aftermath of the crisis. The most important reform has been to require more capital, largely in the form of equity (or shares) but also in the form of bonds that can be converted into shares at times of crisis (known as cocos in the jargon). Roughly speaking, banks are required to hold about three times as much equity capital as before the crisis. There has also been a revival of the old cash ratio (see previous chapter), in the form of a liquidity coverage ratio; the banks need to have a rainy-day fund to meet the kind of emergency they faced in 2008, when it was difficult for them to borrow in the markets.

On pay, regulators have tried to ensure that bonuses are in the form of deferred remuneration, not cash. The aim is to ensure that bankers have an interest in the long-term health of their bank and in the deals they do; that they are not just trying to make a quick buck. Why not eliminate bonuses altogether? Bonuses are a very flexible way of rewarding staff; they can be cut dramatically in bad times. If they were abolished, banks would simply increase the basic pay of their key staff, making the bank more likely to lose money in bad times. That said, there have been occasions when banks have lost billions of pounds and were still able to pay bonuses to key staff. The rationale was that the banking business is very patchy; a bank can lose a fortune in, say, mortgages, while doing extremely well in merger advice. If the bank penalizes the mergers team for mistakes in the mortgage department, those staff will go elsewhere and the bank will become less profitable.

Some have argued that much more radical reform is needed. One option is to separate commercial and investment banking completely; this was the response to bank failures in the 1930s, when America passed the Glass–Steagall Act. The worry then was that the deposits of ordinary consumers were put at risk by the speculative activities of the investment banks. Separation was maintained until the 1980s but the distinctions became more and more blurred, and were finally abolished in the late 1990s. Small wonder, critics say, that a crisis happened soon after the two sectors became entwined.

But things are not quite that simple. Many of the banks that collapsed did not blur commercial and investment banking: Northern Rock in the UK had no investment-banking arm and Lehman Brothers in the US did not take customer deposits. Even without deposits, Lehman's collapse proved calamitous because of the way the bank was intertwined with the rest of the finance sector.

The fundamental problem is that governments feel obliged to insure the deposits of retail banks, because of the economic damage that might be caused if ordinary people lost confidence in the banking system. But the effect is to make depositors less cautious about leaving money in their banks. As a result banks have access to cheap funding (in the form of deposits) that they can use to take speculative bets – whether by lending recklessly in the property market or trading in derivatives. This requires the government to bail them out when they fail; the privatization of profits and the nationalization of losses, as it has been described. This is a classic example of 'moral hazard'; if the government provides a sector with protection, it is likely to act more recklessly.

A report by the Vickers commission in 2011 suggested a halfway house: retail and investment banks can exist within the same group, but the retail arm would have to be ring-fenced, with specific capital standing behind it, to protect the deposits of retail customers. The British government accepted the report, although the banks have until 2019 to implement the details.

Longer term, the problems of the sector in 2007–8 have prompted a debate about whether the banks are fulfilling their economic function – to channel funds from savers to borrowers. In the wake of the crisis, savers have earned very low returns on bank deposits (indeed, if one allows for inflation, returns have been negative) while small businesses have found it very difficult to get loans.

Banks are being bypassed in three ways. First, more and more companies are turning to the bond market, instead of the banks, to borrow money. That option is not available to small companies but there is talk of creating a securitized market for small-business loans, under which a group of loans will be bundled together and used to back a bond. In some ways, this is good; companies will have access to a wider range of investors. But the risk is the creation of new forms of financial institutions, dubbed shadow banks, which perform some of the roles of the sector but are not regulated as tightly. The more regulators clamp down on the traditional banks, the better the shadow banks will do. That may create the seeds for the next crisis.

Second, there is a fast-growing sector called peer-to-peer lending, through platforms such as Zopa and Lending Club. These platforms link together savers and borrowers; a saver with, say, £2,500 in cash can lend £25 to each of 100 borrowers so as to spread the risk. The saver can earn a higher return than a bank deposit can provide, while the borrower pays a lower rate than the bank would charge. The test for these platforms will come when there is a big wave of defaults and some of them find they lose money; peer-to-peer loans are not covered by deposit insurance.

A third challenge is to the role that banks play in the payment system. No longer are consumers limited to cash, debit and credit cards for payment. Over the internet, they can use PayPal, which is owned by eBay, the auction site, or they can use services on their mobile phones like Square. Ultimately, these services still use the payments mechanism established and maintained by banks; nevertheless, the effect is to reduce bank revenues. Electronic forms of money have also been created; the most famous example is Bitcoin. These are maintained via computer networks, rather than the banks. Media interest in Bitcoin has been high, thanks to some spectacular rises and falls in its price. That turbulence, however, may prevent its widespread use; why spend money if you think it might jump in value the next day? But in the long run, the idea of electronic money that can be used to avoid bank charges and currency conversion costs looks very appealing.

BUILDING SOCIETIES

Building societies face a threat to their long-term survival. In retrospect, the decision of a number of the biggest societies to turn into banks looks like a mistake. All those societies that did so have either gone bust, or been taken over by high-street banks. Those who received 'windfall shares' at the time of flotation may feel it wasn't much of a windfall at all.

For a long time, however, societies were perceived as one of the most consumer-friendly elements of the financial system. They were the repositories of the small savings of millions of people and the providers of finance for the vast majority of home purchases. Few folded because of financial mismanagement.

Over the years, societies have grown closer and closer to banks in any case. In the old days, they talked of surpluses, now they talk of profits. They compete with banks in terms of offering current accounts, cheque books, cashpoint cards, personal loans, foreign exchange, unit trusts and life assurance.

Only in structure are they different. Societies are mutual societies, owned by their members (savers), rather than public companies with shareholders.

ORIGINS

The original building societies were literally that – groups of individuals who subscribed to a common fund so that they could buy or build themselves a house. Once the house or group of houses were built, the societies were folded up.

After a rather shaky period in the late nineteenth century, when a spate of society collapses sapped public confidence in the movement, the building societies established an important place in the financial community.

The scramble for personal savings increased in the 1980s when the Building Societies Association's control over the mortgage and savings rates charged by members gradually weakened. The result was that building societies began to compete more aggressively among themselves for funds, with extra interest accounts offering instant withdrawal without penalty for the saver. Rates will vary depending on the amount of money invested, the notice needed before withdrawals and the frequency of interest payments.

A SHRINKING INDUSTRY

Even before the wave of mergers in the mid-1990s, the industry had experienced a long period of consolidation. The total number of societies fell from 2,286 in 1900 to 273 in 1980 and 45 by 2013. The largest society, Nationwide, had £191 billion of assets in 2013, over five times more than the next biggest, Yorkshire, with £35 billion. The smallest society, City of Derry, had assets of just £46 million.

In some ways, the building society industry was like many others. Economies of scale helped societies reduce costs and that enabled them to offer better rates, pull in more depositors and achieve greater economies of scale.

But greater size brought its own dangers. At the start of the 1980s, building societies were still very small compared with the big banks, but their success encouraged banks to enter the mortgage market. Competition between the banks and the societies became intense and has remained so now that many former societies have converted.

Increased competition in the mortgage market meant that societies had to look elsewhere for profits. In the 1980s, there was a big drive to sell endowment mortgages, loans linked to an insurance policy which would grow sufficiently (in theory) to repay the capital. Endowments earned high commissions for the societies. In the 1990s, endowments became less popular and attention switched to building and contents insurance.

In the savings market, competition has forced societies to abandon some of their long-held customs. In November 1984, the Building Societies Association Council decided to stop recommending specific interest rates to its members, bringing an end to the interest-rate cartel which the societies had practised for so long. The resulting competition has led societies to increase the number of so-called 'premium' accounts which grant savers extra interest if they fulfil certain conditions. They also attacked the banks head on by offering withdrawals from automated teller machines, chequing facilities and home banking; no longer is it the case that banks are for current accounts and building societies for savings accounts.

Conversion into banks created an initial bonanza for building society members and put pressure on other societies to convert. The Nationwide, the largest remaining society, narrowly fought off a call for conversion in the summer of 1998. It subsequently made clear that new investors would not be rewarded in the case of conversion – an attempt to discourage 'carpet-baggers', savers who deposit small sums in a number of institutions in the hope of benefiting from a spate of windfalls. Other societies imposed minimum investment levels to prevent carpet-baggers cashing in.

Enthusiasts for the sector still hope that it can survive. Traditional building societies are mutual organizations, that is they are owned by their savers and borrowers rather than shareholders. That has some advantages to the savers and borrowers. Instead of paying out profits to shareholders, the profits can be used to increase (or for borrowers, reduce) the societies' interest rates.

There are some hopeful signs for building society fans; the Northern Rock debacle may make the building society structure look more attractive. If societies can pay rigorous attention to the interests of their members by keeping down their costs, offering competitive rates to savers and borrowers and refusing to sell unsuitable add-on policies just because it earns them commission, then there should be a place for them in the twenty-first-century financial system.

THE MORTGAGE BUSINESS

As noted in the Introduction, building societies perform a piece of financial magic by turning customers' deposits, which can be withdrawn at any time, into home loans, extending up to thirty-five years. To guard against sudden shortfalls in deposits, they also have limited investments in safe short-term instruments like short-dated gilts. For much of the twentieth century, the business of building societies was extremely sound because of the credit record of its borrowers. Most people made every effort they could to keep up the payments on their mortgage; and since inflation tended to erode the value of the debt, it was relatively easy for them to do so.

But the 1980s and the early 2000s saw house price bubbles. The profits made by some people from their properties drew more and more people into the housing market. Competition from other lenders caused build-ing societies to lower their credit requirements; some people were allowed to buy homes on 100 per cent loans, that is without putting up a deposit, and were lent large sums in proportion to their incomes. (Incredibly, a few were allowed to borrow more than the value of their house.)

All this activity was built on the assumption that house prices would rise for ever. But one bubble eventually burst in the early 1990s, and the same process seemed to repeat in early 2008. Eventually, prices rise (or interest rates go up) so far that first-time buyers are shut out of the market. As the prospect of easy profits vanishes, speculators also lose heart. And the banks and building societies also become more cautious about lending. As house prices fall, many mortgages become worth more than the homes they are secured on – a state known as 'negative equity' (see Chapter 15).

Negative equity faces lenders with a tricky dilemma. Once borrowers default on their interest payments, societies have the right to reclaim the asset, i.e. the house. But selling the house would not provide enough cash to pay off the loan. Furthermore, the more homes the societies repossess, the more empty homes there are on the property market, depressing house prices and giving an extra twist to the downward spiral.

THE MORTGAGE RATE

The mortgage rate goes up or down with the general level of rates in the economy. The building societies cannot stay separate from the other financial institutions, since they must compete with them for depositors and they must sometimes borrow from them. As the cost of raising their funds rises and falls, so must the mortgage rate. In general, however, the mortgage rate is slower both to rise and to fall than bank rates.

As interest rates rise and fall, societies switch their concern between savers and borrowers. In 1990, when base rates were 15 per cent, the typical mortgage rate was just a fraction above that level, at 15.4 per cent. Societies were holding down the rate to prevent any more pain being inflicted on homeowners. In late 2001, when the Bank of England cut rates to 4 per cent, many building societies were charging 5.5 per cent, a margin of 1.5 percentage points. The societies had switched their concern from borrowers to savers.

A big change in the 1990s came with the development of fixed-rate mortgages. These promise borrowers a set rate for several years at a time, allowing them to plan their budgets and avoid the danger of a sudden jump in rates. The catch is that borrowers do not benefit if rates fall and, if they try to repay the loan ahead of time, they face heavy redemption penalties.

Building societies fund fixed-rate deals by borrowing in the wholesale markets. The problem that emerged in 2008 was that wholesale markets were either closed to new borrowing, or extremely expensive to access. The result was that homebuyers seeking fixed-rate mortgages found that loans were either withdrawn from the market or became a lot more expensive. That did not help a housing market that was already struggling.

By early 2014, the housing market was booming again, particularly in London. The introduction of a government 'help to buy' scheme had proved controversial. The government's aim was to help first-time buyers get a foot on the housing ladder; with an average house price of £172,000, few could afford a 20 per cent deposit (£34,400). But the policy seemed to encourage a return to the bad old days of lending people more money than they could afford. The best answer would be to build more houses and flats so as to bring prices in line with demand, but thanks to planning rules, that was proving very difficult.

Most people have a pretty clear idea of what retail banks do: take deposits and make loans. But the public understanding of investment banking is far less developed. Perhaps the first time they really hit the headlines was in the crisis of 2008, when in effect, independent investment banks disappeared. Three of the leading five banks in the US lost their independence (or went bust) within six months; the other two (Morgan Stanley and Goldman Sachs) applied for commercial banking status.

But while the banks may have vanished or mutated, the business of investment banking goes on. In Britain, the sector used to be known as merchant banking; investment banking was the American term. Investment banking is only part of the activities of the likes of Merrill Lynch and Goldman Sachs, which are also known as broker-dealers, and larger banking groups such as Citigroup or Union Bank of Switzerland have their own investment banking arms.

The key change of the last twenty to thirty years has been that investment banks no longer depend on fee income for the bulk of their profits. Now they put their capital at risk through trading and underwriting. This has hugely increased their importance and, as we saw with Bear Stearns and Lehman Brothers in 2008, the risk posed both to their own financial health and to the system.

Broadly speaking, the investment banks earn their money from four areas: advising clients on everything from takeovers to how to handle currency risk; broking (connecting buyers and sellers in return for a fee); trading in the markets; and asset management (looking after other people's money).

The roots of the industry grew out of trade. Before the development of a worldwide banking system, much international trade depended on trust – trust that goods would be delivered and that they would be paid for. It was much easier for overseas clients to trust merchants with whom they had traded before or those with whom their friends had traded. Thus, the larger and more well-established merchants found it easier to trade than their smaller and less familiar competitors.

The smaller firms needed some way both of assuring their clients that they were trustworthy, and of raising money to cover the interval between the time goods were delivered and the time they were paid for. The normal method for raising finance in this period was for the exporter to draw up a bill of exchange, whose value was a large proportion of the value of the goods being sold. The exporter could then sell the bill to a local banker at a discount and receive a substantial proportion of the money in advance. The extent of the bank's discount would represent two elements: a charge equivalent to interest on what was effectively a loan, and a charge reflecting the risk of non-payment.

Small exporters found the banks would often charge a very large discount to advance money on their bills, if they agreed to do so at all. So the smaller merchants began to ask their larger brethren to guarantee (or accept) their bills. In the event that the small merchant failed to pay up, the large merchant would be liable. In return for the service, the large merchants charged an acceptance commission, based on a percentage of the size of the bill.

Eventually, some of these large merchants found that they could earn more money from their finance activities than from their trading and became full-time merchant banks or accepting houses. For a long time, their business was centred around the financing of trade but gradually, as they developed a reputation for financial acumen, they increased the corporate finance side of their activities.

Many merchant banks were begun by immigrants, refugees or Jews, shut out of the rather stuffy world of the clearing banks. The wheeling and dealing involved appealed to the more adventurous spirits. However, the business was so lucrative that the merchant banks became absorbed into the mainstream establishment.

From the 1950s onwards, merchant or investment banks used their financial expertise to help their corporate clients, advising on share issues, bond issues and takeovers. For this, they were rewarded with fee income, a very good business in boom times. Unlike their commercial banking rivals, they had no need to maintain a vast branch network. Their fixed costs were low; their profits-per-employee high.

But, as we saw in Chapter 1, the international financial markets changed in the 1980s. Large companies no longer needed advice alone; they needed banking advisers who could commit capital to deals. The clients wanted the assurance that, if things went wrong, the investment bank could ensure that the money was still raised.

That spelled the end for the old British-style merchant bank, which was often a private business, run by a small group of partners. It also meant that, having raised large amounts of capital, investment banks started to move into new areas. They used their expertise to deal on their own behalf, through proprietary trading desks. They sold their expertise to clients as asset managers. They dreamed up exotic new products, particularly in the derivatives markets, and sold them round the world. They lent money to favoured clients such as hedge funds and private equity groups (see Chapter 9).

Broadly speaking, the activities of investment banks can be divided into three: front office, middle office and back office. The front office deals with clients or counterparties. This includes the traditional investment bankers, who advise companies on takeovers or new issues of debt and equities. Then there are the traders, who buy and sell shares in the market, and the research department, which advises investors (dubbed the 'buy side', with investment bankers as the 'sell side') on which shares or bonds to buy.

Those who work for this last group are the strategists and analysts you might see quoted on the ten o'clock news, opining about the economy, or hear on the BBC *Today* programme talking about the prospects for Tesco or BP. Top-rated analysts have a lot of influence on the markets, and their buy and sell recommendations can move prices significantly. They try to forecast the level of profits for companies over the next quarter or year, based on their analysis of the industry and on talking to the companies concerned. If investors find their research useful, they reward the banks by placing their buy and sell orders through the bank's dealing department. But this is a tricky issue. Many investors are acting on behalf of others (pension fund members or mutual fund holders, for example). When they deal in shares and bonds, they should surely have an obligation to get the best price. If they want to pay for research, that should be a separate and open transaction.

The middle office of a bank has functions that tend not to deal with the outside world: risk management, treasury and compliance, for example. In a sense, this part of the bank acts as the parent, or the conscience, of the front office. It makes sure that the bank has enough money to meet its needs, that the bank is not exposed to a sudden collapse in the markets and that the traders or analysts are not involved in any questionable activities. This can lead to conflict; traders may feel that the risk management team is stopping them from making money. As 2006 and 2007 shows, the greatest danger appears at the end of a long period when the traders have been doing well; the risk managers can be overruled because the bank's top brass want the trading profits to keep rolling in.

Finally, the back office handles the plumbing of the system. It makes sure the technology keeps working and that the deals made are cleared or settled in the markets; that the right amount of money comes in one door and goes out the other. This is the least glamorous part of banking but if it goes wrong, the whole operation can unravel.

While the functions of an investment bank can be divided into front, middle and back office, this is not usually how a bank is formally constructed. The divisions tend to be based on products – FICC, which deals with trading in fixed income, currencies and commodities, for example, or DCM (debt capital markets), which advises on bond issues and loans.

The expansion of investment banking has been hugely lucrative. But it has also brought such banks to the heart of the global financial system. It was significant in March 2008 that the US Federal Reserve felt obliged to help with the rescue of Bear Stearns, an investment bank. The bank had no retail depositors. There would have been no queues of worried consumers, as there were at the British bank Northern Rock. Nevertheless, Bear Stearns was deemed too big to fail (TBTF in the jargon), or even TCTF (too complex to fail).

Bear Stearns was a participant in a multitude of complex deals, in which investors and companies took positions on everything from exchange-rate movements through commodity prices to the possibility of corporate failure. Had it defaulted, it could have taken ages to sort out the mess because markets are so interconnected. Some banks might, for example, have taken a position betting on a rising dollar with Bear Stearns and then hedged that by betting on a falling dollar with someone else. The failure of Bear Stearns would thus have given such banks a currency exposure they did not desire. While everyone involved tried to work out their exposure, the markets could have been frozen.

When the US authorities changed tack in September 2008 and allowed Lehman Brothers to fail over a weekend, the consequences were immediate. Merrill Lynch decided not to take the risk of depending on market support and opted for a takeover by Bank of America. A lack of investor confidence caused AIG, a huge insurance company, to have trouble raising capital, sending it into the arms of the US government. The cost of borrowing money in the banking sector soared, and share prices of the remaining investment banks came under attack. The US Treasury was forced to dream up a $700 billion bailout plan to buy the mortgage-related assets that were undermining bank balance sheets. For a few weeks the financial markets seemed to freeze completely.

In short, the huge change in the international financial markets, which has allowed capital to flow freely across borders, made investment banks just as important as commercial banks. Indeed, investment bankers often make the system tick by acting as market markers; they offer to buy or sell shares and bonds at a given price in the market.

In theory, market markers can make money through the spread – by buying shares or bonds at a lower price than they sell them. But in an electronic market with thousands of players, it can be quite difficult to make a lot of money this way. So they end up betting on trends in the markets – trends that can go wrong.

The risks were increased by the high level of leverage (use of borrowed money) employed by the banks. They used gearing ratios of 25 or 33 to 1, meaning their assets were many times their core capital. In such circumstances, a fall of 3 or 4 per cent in asset prices could wipe them out. Of course, the investment banks employed highly sophisticated models (devised by PhDs in maths and physics) to monitor those risks. But either these models were flawed or the risk managers were simply overwhelmed by the power of the traders, who could point to the short-term profits they were generating.

Top traders can take home earnings (including their bonuses) that easily stretch into six figures and often top a million. If not properly monitored, however, their activities can endanger the health of the bank, as Barings found with Nick Leeson and the French bank Société Générale found with Jérôme Kerviel. Derivative instruments, such as futures and options, can be difficult to understand and can behave in unpredictable ways. It can be easier to disguise losses for long periods.

Even when traders are not careless or fraudulent, they can just be wrong. When markets fall sharply, banks often face losses from their proprietary trading activities. Even the more standard activities of arranging new issues and takeovers can be highly volatile; when markets are in the doldrums, few companies use the stock market to raise capital and few bids are announced. Market downturns in the early 1990s or in 2000–2002 caused a number of banks to announce write-offs to profits.

But in the good years, the best investment banks earned very high returns on capital. It is rather like the film business. A lot of films lose money and it costs a fortune to hire a Hollywood star; but get the right picture (such as *Titanic*) and the profits are huge.

In particular, the returns on capital can be very high. That explains why investment bankers can earn enormous amounts, in return of course for working very long hours. The annual bonus round is the most important time in an investment banker's year. A big payment may mean a new house, or financial independence. But this is a relative, as well as an absolute, contest. Bonuses are supposed to be private but the best rewarded can rarely avoid boasting about their gains. And nothing spoils the pleasure of a £250,000 bonus more than knowing your colleague got £500,000.

It is a tricky decision for an employer. Make the bonus too small and the employee will leave in disgust. Make it too large and he may leave anyway, because he has already lined up another job on the quiet. In addition, it may well be that the employee's success is down to luck, not skill, particularly if he is a trader. When traders lose money, they may get fired but don't have to pay past bonuses back. That creates skewed incentives.

The demise of Bear Stearns and Lehman Brothers illustrated the problems. It was not that the bankers didn't suffer; a lot of them had their wealth tied up in company shares, which were virtually wiped out. But the bonus culture may have encouraged them to dream up complicated instruments like derivatives that earned high fees in the short term but were very dangerous to the health of the banks in the medium term.

Their key weakness proved, like Northern Rock (see Chapter 3), to be their dependence on the wholesale markets for capital. The markets proved to be ruthless in withdrawing their money from faltering institutions. That forced them into the arms of the big commercial banks, which had more stable sources of funds from retail depositors.

The irony is that, after the crash of 1929, regulators decided it was too risky to let investment and commercial banks be part of the same group. The Glass–Steagall Act of 1933 separated the two, so that the funds of ordinary Americans would not be put at risk. The response to the 2007–8 crisis has been to push the two together again.

One further point is worth exploring. The biggest investment banks are all-singing, all-dancing institutions which play almost every role in the financial system. For example, many have fund management arms, which manage money on behalf of small pension funds or charities, or the savings of private investors, via unit and investment trusts.

The banks also have their own teams of investment analysts who pore through the accounts of companies listed on the market and make recommendations about which shares are attractive or overvalued.

This raises a number of conflicts of interest. Suppose a corporate finance team is arranging a takeover for a client, which involves that company using its own shares. What if the analyst covering the company thinks the shares are overvalued? That would send out a bad message to the market. But if the analyst changes his view and starts singing the praises of the shares, his clients are entitled to be cynical. And what if the bank's fund management arm buys shares? Is it doing so because of a dispassionate analysis of the company's merits or because the purchase will help the deal go through?

This issue came to the fore during the dotcom boom of the late 1990s when analysts touted the attractions of companies which had never made a profit and had little even in the way of revenues.

It became clear that analysts were far from unbiased and were motivated by the need to 'do deals' – to persuade companies to hire the analyst's bank as managers for the company's flotation. The more optimistic the analysts were prepared to be, the more likely it became that his or her bank would get the deal.

Analysts face a further problem. Companies do not like to hear that their shares are overvalued, any more than actors or writers like to receive a bad review. Analysts who tell their investment clients that they should sell a company's shares may find that the company's management refuses to speak to them. That can be a real problem for an analyst seeking to prepare an in-depth report on a company's finances.

The net result of all these pressures is that analysts make very few sell recommendations – according to one survey, buy recommendations exceed sells by 9–1. Many of the big institutional investors now employ their own analysts to get round this problem of biased advice.

Other conflicts of interest emerged in the wake of the 2008 crisis. The borrowing costs of many companies were set with reference to LIBOR, or the London Interbank Offered Rate. This was supposed to be the rate that banks paid to borrow in the markets; their corporate customers paid a margin over this. On the surface, the system seemed transparent. A panel of banks submitted their numbers for LIBOR to Thomson Reuters, an information group, every day; the extreme estimates were thrown out, and the remaining estimates averaged to arrive at the quoted number.

In fact, it turned out that these numbers were often estimates, rather than records of actual loans. And investigations revealed that banks colluded to manipulate the rates they submitted; in some cases, this was to reduce their borrowing costs so as to make them look less risky, in other cases it was to make profits from trading in the market. The scandal seemed to centre on those universal banks that had both commercial and investment banking arms. Later on, there were allegations that prices were rigged in both the foreign exchange and the gold markets.

This did suggest that there was an inherent problem with the new investment banking model. When investment banks were just giving advice, they had every incentive to do the right thing by clients; otherwise their reputations would suffer. But to a bank that is taking a position in the markets, clients may look like easy meat. Economists talked of 'information asymmetry' in which banks, equipped with complex models and knowledge about order flows, dealt with customers who were much less well informed.

The future of investment banking is open to question after the events of 2008. Niche advisory groups, dubbed boutiques, have emerged in reaction to the sheer size, and embedded conflicts of interest, of the big investment banks. But the big battalions are not going away. The best-known investment bank, Goldman Sachs, remains highly controversial; *Rolling Stone* magazine described it as a 'giant vampire squid' in a hard-hitting article. In 2010, the group had to pay a $550 million fine to the US regulator relating to some of its activities in the subprime mortgage market. Nevertheless, the group is generally perceived to be highly professional, employing some of the brightest people of their generation. Its alumni have moved into positions of power, including two (Robert Rubin and Hank Paulson) who became Treasury secretary in the US and another (Jim Corzine) who was both governor of New Jersey and a senator.

For many, investment banks are the unacceptable face of the finance sector. They pay the highest bonuses and operate in fields that can be dubbed 'casino capitalism'. By the same token, however, they are a very important part of London's finance sector; the willingness of Goldman Sachs, Morgan Stanley and others to base themselves in the City gives the financial centre critical mass. Without the investment banks, London would have a smaller share of the business of bond and loan issuance; that would mean less work for British lawyers and accountants, and a smaller tax take for the UK Treasury. But what we have learned from the crisis of 2007 and 2008 is that investment banks are just as important as commercial banks to the health of the financial system. They are at the heart of the markets, involved with deals with big companies, governments, pension funds and charities. When they fail, confidence in the system fails. And that is disastrous for the economy.

5   The Bank of England

The Bank of England has been, for three centuries, the centrepiece of the British financial system, an institution which in the past has been able to influence the markets with a twitch of its governor's eyebrow. Today, having been given effective independence on monetary policy, the Bank is more important than ever.

The Bank was founded back in 1694, when King William III needed money to fight Louis XIV of France. A Scottish merchant, William Paterson, suggested that a bank should be formed which could lend money to the government. Within fifteen years, the Old Lady of Threadneedle Street, as it became known, was given the monopoly of joint-stock banking in England and Wales. That ensured that it remained the biggest bank in the country since those banks which were *not* joint-stock could by law have no more than six partners, severely limiting their ability to expand. However, that monopoly was eroded by Acts in 1826 and 1833 and the Bank's pre-eminent position was not really cemented until the Bank Charter Act of 1844. The Act followed a succession of banking failures, which was blamed on the overissue of banknotes. Until 1844, any bank had the right to issue its own notes, opening up the risk not only of fraud but also of inflation. The Bank Charter Act restricted the rights of banks other than the Bank of England to issue notes, a restriction which became total (in England and Wales) in 1921. Scottish banks can still print notes.

By that time, the Bank's position as one of the country's most prestigious institutions had been established and the interwar governor, Montagu Norman, was one of the most influential men of his age. Such was the power of the Old Lady that the Attlee government thought it right to nationalize it in 1946.

The election of the Labour government in May 1997 ushered in a new phase in the Bank's history. One of the first acts of the Chancellor, Gordon Brown, was to give the Bank the power to set interest rates. Now every month, traders wait anxiously to see what the Bank has decided.

Gordon Brown's decision owed a lot to the rather unhappy history of UK economic policy during the war. Britain suffered from a much higher rate of inflation than many of its competitors and the pound endured a seemingly relentless decline (see Chapter 14).

Many people felt that one reason for the country's poor performance was the control that politicians exercised over interest rates. When inflation started to pick up, politicians proved reluctant to raise rates, especially if a general election was in sight, because of the unpopularity with the voters that would result.

In theory, a central bank consisting of 'dispassionate' professionals who did not have to face the electorate would not face the same pressures. Economists noted that independent central banks in the US (the Federal Reserve) and Germany (the Bundesbank) had been much more successful in controlling inflation.

For a time, under the Conservative government of 1992–7, a hybrid system was in place in which the Chancellor met the Bank of England governor every month and the former then made a rate decision, based on the latter's advice. Although the minutes of the meetings were published in a bid to create transparency, the system was not entirely successful; when the governor proposed rate increases in the run-up to the 1997 election, the then Chancellor Kenneth Clarke turned him down.

The new system leaves rates to be set by a monetary policy committee, which meets monthly, chaired by the governor. The current occupant, Mark Carney, was recruited at great expense from Canada, where he had been governor of its central bank. The decision resembled the appointment of a foreign manager to run England's football team.

But the Bank's new interest-rate powers were offset by a substantial loss of influence elsewhere. Supervision of the banking sector was transferred to the Financial Services Authority (FSA), which has subsequently been replaced by the Financial Conduct Authority (see Chapter 16). Rather awkwardly, while the FCA watches over individual banks, the Bank of England still has responsibility for what is called 'macroprudential policy', making sure the whole system does not collapse. This it does through a new arm called the financial policy committee, which has 'a primary objective of identifying, monitoring and taking action to remove or reduce systemic risks with a view to protecting and enhancing the resilience of the UK financial system'.

Giving the Bank ultimate responsibility for the financial system makes some sense. When collapse threatens, only a central bank has the resources to provide unlimited credit (at least in the short term). That lesson was made clear in 2008. The Bank is the lender of last resort for the banking system in times of crisis. But the crisis also made it clear that the division of authority between the Bank and the FSA could lead to a loss of clarity. Having two committees, the monetary policy committee and the financial policy committee, also creates scope for confusion; what if the latter wanted to raise interest rates to stop speculation in the banks, but the former resisted a rate rise because of a weak economy?

How does the bank exercise its power? It has two main tools: the level of interest rates (the price of money) and the size of its balance sheet (the quantity of money). Each month, the monetary policy committee meets to decide the bank rate. This rate is important because of the Bank's role as the lender of last resort – it is the rate it will charge banks that need loans. In effect, it sets the floor for rates in the markets.

At the time of writing, however, the bank rate had not been changed in more than five years. In the wake of the financial crisis, the rate was cut to 0.5 per cent, far lower than it had been at any previous stage in the Bank's history. With consumers and borrowers reluctant to borrow, and with many burdened by debts taken out before the crisis, the Bank wanted the cost of debt service to be as low as possible.

This has been a controversial policy. Low rates for borrowers also mean low returns for savers, many of whom are elderly people relying on income from banks and building societies to keep them going. But the Bank's argument was that higher rates would force the economy into a deep recession.

Indeed, the Bank followed up low interest rates with an even more controversial policy known as quantitative easing (QE). This involved the creation of new money to buy assets, primarily government bonds. No extra money was printed; the whole process was electronic. When the Bank bought bonds, it credited the bank accounts of the seller with new money. The result was a bigger balance sheet for the Bank of England; it owned assets in the form of bonds and had liabilities in the form of new reserves, held by the commercial banks.

The aim of QE was twofold. First, the Bank wanted to stop the money supply from shrinking. When that happened in the US in the 1930s, the result was the Great Depression. If there is less money to go around, there is less for consumers to spend and thus lower revenues for companies, which can in turn afford to employ fewer workers. Second, by buying bonds, the Bank hoped to drive down the cost of long-term borrowing. Many companies issue bonds and these tend to have an interest rate that is slightly higher than that paid by the government; lower government bond yields tend to mean lower corporate borrowing costs.

QE was controversial because it seemed to smack of the policies followed by the Weimar Republic in the 1920s, when the central bank printed money to pay the government's bills and hyperinflation resulted. The Bank was very adamant that this would not be the case; it would still keep inflation under control. However, inflation was consistently above target for the first four years of QE, reaching as high as 5 per cent, and the Bank did nothing.

At the time of writing, the Bank owned £375 billion of government bonds (or gilts) as a result of the QE programme. In 2013, it agreed to hand back the interest on those gilts to the Treasury, which used the money to pay down the deficit. And in 2014, Mark Carney indicated that the Bank was unlikely to sell all those bonds any time soon; it would have a much bigger balance sheet for the foreseeable future. So, in effect, the Bank had given the government a long-term interest-free loan. The difference between such an arrangement and monetization of the debt is hard to spot.

So why hasn't QE led to the kind of hyperinflation seen in the 1920s? The main reason is that the central bank is not the main creator of money; that is the commercial banking system. As noted in the last chapter, commercial banks create money when they make loans (expand their balance sheet). Since 2008, banks have been reluctant to make loans, i.e. they have been shrinking their balance sheets. This has tended to shrink the money supply. So while the Bank of England has turned on the monetary taps, the commercial banks have pulled out the plug; the two effects have balanced each other out.

Still, there are some tricky issues ahead. By mid-2013, the UK economy was showing signs of recovery. That led to speculation that the Bank might have to start to tighten monetary policy by raising rates. In response, Mark Carney instituted a programme of 'forward guidance', letting the market know that rates would stay low. But by mid-2014, the Bank had reversed itself, indicating that rates would rise more quickly than the markets expected.

As a result, the Bank's procedure for setting monetary policy looks a bit more confused than before. In theory, this is how it works. The committee consists of nine people, five from within the Bank and four from outside (usually academic economists). It meets, normally on the second Wednesday and Thursday of each month, and announces its decision at noon on the second day. The minutes of the meeting are published two weeks later, with details of how each member voted. Every quarter, the Bank publishes an inflation report, which reviews the progress made in combating inflation and forecasts the likely level of inflation over the next two years. And the Bank goes to Parliament on a regular basis to explain its actions to MPs.

The initial target set by the Chancellor for the Bank was to keep the inflation rate at 2.5 per cent. This was not the retail prices index that had been the traditional measure of inflation for decades but the 'underlying' rate, which excluded mortgage interest payments. This may seem a bit of a fiddle; most of us have mortgages and thus a rise in the interest rate reflects an increase in our cost of living. But if the Bank had included mortgage payments, it would have faced a paradox. Every time it increased rates to target inflation, the effect would have been to push up the headline rate. By stripping out mortgages, it could have a clearer picture of what was going on in the underlying economy. In 2003, the Bank was asked to target a different measure, the harmonized index of consumer prices (HICP), which has since been renamed the consumer price index (CPI). The new measure excluded other housing costs such as buildings insurance and council tax and generally ran at a lower rate than the old measure. As a result, the Bank was asked to aim for 2 per cent rather than 2.5 per cent.

As before, the governor is required to send a letter of explanation should the rate deviate by more than 1 percentage point on either side of the target. The aim is to avoid either excessive inflation or deflation, a state of falling prices which is normally associated with economic contraction.

The Bank has actually been pretty poor at forecasting inflation, and it is not hard to feel that, since 2009, it has focused more on avoiding recession. However, there has been no sign that the British government is unhappy about this policy, and other central banks, notably the Federal Reserve in the US, have followed a similar path.

Nevertheless, there are lots of question marks. Can forward guidance be convincing, given that the Bank has already reversed policy, and given that membership of the monetary policy committee is subject to regular change? Can one committee bind its successors? If it can, what is the point of the monthly meetings? And if it can't, why should the markets rely on forward guidance?

The Bank now has enormous power. Its QE programme has pushed up the stock market because investors in low-yielding bonds have bought equities in search of higher returns. Since equities tend to be owned by the better-off, this has boosted the income of the rich, while the low-rate policy has penalized small savers. In effect, an unelected body is redistributing income.

Another issue is the housing market. Low rates have seen a revival of house prices and, by 2014, an enormous boom in London. To give an idea of its scale, London house prices have averaged around five times the income of a first-time buyer, according to the Nationwide building society. In 2007, when the market was peaking, this ratio reached 7.2; although house prices fell, this ratio never fell back to its long-term average. By 2014, it was at a new record of 8. Raising interest rates to deal with this issue might damage the rest of the economy. So what about macro-prudential policy? The Bank of England could insist that banks be more cautious about making loans. In July 2014, the Bank took a tiny step in this direction by limiting the amount of loans that banks could make at a multiple of 4.5 times the buyer's income. But banks were below the limit, so the policy had no immediate bite. And it is hard to see why banks should make *any* loans of that size; they sound very risky.

What checks are there on the Bank's power? In theory, the government could dismiss the governor of the Bank of England, but it is hard to see that happening since the government went to great pains to recruit Mr Carney and the Bank's purchases of bonds have been so useful. Arguably, Mr Carney is far more powerful than any politician.

BANKNOTES

As well as its responsibility for monetary policy, the Bank still retains one of its oldest jobs; looking after banknotes. The Bank decides which denominations to issue and whose face goes on the reverse of the notes (the monarch is on the front). That led to some controversy in 2013, when the Bank announced that prison reformer Elizabeth Fry was being removed from the £5 note in favour of Winston Churchill. As a result, all the historical figures on notes would be male. After a campaign on social media, it was announced that, as of 2017, Jane Austen would replace Charles Darwin on the £10 note.

Another important aspect of banknote design is the prevention of counterfeiting. Over the years, a number of features have been added to notes, including a watermark, metallic thread and holographic image. The next stage will be to move from paper notes to polymer or plastic notes, starting in 2016 with the fiver. The Bank says the polymer notes are more durable and harder to counterfeit, although they may have a tendency to stick together when new. No doubt people will grumble when the new notes appear, but twenty-five countries already use them.

6   The Money Markets

The primary aim of most financial institutions is quite simple. They need to borrow money more cheaply than they can lend it. The most obvious illustration of this principle is the commercial banks. They bring in billions of pounds from customers putting money into their current accounts; those accounts usually pay a token amount of interest but the money can be withdrawn at any moment. They lend out such funds at market rates of interest. Because depositors can demand their money immediately, the banks want to keep a substantial proportion of their money in liquid form. This they do by lending it to other financial institutions in the so-called money markets.

Banks can also find themselves short of the cash needed to meet their obligations and thus have to *borrow* in the money markets. The markets are therefore one of the main channels through which banks can iron out day-to-day fluctuations in their cashflow. For the investment banks, the money markets are a very important source of funds since they do not possess the customer deposits of the clearing banks. To distinguish them from the retail markets, the money markets are often known as the *wholesale markets* and the deposits or bills involved are usually denominated in large amounts. A typical deal might involve a loan of tens of millions of pounds.

Investors in the markets tend to be anyone with short-term funds – banks, companies and fund management companies. Retail investors can get involved via money market funds – unit trusts which offer returns that are competitive with bank and building society accounts. This is a huge business which normally works very well, but broke down spectacularly in the summer of 2007.

Transactions in the money markets were traditionally in the form of either deposits or bills, although nowadays money is lent and borrowed in a wide range of ways. Deposits are made (with the exception of money-at-call) for set periods of time at an agreed rate of interest. Bills are pieces of paper which are issued at a discount to their face value. The bills can then be traded by their holders after issue.

The practice of discounting bills was the main activity of a group of institutions called the discount houses. The discount houses were for a long time the main link between the Bank of England and the money markets.

THE MONEY MARKETS

What instruments are traded in the money markets? Much trading is in short-term bank deposits. Interest rates were quoted as the spread between the bid and offer rates. The bid rate is the rate which a bank is prepared to pay to borrow funds; the offer rate is the rate at which it is prepared to lend. As mentioned in Chapter 4, the average of the offer rates, the London Interbank Offered Rate (LIBOR), is an important benchmark for other loans, although its reputation has been severely damaged by the fact that it was manipulated in 2008. Responsibility for the benchmark has moved from the British Bankers' Association to NYSE Euronext, a stock exchange group, and the system has been simplified. The hope is that LIBOR will still be used as the benchmark for corporate borrowing. Companies will normally pay a spread over LIBOR, depending on how risky the lender feels them to be.

In this huge market, currencies are borrowed for a whole range of maturities from overnight to one year and beyond; rates for the major currencies are quoted every day on the currencies and money page of the *Financial Times*. With the growth in the size and depth of the market, many billions of dollars can be moved between banks in anticipation of tiny changes in rates.

Another important instrument is the Treasury bill, although its importance varies with the government's financing needs. Treasury bills are a vital component of the market, being highly secure. The government is not likely to default and inflation will not erode the value of a bill that matures in weeks or months. Such was the appeal of US Treasury bills during the 2008 crisis that they occasionally offered negative interest rates; i.e. investors were prepared to suffer a small loss for holding them.

Treasury bills and other government debt are also used as the basis for the repurchase or repo market, which is a huge component of the money markets. One party sells the bonds or bills to another, in return for cash, with the promise to buy those securities back at a higher price after a set period; this price difference is the equivalent of interest. The bonds or bills act as collateral for the lender. This is a huge market; it is estimated that every day, some $1.6 trillion of repos are arranged in the market.

Central banks have also played a huge part in the financial market since the crisis. If a commercial bank runs short of money, even overnight, it risks going bankrupt, with potentially huge effects on the rest of the economy via frozen payments and lost confidence. Central banks accordingly stand ready to lend money to commercial banks when they need it, at extremely cheap rates. The European Central Bank lends money for up to three years via its long-term refinancing operations (LTRO).

Commercial bills are also an important part of the money market. In the old days, commercial bills could refer to a particular transaction. When a supplier sold a customer some goods, he might be paid in the form of an IOU. This 'promise to pay' could be traded for cash upfront. Nowadays, however, commercial bills are just the equivalent of Treasury bills, short-term corporate debt.

As well as commercial bills, many companies borrow money in the form of commercial paper. Commercial paper facilities can extend to the hundreds of millions of pounds and are used by companies to fund their short-term financing needs, such as acquisitions.

In addition to Treasury and commercial bills, another widely used instrument in the money markets is the certificate of deposit. The simplest definition of a certificate of deposit (CD) is that it is a tradeable document attesting that the holder has lent money to a bank or building society.

CDs are a highly important form of investment in the money markets. If an investor puts his or her money into a term loan, it cannot be withdrawn until the loan matures. A CD, however, can be sold by an investor if the funds are needed suddenly. They are dealt with on an interest-accrued basis (i.e. the money that the CD would have earned is added to the CD's face value). However, the rate which the investor will effectively have earned will depend on the way that interest rates have moved since the CD was purchased.

For example, an investor buys a three-month CD for £100,000 at an interest rate of 10 per cent. If the CD is held until maturity, the bank would repay the investor £102,500. That sum will be repaid to whoever holds the CD when it matures. After a month, the investor decides to sell the CD. Its price will not necessarily be one-third of the way between £100,000 and £102,500 (i.e. £100,833); it will be so only if interest rates have stabilized and if investors expect interest rates to stay at 10 per cent. If rates have dropped (or are expected to drop), the price will be more than £100,833 because it will be more attractive to other investors. If rates have risen (or are expected to rise), then the price will be less than £100,833 because investors will be able to get more attractive interest rates elsewhere. In either case, the price will settle at the level where it is equivalent to other prevailing market rates.

In return for receiving the extra liquidity that the CD provides, investors are ready to accept a slightly lower interest rate than on the equivalent term deposit. Borrowers (which are mostly banks) get the benefit of the slightly lower interest rate and are still guaranteed that the money will not have to be repaid until the CD matures.

CDs may be issued for periods up to five years and are normally issued in amounts ranging from £50,000 to £500,000. In the UK, the size of an individual certificate is at least £10,000. In the US, however, they have been issued in smaller denominations in order to attract individual investors.

Another component of the money markets are gilt-edged securities near the end of their life. Since the gilts are about to be repaid, they start to resemble the other instruments prevailing in the markets.

All these instruments share a feature noted in the Introduction to this book – their price changes when interest rates move. If short-term interest rates fall, then CDs, etc., which pay a higher rate, will be more valuable and will rise in price. If interest rates rise, then the price of previously issued instruments will fall. Conversely, those who invest in the money markets tend to hope for interest rates to fall, since they then make a capital gain on their investments.

Not all instruments in the money market are tradeable. Local authority loans form one of the oldest sectors of the money markets. Lending money to local authorities is a steady and unspectacular business but the 1980s storms over rate-capping highlighted the fact that local authorities look to the City for funds.

THE PLAYERS IN THE MARKETS

The bulk of the activity in the markets consists of banks borrowing and lending to and from each other, sometimes with the assistance of a broker. Most of the loans have maturities of three months or less.

Much of this trading takes place electronically or via the telephone. Each trader will be seeking to manage the bank's money for profit. He or she will attempt to do so in one of two ways. As in the foreign-exchange markets (see Chapter 14), dealers charge a spread between rates. They will lend at a slightly higher rate than the rate at which they will borrow. The spread may be as small as a few hundredths of a percentage point. Because of the size of the deals involved, the cumulative effect of spreads can add up to a sizeable profit.

However, the dealer cannot rely on the spread alone. Interest rates are constantly fluctuating. This can wipe out the dealer's spread. For example, a dealer may agree to lend at 8.04 per cent and borrow at 8 per cent. He accordingly lends money at 8.04 per cent. While he is making the deal, the market moves to a spread of 8.06–8.10 per cent. If the dealer now borrows the money the bank needs to cover the loan, he or she will have to pay 8.06 per cent, 0.02 per cent more than the bank is receiving, even allowing for the spread.

The second way that money market dealers make money, therefore, is by trying to anticipate these moves in rates. If they expect rates to rise, they will borrow more than they lend (in market parlance, 'go short'). If they expect rates to fall, they will lend more than they borrow ('go long'). So in the above example, the dealer went long at the wrong time – when markets were rising. Had he or she gone short and borrowed at 8 per cent, then when rates rose the dealer could have lent the bank's money at the new higher rate.

MONEY BROKERS

Linking the activities of the money market dealers are the money brokers. They wheel and deal on the telephone, linking lenders and borrowers in return for a commission. Unlike the dealers, they do not lend and borrow themselves. They depend on high turnover to make money. Fortunately for the brokers, turnover has grown considerably over the past few years as interest rates have fluctuated more violently. The commission the brokers earn is tiny (less than 0.02 per cent). However, all those small percentages add up to a lot of money when the principal sums involved are so large. Even the advent of negotiated commissions at the start of 1986 did not prevent the larger brokers from maintaining their profits.

The real importance of the money markets is that they react very sensitively to economic changes. Rates will rise very quickly if, for example, dealers think that inflation is increasing or that the pound is about to fall. Foreign investors can quickly withdraw their funds if they are worried about the UK economy. The flight of this so-called 'hot money' can put real pressure on a government.

The money markets were at the heart of the credit crunch. Banks became reluctant to lend to each other, and outside investors (such as money market funds) were also unwilling to lend to banks. The result was that LIBOR rose sharply. Instead of being a few hundredths of a percentage point above base rates, LIBOR was two or three percentage points higher. This raised the cost of borrowing for everyone, and prompted central banks to lend directly in the money markets to try to ease the pressure.

The central banks had some limited success but the difficulty of obtaining money at a reasonable price was one reason why the credit crunch became so serious. Companies struggled to refinance themselves; speculators who had borrowed money to buy assets were forced to sell, sending asset prices sharply lower. The money markets are the plumbing of the financial system; when they get blocked, the result is an almighty stink.

7 Borrowers

The financial institutions described in the last few chapters perform the function in the economy of channelling funds from those who wish to lend to those who wish to borrow. Of course, the banks borrow money themselves, as we saw in previous chapters. In this chapter we will look at the other borrowers. There are three main groups in the economy: individuals, governments and companies.

INDIVIDUALS

Individuals borrow for a host of different reasons. Perhaps the most common is that income and expenditure are rarely synchronized. Christmas comes but once a year, but drives many people into overdraft. Few people can afford to buy larger consumer durables (like cars) without borrowing the funds involved. Unplanned events such as illness or redundancy can reduce income without a corresponding effect on expenditure. Food must still be bought and rent and mortgages must be paid.

Most people borrow by taking out an overdraft from a bank or carrying a credit-card balance. Banks will also lend money for more specific projects, like study courses or home improvements. Finance companies and big businesses will lend money to those buying expensive goods. However, the most important debt which most people incur is to buy a home with a mortgage.

GOVERNMENTS

British governments have historically spent more than their incomes and, like anyone else, they have to borrow to cover the difference. They borrow in the form of long-dated securities called gilts and short-dated securities called Treasury bills. Money is also borrowed direct from the public through the various national savings schemes on offer (see Chapter 15). The government can give itself a built-in advantage in the market for personal savings because it can allow savers to escape tax. It does so on some schemes. However, the loss of tax income increases the government's effective cost of borrowing. As a result, it tries to maintain a balance between the amount it borrows in the form of savings schemes, bills and gilts.

The total amount that most governments have had to borrow has increased in the last few decades, because of the growth of welfare economies in the West with the resulting inbuilt increases in expenditure. The result has been a steady rise in the tax burden and regular battles between the Treasury and spending departments like the Ministry of Defence.

The difference between the government's total revenue and its expenditure is known as the public-sector borrowing requirement (PSBR) or more recently the Public Sector Net Cash Requirement. Reducing this deficit was one of the main aims of the Conservative governments of 1979–97.

In the early days of Margaret Thatcher's administration, the economic rationale behind the government's desire to reduce the PSBR was that a fall in government borrowing would stimulate the economy. If the PSBR is too high, it was reasoned, the available funds for investment will flow to the government (a safe credit) rather than to industry. Companies will be able to borrow only by offering investors penally high rates of interest, discouraging them from investing in new plant and machinery. Without new investment, the economy will not grow. The government will effectively have 'crowded out' private-sector borrowing. A low PSBR, the government argued, would result in low interest rates. Businesses would be encouraged to invest and the economy would grow.

The drive to cut government deficits spread more widely in the 1980s and 1990s. The heavy defence expenditure incurred by the US during the Cold War had caused its deficit to rise sharply. Tax rises and some spending cuts imposed by Presidents Bush and Clinton helped bring down the shortfall in the 1990s.

In Europe, an annual deficit of less than 3 per cent of gross domestic product was one of the key 'Maastricht convergence criteria' that countries had to meet in order to qualify for the single currency. Governments duly cut back, albeit with the help of some dodgy accounting tricks. These were exposed in the euro crisis of 2010 and 2011, as budget deficits soared.

This attention to deficits owes something to a general realization by politicians that running up debts on the never-never is a short-sighted strategy. Gradually, interest payments on previous debts consume an increasing proportion of the annual budget. After the financial crisis of 2008, it became impossible for governments to avoid deficits as their tax revenues plunged and expenditure on unemployment benefits rose. In the short term, this acts to cushion the economy.

Until recently, the rise of the so-called 'bond market vigilantes' has also made it more difficult for profligate governments. Countries have to raise money from the international markets and in these days of free capital flows, investors will be quick to sell the government bonds of a nation if it suspects its finances are deteriorating. That will increase the cost of raising new money and make the government's finances even worse. But the willingness of central banks to buy government bonds through quantitative easing programmes (see Chapter 5) has made it easier for governments to keep spending during the recession.

A lot depends on the currency in which the debt is denominated. If a country has borrowed in its own currency, like the UK, then the central bank can create the money to buy its debt (eventually, this will lead to rapid inflation if taken too far). But if the country has borrowed in another currency, like Latin Americans who borrowed in dollars in the 1980s, that option is not open. Countries that joined the euro are in a similar position; they do not control their currency. They have thus relied on their EU partners and the European Central Bank to help them out.

If a country's position gets really bad, it will be forced to go to the International Monetary Fund for help – but the IMF will impose tough conditions in terms of spending cutbacks and tax rises. The option of default – refusing to pay the nation's debts – will cut the country off from international capital for a long time, and lead to further economic hardship.

The bonds issued by the UK government are called *gilt-edged securities,* or gilts, because of the near certainty that they will be repaid.

They fall into three categories, conventional, index-linked and the irredeemables. Conventional gilts pay a fixed rate of interest twice a year and have repayment dates varying from five to thirty years.

Index-linked gilts pay a low rate of interest (1–4 per cent) but this interest, and the repayment value of the bonds, is linked to the retail price index. If prices double over the lifetime of the bond, then those who bought when the bond was first issued will be repaid twice their original investment.

Irredeemable issues are a bit of a historical throwback. They are literally issues that will not be repaid. Some were issued in the nineteenth century on very low rates of interest and now trade well below their face value. But their yield (the interest rate divided by the face value) is at around the same level as other issues in the market. Examples of irredeemables include Consols and War Loan.

A new type of gilts trading has also been introduced, called *strips*. Under a strip, a gilt issue is separated into a series of different payments; all the interest payments between now and the repayment date and the final repayment value. These separate units offer an interesting investment opportunity; they have a certain final value but pay no income in the interim.

Of course, the UK government bond market is not the largest in the world. By far the biggest, and most important, is the US Treasury bond market. Even though the US has had a long-running tendency to budget deficits, its government bonds are the most liquid and are seen as a 'safe haven' when other markets are in turmoil. The Japanese government bond market is also important, and notable in the late 1990s for temporarily offering yields of less than 1 per cent; the European bond market may eventually rival the US.

COMPANIES

Why do companies borrow? Unlike individuals, for whom borrowing is often a sign of financial weakness, borrowing is a way of life for most corporations, no matter what their prospects. Firms which are very successful often have substantial amounts of debt. There obviously comes a point beyond which companies can be said to have borrowed too much, but frequently, corporate borrowing merely indicates a willingness to expand.

What routes are open to a company which wishes to finance expansion? It might be imagined that the ideal method would be to generate the funds from past profits (retained earnings). In other words, the company would finance itself and thus reduce its costs by avoiding interest payments. However, self-financing is not always possible. While companies are in their early years, they have little in the way of previous profits to draw on, since many of their investments will not yet have generated a return. Nevertheless, in order to establish themselves, companies must continue to invest in further projects, necessitating capital outlay. If they were forced to wait until funds were available internally, they might miss profitable opportunities and spoil their long-term prospects in the process. Company results are often judged by their profitability in relation to their equity base (the value of the combined shareholdings). Debt can be used to increase the return on equity (a process known as *leverage* or *gearing*) by allowing companies to seek profitable investment opportunities when retained earnings are insufficient.

Another way that a company could generate cash for expansion would be to sell existing assets or alternatively not to replace old and worn-out assets. Both, however, are one-off ways of raising money and are more indicative of a company which is winding down than of one which is expanding.

A company could increase its capital base by issuing new shares or equity. However, it might not wish to do so because that would weaken the control of the existing shareholders. In companies where control is exercised by a small majority of shareholders' votes, that could be particularly important.

It is also possible for a company to have too much equity. It is in the nature of equity (see Chapter 9) that, unlike debt, it cannot be redeemed. If the company issued more equity and then failed to expand, it would be left with large cash balances. Paying those balances back to shareholders in the form of increased dividends would have severe tax disadvantages.

In the 1990s and 2000s, many companies moved to return cash to shareholders by buying back their own shares, rather than paying dividends. This had the effect of pushing up share prices (the same level of demand was chasing a smaller supply) and was one of the factors behind the long bull market.

Debt, as a financing technique, has some distinct advantages. Interest is tax-deductible from company profits, so the effective cost of borrowing is reduced. In addition, debt is reversible. If a company finds itself flush with cash or lacking in investment opportunities, it can repay some of its borrowings. Most shareholders will accept the need for a company to borrow, provided that they expect that the project in which the borrowed funds will be invested will yield a higher return than the cost of borrowing the funds. As already noted, a company can be described as being inefficient if it achieves a very low return on equity – borrowing can increase that return.

Company analysts tend to watch the debt–equity ratio, which is very roughly defined as the company's borrowings relative to its shareholders' funds. Ideal debt–equity ratios vary from industry to industry, but most companies start to look a little exposed if their debt exceeds their equity capital – in other words, if the ratio is larger than 1.

HOW COMPANIES OBTAIN EXTRA FINANCE

Which are the debt instruments most used by companies? Some small firms start out with a bank overdraft. The overdraft has built-in advantages – it is very flexible and easy to understand. An upper limit is agreed by the bank and the borrower: the borrower may borrow any amount up to that limit but will be charged interest only on the amount outstanding at any one time. The rate charged will be agreed at a set margin over the bank's base rate and thus the cost of the overdraft will move up and down with the general level of rates in the economy.

The overdraft is a very British institution. In the US, it is virtually unknown. American companies use term loans – the amount and duration of which are agreed in advance – and interest is charged on the full amount for the full period of the loan.

Companies have found that the 'hard core' element of their overdrafts has increased over the years, suggesting that they are funding their long-term needs with short-term loans. Accordingly, many companies have begun to switch to funding with term loans from banks instead of overdrafts. Term loans are normally granted by banks for specific purposes such as the acquisition of machinery, property or another company, rather than for the financing of working capital needs such as the payment of wages or raw-material costs.

Overdraft financing was probably the only source of funding for the smaller companies up to twenty years ago. Many companies now borrow in the money markets, often using the services of a money broker to find a willing lender, which is likely to be a bank. In return, the broker (who never lends or borrows money himself) receives a commission. Money market loans are for set amounts and periods and are therefore less flexible than overdraft facilities. However, interest rates in the money markets are generally below those for overdrafts.

Larger companies borrow hundreds of millions, or even billions, of pounds from groups of banks in the form of syndicated loans or loan facilities (see Chapter 11).

Longer-term finance for large firms is most frequently obtained by the issue of bonds which pay a fixed rate of interest to the investor. Such bonds usually have maturities of over five years. Multinational firms which have very large financing needs may turn to the international and Eurobond markets (see Chapter 11). Those markets give firms access to a very wide investor base and allow companies to raise tens of millions of pounds at a stroke.

The more sophisticated financing techniques of the Euromarkets are not open to the small and medium-sized British firm. Their long-term financing needs are normally satisfied by some kind of bank loan. However, there are a variety of options open to firms seeking shorter-term finance. One in particular is the acceptance credit or banker's acceptance. A bank agrees that it will accept bills drawn on it by the company, in return for a commission. When the company needs funds, it will send the bills to the bank, which will then discount them – that is, pay the company less than the full amount of their value. The amount of discount is equivalent to the rate of interest charged by the bank. So, if the company sent the bank a three-month bill with a face value of £100 and the interest rate on such bills was 12 per cent a year, the bank would discount the bill to £97. As with other loans, the credit rating of the company will affect the cost of the borrowing: the poorer the credit rating, the bigger the discount.

THE FINANCING OF TRADE

Many of the more specialist methods of raising finance revolve around the financing of trade. The key principles are that it is better to be paid by debtors as soon as possible and pay creditors as late as possible. It is also important to ensure that debtors settle their debts. This is a particular problem for exporters who are dealing with customers out of reach of the UK legal system.

There are four main methods of payment for exports: (1) cash with order; (2) open account trading; (3) bills of exchange; (4) documentary letters of credit.

The best method for the exporter is cash with order. That way the exporting company already has the money before it sends off the goods; however, importers can obviously not be so keen to pay by this method and it is rarely used. Open account trading is the opposite end of the scale – the exporter sends the client the goods and then waits for the cheques to arrive. It offers the least security of all the payment methods but is still the most widely used, at least in trade between industrialized countries.

Bills of exchange offer rather more security to the exporter. The firm will send the bill ('draw' it) to its foreign customer with the invoices and the necessary official documentation (referred to as a *documentary bill*). Then the firm will inform its bank, telling it to obtain the cash from the client. The bank will send the documentary bill to a bank in the importer's country. Under some arrangements, the buyer pays for the goods as soon as he receives the documents. Often, however, he is given a period of credit. He must accept the bill (otherwise he will not get the goods), and accepting a bill is proof of receipt of goods in law. When the credit period is up, the bank presents the bill to the buyer once again.

Bankers' documentary credits, normally known as letters of credit, are the most expensive of the forms of payment but offer a greater measure of security. The onus is on the *importer* to open a credit at his bank, in favour of the exporter. The importer's bank then informs the exporter's. The credit tells the exporter that if he presents certain documents showing that the goods have been shipped, he will be paid.

There are many different types of letters of credit. *Revocable* credits can be cancelled or amended by the importer without the exporter's approval – they are therefore very risky for the exporter. *Irrevocable* credits, despite their name, can be altered, but only with the approval of both parties. *Confirmed irrevocable* credits are guaranteed by the exporter's bank, in return for a fee – as long as the exporter has kept to his side of the bargain, the bank will ensure that he is paid. If the importer fails to pay, it is the bank's job to pursue the debt. These credits are the normal method of payment for goods shipped to risky countries. *Revolving* credits allow two parties to have a long-term relationship without constantly renewing the trade documentation. *Transferable* credits are used to allow goods to be passed through middlemen to give security to all three parties – exporter, middleman and importer. With all these payment instruments, the finance comes, in effect, from the exporter or his overdraft. If he has to wait for, say, sixty days before being paid, he is, in effect, making an interest-free loan to his customer. Only when the credit is medium term (more than six months) will the customer normally be expected to pay interest.

There are three further methods of trade finance which involve the exporter in passing to another institution part or all of the responsibility for collecting its debts. One is to use an export credit agency in return for a premium. The other two are factoring and forfaiting.

A company which is involved with all the problems of designing, producing and selling a range of products may feel that it has enough to do without the extra burden of chasing its customers to settle their debts. Instead, it can call on the services of a factor. Factors provide both a credit collection service and a short-term loan facility. Their charges therefore have two elements, the cost of administration and the charge for the provision of finance. Most factoring covers domestic trade but it has a distinct role in exporting.

Companies which have called on the services of a factor will invoice their clients in the normal way but give the factoring company a copy of all invoices. The factors will then administer the company's sales ledger, in return for a percentage of the turnover. They will despatch statements and reminder letters to customers and initiate legal actions for the recovery of bad debts. In addition, some companies will provide 100 per cent insurance protection against bad debts on approved sales.

Factoring is a particularly important service for expanding companies which have not yet developed their own full accounts operations. Factors will also provide short-term finance to corporations short of cash. When the company makes out its invoices, it can arrange to receive the bulk of the payments in advance from the factor. Effectively, the factor is making the company a loan backed by the security of the company's invoices. In return, the factor will discount the invoices, paying, say, only 90 per cent to the company. The extra 10 per cent covers both the factor's risk that the invoices will not be paid and the effective interest rate on the 'loan'.

Like factoring, forfaiting is a method of speeding up a company's cash flow by using its export receivables. Forfaiting gives exporters the ability to grant their buyers credit periods while receiving cash payments themselves. While factoring can be used for goods sold on short-term credit, such as consumer products or spare parts, forfaiting is designed to help companies selling capital equipment such as machinery on credit periods of between two and five years.

Suppose that a UK company has sold goods to a foreign buyer and has granted that buyer a credit period. A forfaiting company will discount an exporter's bills, with the amount of discount depending on the period of credit needed and the risk involved to the forfaiting company. In order for the company to make the bills more acceptable to the forfaiting company, it will ask the buyer of the goods to arrange for the bills to carry a guarantee, known as an *aval*, from a well-known bank. The more respected the bank involved – and the less risky the country it is based in – the cheaper the cost of forfaiting. Unlike factoring companies, forfaiters often sell on these bills to other financial institutions. Their ability to do so helps reduce the cost of the service. (In general, the more liquid the asset, the lower the return.)

This chapter has discussed the needs of the major borrowers in the UK economy. In the next chapter we will look at those individuals and institutions with funds to invest.

8   Investment Institutions

Nowadays the majority of the nation's shares are held not by wealthy individuals but by institutions – pension funds, life assurance companies, unit and investment trusts and the new powers on the block, hedge funds and private equity (see Chapter 9). These institutions are also the biggest holders of gilts and wield significant power in the property market. In an age of international capital flows, many of these institutions are from overseas; at the end of 2012, 53.2 per cent of the UK stock market was foreign-owned, up from 30. 7 per cent in 1998.

The institutions had already become powerful in the 1980s when the City was forced into the 'Big Bang' in order to meet their needs. The abolition of fixed-minimum commissions dramatically brought down the costs of share-dealing to the big investors. Previously they had shown signs of being enticed away from the Stock Exchange and into the telephone-based, over-the-counter markets made by the big securities firms.

Most fund managers do not feel very powerful, however. Each of the investment institutions has outside forces to which it is beholden. Pension fund managers must look to the trustees of the companies whose funds they administer, life assurance and insurance companies to their shareholders and policyholders, and unit and investment trusts to their unit and shareholders respectively. Conspiracy theorists can follow the chain of ownership back and back without finding a sinister, top-hatted capitalist at the end of it (although when it comes to hedge funds and private equity, it may be a different matter).

Some people, particularly company executives, worry that investment institutions will gang together and try to alter the policies of the companies in which they have substantial holdings. This is happening more than it used to, with so-called activist investors often demanding that companies take action to create 'shareholder value' and other ethical investors demanding that companies respect the rights of workers in developing countries, adopt sound environmental policies and so on.

In the majority of cases, however, institutions do not exercise their power to intervene in the day-to-day running of firms. One reason is that they do not have the time or the expertise to do so. Another is that investors will not necessarily agree on the action that needs to be taken. In other countries, even in America, their right to intervene may be restricted.

There is also an alternative to intervention: if institutions dislike a company's policies, they will sell their shares, bringing down the price in the process. Too low a share price will attract predatory rivals, who will buy up the company, and the management will lose its cherished independence.

The time when institutional investors are most powerful is during takeovers, when both sides vie for the institutions' favours. Traditionally, the sizeable holdings of the institutions mean that the way they jump will decide the success or failure of the bid. In recent years the institutions have shown little tendency to be loyal to existing managements and appear to be more than willing to sell out to the highest bidder. Often, indeed, they sell out quickly and hedge funds end up holding the balance of power.

THE GROWTH OF THE INSTITUTIONS

The extraordinary growth of investment institutions is due in part to the increased wealth and longevity of the population. Before the twentieth century, few people survived into old age, and those who did often had independent means. As people have lived longer there has been a greater need for pensions. The pension provided by the state offers not much better than a subsistence income, so occupational pension schemes have evolved, with both employees and employers making tax-free contributions.

Occupational schemes come in two kinds. Defined benefit schemes contract to pay employees a set sum based on their final salary. The employer is responsible for making up any shortfall in the fund; there is rather more debate about who is entitled to any surplus. In a defined contribution scheme, the employee and employer put in monthly payments but the pension is entirely dependent on the investment performance of the fund. In short, in a defined benefit scheme, the employer takes the risk; in a defined contribution scheme, the employee does so.

Defined benefit pension funds are run by a trust, which can either manage the funds itself or (in the vast majority of cases) appoint outside fund managers. The outsiders are normally specialist fund management companies. The pension fund trustees, usually acting under the guidance of actuaries, often split up the fund between several managers to ensure that a bad set of decisions by one manager does not affect the solvency of the whole fund. In defined contribution schemes, employers will usually offer a range of funds for employees to choose from; most will opt for the default fund, which will invest in a range of assets.

Another set of institutions is the insurance companies. Many people will have some form of life insurance. These policies can be divided into two: term policies, which will only pay out if the policyholder dies during a set period; and savings-related policies, under which policyholders pay regular premiums in return for a lump sum at the end of a set period. These policies contain an element of insurance, since if the policyholder dies before completing the payments, an agreed sum will be paid immediately to his or her dependants.

For much of the 1980s and 1990s, the UK savings market was dominated by the endowment policy, which was taken out by people when they applied for a mortgage. The idea was that, with the benefit of regular savings, the policy would grow sufficiently to repay the mortgage (normally after twenty-five years). Endowment policies came in two forms: with-profits or unit-linked. The former offers a smoothed investment return; the latter a return which is more directly linked to the market.

The problem with such policies was that they had high charges and offered poor value to those who surrendered them in their early years. In addition, a fall in inflation during the 1990s meant that many policies did not grow sufficiently to repay the mortgages. Endowment mortgages are rare nowadays. Nevertheless, the life insurance companies still have plenty of assets under management, thanks to other products such as pensions and savings bonds.

Added to this group are the general insurance companies (see Chapter 12) which collect premiums in return for insuring property holders against risk. Car insurance, travel insurance, even pet insurance – the small sums paid by policyholders every month or year eventually add up. These three sets of institutions – pension funds, life and general insurance companies – make up a distinct branch of the institutional investment family.

They all have essentially long-term liabilities – pensions to be paid, life assurance policies to mature. They create portfolios of assets with the contributions they receive – portfolios which are designed both to be safe against loss and to provide capital growth. If the institutions invested only in one company or in one type of security, they would be exposed to the chance of heavy losses.

PORTFOLIO INVESTMENTS

What are the ingredients of these portfolios? A significant proportion, which has been increasing in recent years, is invested in government securities. Government regulations require insurance companies to hold a certain number of gilts as reserves to ensure they can meet claims when they occur. Bonds tend to be more stable in price than shares.

UK government bonds or gilts can be used to match long-term liabilities because of their long-term maturities, which stretch out for fifty years. Index-linked bonds, which compensate investors for higher inflation, are seen by many observers as the closest match for pension liabilities. Gilts also offer a high level of income and this can be extremely useful for pension funds where most of the members are retired. The government would have enormous difficulty in funding itself without the gilt purchases of the institutions.

A further chunk of the funds' investments goes into property – buying land or buildings that are used for factories, offices and shops. Property investment goes in and out of fashion; popular in the 1970s and early 1980s, it was out of favour by the 1990s. Ironically, that turned out to be a pretty good time to buy. The plus side of property is that it has a tradition of being a good long-term investment, with an attractive yield and a record of more than keeping pace with inflation. The negative side is that property is illiquid; it is most difficult to sell at the moment you really want to (when its price is falling). There also can be a lot of administrative hassle (finding tenants, maintaining buildings) involved in owning property directly. As a result, in recent years, there has been a growing trend for institutions to invest in property funds run by fund management companies.

The biggest proportion of institutional investment goes into equities, and in Chapter 10 we examine the effect of institutional investors on the share market. Equities have historically offered much better returns than bonds or money market instruments and thus have greatly benefited the institutions. However, the long bull market of the 1980s and 1990s caused investors to overcommit to the stock market, leaving them very exposed when the dotcom bubble burst in 2000. As share prices fell, many defined benefit pension funds went into deficit, forcing the companies that sponsored them to cough up more cash.

In the aftermath of the 2000–2002 bear market, many pension funds decided they had staked too much on the success of the stock market. They decided to diversify into alternative asset classes such as commodities, hedge funds and private equity. The hope is that a diversified mix of such assets can deliver better returns than government bonds, but with less volatility than equities. The spare cash of the investment institutions goes into the money markets. Although their immediate outgoings are usually met by the premiums and contributions, the institutions still need liquid funds to meet any disparities. So they invest in bank certificates of deposit and money market funds. At certain times, when shares seem unsafe investments, the proportion invested in the money markets increases.

OVERSEAS INVESTMENTS

Nowadays, institutional portfolios are very international. In 1979, the government abolished exchange controls. This allowed the institutions to invest substantial sums abroad. In 1979, the proportion of pension fund portfolios held in the form of overseas equities was 6 per cent; by 2008, it was almost 30 per cent.

The amount of money that pension funds invest depends on a variety of factors. First of all, the fund managers must decide whether overseas markets look more attractive than the UK, perhaps because the prospects for economic growth and corporate profits look better, perhaps because overseas shares look better value, relative to company profits and assets. They also must allow for the fact that UK-listed companies earn only a small part of their living from the UK in any case; a study found that more than three quarters of the revenues of companies in the FTSE 100 comes from overseas.

Secondly, the managers must decide whether sterling is set to rise or fall. If the pound rises, then the value of overseas assets, when translated back into sterling, will reduce; if the pound falls, then the value of such assets may rise. They can separate these two decisions, by buying shares in the US and then hedging the risk that the dollar will fall against sterling.

Thirdly, managers must pay attention to matching their assets and liabilities. The beneficiaries of the funds (future pensioners) will use the money they receive to buy goods and services in the UK, so it makes sense for the fund to have a significant UK element. Many UK companies already receive a large proportion of their income from abroad, so investors can get a reasonable amount of diversification without leaving the London stock market.

The overseas diversification of funds used to come under some criticism from the left but with the increasingly free flow of international capital, the complaints have died down. There is little evidence that UK companies are short of capital and US and European investors are active in the UK market.

Just as UK institutions invest overseas, overseas institutions buy into the UK market. Other countries have their own pension funds and insurance companies, of course. They also have mutual funds, the equivalent of unit trusts (see below). A fast-growing group of investors are so-called sovereign wealth funds. These are funds accumulated by overseas governments, such as China, Russia, Norway and the Middle Eastern oil producers. All these countries have accumulated trade surpluses. This allows them to build up reserves. Traditionally, a lot of this money was held in the form of deposits or government bonds. But the countries have become more adventurous, buying equities and sometimes whole companies. This has created some controversy, with commentators worrying about 'back door nationalization' and about the potential influence that overseas governments can hold over the UK economy.

FUND MANAGEMENT COMPANIES

Much of this institutional money is run by professional fund management companies, which look after the portfolios in return for an annual fee. These managers run the portfolios of pension funds, charities, unit and investment trusts (and manage money directly on behalf of rich individuals as well).

Fund management is a fairly reliable business, since the annual fee tends to rise when markets do. The likes of Fidelity manage many hundreds of billions of dollars. They live and die on performance, with individual managers trying to pick the stocks that beat the market average. Some travel the world, meeting company managers and poring over balance sheets in an attempt to outperform; others rely on computer programs to identify attractive stocks.

The reputation of individual fund managers can rise and fall with the markets. In the late 1990s, the institutional market was dominated by four groups: Gartmore, Schroders, Phillips & Drew and Mercury. Two of those companies have been taken over; Mercury is now part of Blackrock, a big US group. Phillips & Drew lost business in the late 1990s because it was sceptical about the dotcom boom. Although it was proved right in the long term, it lost clients in the short term and was taken over by UBS, the Swiss bank. In the US, by contrast, Janus was a fund management group that rode the technology bubble and then suffered heavily when the market collapsed.

The different fund management houses have different styles. Some emphasize the importance of individual star managers who have shown the ability to beat the market. The danger is that, if the star gets dissatisfied and leaves the company, the clients may go with him. Others emphasize a team approach, with decisions made by the leadership or with the help of analysts. Some firms offer a complete gamut of funds, both geographically and by sector; others focus on particular countries or on particular styles.

While the fund management groups can seem very powerful, with hundreds of billions in assets, it is worth emphasizing that they do not own the assets themselves. They are acting on behalf of clients, who can move swiftly if dissatisfied. Managers are always worried about bad publicity, or about a period of underperformance.

Investors can buy the shares or bonds of individual companies or they can buy into a pool of assets known as a collective fund. These come in various guises; unit trusts, investment trusts, mutual funds, exchange traded funds, or have bewildering acronyms like OEICs (open-ended investment companies) or UCITS (undertaking for collective investment in transferable securities). The structure is different but the idea is the same. By owning a wide range of assets, investors reduce the risk that any individual asset collapses. Each share or unit of the fund rises and falls with the value of all the assets in the fund.

TRUSTS

The oldest of these collective funds is the investment trust.

A trust is a public company like any other company except that its assets are not buildings and machinery, but investments in other companies. Investors buy shares in the trusts and rely on the expertise of the fund managers to earn a good return on their investments.

The origins of the investment trust movement lie in Scotland. Many of the entrepreneurs who made money out of the Industrial Revolution found themselves with surplus funds which could find few profitable homes in their locality. So they looked for advice to help them invest elsewhere and turned to their professional advisers – the lawyers and accountants. A few smart people from both professions realized that they could pool the funds of their clients and invest larger sums. That early development was complemented by the growth of Scottish life assurance companies and pension fund managers, and today Edinburgh is still a very significant force in international fund management.

Nowadays all investment trusts must be approved by the Inland Revenue. They raise money through preference shares and loan stock as well as through ordinary shares. At the end of June 2014, there were 278 investment trusts, with assets of nearly £66 billion.

There are a few restrictions on the way in which trusts can invest. No single holding can constitute more than 15 per cent of their investments. Capital gains must be reinvested in the business and not distributed to shareholders.

Those restrictions aside, the trusts appear in a wide variety of forms.

Some, including the largest, Scottish Mortgage, invest across the world; others confine themselves to a single country, such as Brazil, or a specific sector of the market, such as property or mining.

The structure of trusts also gives them enormous flexibility. For example, they can borrow money to finance their investments, and the interest on their borrowings can be offset against tax. This is known as *gearing* and relies on the rate of return on the trusts' investments exceeding the cost of borrowing. If it does, the trusts' profitability increases substantially; if it does not, losses multiply.

Split capital trusts use a different approach. Most trusts offer investors a mixture of income and capital gains. A split capital trust separates the two. All the revenue of the trust is paid as dividends to the income shareholders; however, they will usually receive no capital gain and, in some cases, can expect a capital loss. The capital growth of the trust is then parcelled among other classes of share: either in a safe and steady form (zero dividend preference shares); or in a more high risk/high reward form (capital shares).

In mid-2001, some split capital trusts ran into difficulty. They had borrowed money to invest in shares, but the decline in the stock market had slashed their ability to repay. Worse still, it emerged that there were a lot of cross-holdings between trusts, so that the problems of one fund were quickly communicated to others. The losses incurred by some investors are likely to dent the popularity of split capital trusts for a while.

One of the problems of investment trusts is that their shares tend to stand at a discount to the net asset value. This means that the total value of their share capital is less than the value of the investments they hold. The discount is a function of supply and demand. There are normally not enough investors wanting to buy the shares to keep them trading at asset value. This discount varies from trust to trust, depending on the nature of the trust's investments and the reputation of the manager.

MUTUAL FUNDS

An investment trust is a closed-end fund; that is, the number of shares normally stays constant. Shares are bought and sold from other investors on the stock market. An alternative structure is what Americans call a 'mutual fund'; units are bought and sold from the manager of the fund and the size of the collective pool alters with demand. In Britain, these funds tend to be known as unit trusts, OEICs and UCITS. Although the names may be different, the basic structure is the same.

Unit trusts are still probably the best known name of the three, thanks to the longer use of the term. Under the old structure, there were different prices for units depending on whether the investor was buying or selling. The gap between the two prices covered the cost of creating or destroying the units (which might involve buying or selling assets.) Nowadays, there tends to be just the one price shown, with any costs treated as an extra charge. The OEICs name comes from the fact that these funds are open-ended, unlike the closed ended investment trusts. Under the single market rules of the EU, officials have been keen for mutual funds to be available in many countries at the same time; the EU rules are known as UCITS, hence the use of that term.

All these structures are very flexible; hence the success of the industry. As of mid-2014, there was some £800 billion of British assets managed in this form, according to the Investment Management Association. Unlike investment trusts, mutual funds always trade at their asset value, which makes them easier for retail investors to understand. They come in many shapes and forms; the IMA has 31 sectors from European smaller companies to money markets. Mutual funds are often bought through tax wrappers such as the individual savings account (ISA) or self-invested personal pension (SIPP).

The industry has its critics, however. With some 2,500 funds and over 104 fund management companies, there are a lot of mediocre products. Fewer than half of all funds beat the index (see Chapter 15), in part because the total charges on such funds are often one to two percentage points a year.

EXCHANGE TRADED FUNDS

These are the new kids on the collective fund block. Like investment trusts, they are traded on the stock market. But rather than being actively managed, they tend to follow an index such as the FTSE 100 or the Dow Jones Industrial Average. Their advantages are that they tend to have very low costs (less than a percentage point per year) and the investors do not have to worry that the manager will pick dud stocks. This has prompted ETFs to grow very quickly, with the main brand name being iShares, part of the Barclays Global Investors range.

The idea of tracking an index is not confined to ETFs. There are lots of unit trusts (and even the odd investment trust) that attempt to mimic a benchmark. As far as investors are concerned, if an ETF and a unit trust are tracking the same index, they should choose the one with the lower fees.

UNDERWRITING

Traditionally, the investment institutions played a key part in the new issues and the rights issues markets by underwriting or sub-underwriting an issue. In return for a fee, they guarantee to buy shares at a set price if no one else will.

Twenty years ago, the institutions tended to be the main underwriters of such issues. That was because they had the capital while the old merchant banks did not. But nowadays, the investment banks like Merrill Lynch and Goldman Sachs can take on this role themselves. The institutions merely act as sub-underwriters, in other words as back-up for investment banks.

A classic case was the rights issue of HBOS (Halifax Bank of Scotland) in 2008. The issue flopped, with just 8.3 per cent of existing shareholders taking up their rights. That was a big problem for the main underwriters, Morgan Stanley and Dresdner Kleinwort. But the two investment banks had arranged for 40–50 per cent of the issue to be sub-underwritten by outside investors. They enforced this agreement, known as the 'stick', thereby limiting their exposure to HBOS shares.

Hedge Funds and Private Equity

Thirty years ago, when the first edition of this book was published, hedge funds and private equity groups were too obscure to warrant a mention. Now they are so important that they deserve their own chapter.

When markets move suddenly, hedge funds are often to blame. If there is a takeover being announced, private equity groups may well be the bidder. The influence of the two sectors is generally accepted in the UK and the US, but still resented in Europe and parts of Asia. Their success has catapulted many of their founders into the ranks of the super-rich; if there is someone buying a Manhattan apartment for $50 million or outbidding a Russian billionaire at an art auction, the chances are it is a hedge fund or private equity titan.

Both industries have their roots in the US and are still more important there than in the UK. But they still wield immense influence in the City, although their offices will usually be in Mayfair rather than the Square Mile.

Hedge funds stemmed from the idea of an American journalist, Alfred Winslow Jones, in the late 1940s. He was good at picking stocks that he thought would do well, but was not good at telling whether the overall market was cheap or dear. So he made use of a technique called shorting, one of the most controversial weapons in a modern hedge fund armoury.

Shorting allows a manager to bet on falling share prices, rather than rising ones. It involves the manager selling shares he does not own. How does he do so? He borrows the shares (at a cost) from an existing investor, promising to return them at a future date. He then sells those shares in the market. If when the time comes to buy back the shares, the price has fallen far enough to cover his costs, then the hedge fund manager has made a profit.

To give an example, say the manager borrowed shares from an investor for three months at an annual interest rate of 8 per cent. He sells 100,000 shares at £6 each, netting £600,000. After three months, the shares have fallen to £5 each. So he buys back the same amount of shares at a cost of £500,000, pays £12,000 of interest to the lender (£600,000 at 8 per cent for three months), and nets a profit of £88,000.

Shorting upsets companies because it tends to drive their share prices down. Short-sellers have been known to spread rumours about a company in an attempt to push their position into profit. At the time of the September 11 attacks on New York and Washington, there was even talk that the terrorists had sold the market short in advance of the event. In the summer of 2008, when bank shares were falling fast, regulators in the US and the UK moved to restrict the ability to sell short their shares.

To go back to Alfred Winslow Jones, he realized that if he bought one group of shares (went long, in the jargon), and went short of another group of shares with the same value, he would be protected against market movements. If the market rose, he would lose money on his short positions but make it on his longs. If the market fell, he would lose money on his longs, but make money on his shorts. His position was hedged. The hedge fund name flowed from that basic idea.

However, this idea needed another twist. Even if Winslow Jones was a very good stock-picker, his long positions might only beat his shorts by 4–5 per cent a year. That differential would not be enough to attract outside investors. The same is true today of a lot of hedge fund strategies. So the fund uses borrowed money to enhance returns. But this is a double-edged sword; leverage enhances losses as well as profits. In 1998, the hedge fund Long-Term Capital Management (LTCM), run by trading legends from the Salomon Brothers investment bank and backed by two Nobel Prize winning economists, needed rescuing after its bets on bond markets went wrong. It had levered up thirty times; in other words, its capital was just 3 per cent of the assets it controlled. Only a small move in markets was needed to cause it trouble.

This use of leverage can make hedge funds risky but it would be wrong to say that all hedge funds are huge risk-takers. Many are very sophisticated about the way they seek to control risk; the volatility of their portfolios will be a lot lower than that of, say, a technology fund. The big blow-ups of recent years have tended to involve funds that invested in riskier assets. In 2006, Amaranth lost 35 per cent in a month after making bad bets in energy futures; in 2007, two Bear Stearns funds lost all their value after investing in securities linked to the subprime mortgage market. In both cases, investors knew they were making such bets, and should have been prepared, if not for the scale of their losses, at least for the possibility of their occurrence.

Another area of hedge fund risk relates to the way they are structured. They are usually registered in an offshore haven like the Cayman Islands to give them tax privileges; they have much greater investment freedom than a mutual fund. But this also means they are very lightly regulated. In the UK, the Financial Conduct Authority looks after the fund managers, rather than the hedge funds themselves; in other countries, there is very little oversight at all.

There have been several examples of fraud, usually when the managers lie about the nature or the value of their investments. The Bernard Madoff case is a slightly unusual one. Technically speaking, Madoff did not run a hedge fund, but hedge funds did give him money to invest. The failure to spot the fraud reflects very badly on those funds that did do so: the authorities try to restrict the damage by limiting the type of people who can invest in them; only the very rich and institutions like pension funds and university endowments can qualify. The idea is that such people can look after themselves.

Gradually, however, hedge funds are becoming open to the wider public. One or two individual funds have listed on European stock markets; once quoted, there is nothing to stop widows and orphans buying shares in such funds. Quite a number of funds-of-funds have listed on the London market.

A fund-of-funds should be less risky – a specialist manager groups together a portfolio of individual hedge funds, having (in theory, at least) weeded out those run by fraudsters or which are taking wild risks. The Financial Services Authority also suggested that retail investors should be allowed to invest in vehicles (so-called FAIFs, or funds of alternative investment funds) that will contain hedge funds within their portfolio.

While hedge funds may be registered in the Cayman Islands, their offices are usually elsewhere. In America, a lot of hedge funds are based in Connecticut, the other side of the Long Island sound from Manhattan; in Britain, the centre for the industry is Mayfair, convenient for the theatres and expensive shops of the West End and a short commute for those who live in Chelsea or Notting Hill. Style tends to be more casual than in the City; it is more common to go without a tie than to wear one.

The hedge fund world is intensely Darwinian; in 2006, while 1,500 funds were set up, some 700 folded. The managers regard themselves as smart people, pitting themselves in daily combat against the whims of the markets. They resent criticism and dislike publicity about their pay packages or their mistakes. But they are not above using the press to promote their positions, particularly in bid situations.

This can lead to a lot of resentment, especially when so-called activist funds start to lobby against the decisions of company managers. The Children's Investment Fund, or TCI, is one prominent example. It campaigned against the Deutsche Börse's bid for the London Stock Exchange, arguing that the German exchange would do better to return cash to shareholders. Not only did the bid fail but the Börse's chief executive Weiner Seifert was forced out. Then TCI took a 1 per cent stake in the Dutch bank ABN Amro, sparking a bidding war that ended with the bank's purchase by Royal Bank of Scotland.

In Europe, where shareholders have traditionally been seen and not heard, this kind of activism was distinctly controversial. Hedge funds were accused of being reckless speculators, only interested in short-term profit and not in the long-term health of the companies they invest in. There were calls for their activities to be restricted. The debate on the issue was much more restrained in Britain, where there is a much longer tradition of corporate takeovers and foreign ownership of big companies. It may help, of course, that Britain has a thriving hedge fund sector.

Another worry about hedge funds is that they might bring the system down; this concern inspired the rescue of LTCM in 1998. The fear is that hedge funds will not be able to repay the money they have borrowed when markets move against them. Since they normally borrow the money from banks, they might bring a bank down with them. This fear was reawakened during the credit crunch, although that episode showed the banks (in theory highly regulated) could collapse of their own accord.

The main link between the banking sector and the hedge funds is the prime brokerage arm of banks. These offer a wide range of services; from lending the funds money, to keeping records of their trades, to setting up the funds in the first place. Hedge funds are fantastic customers of the investment banks, since they trade frequently, earning big brokerage fees. But they are also competitors of the banks; they are trying to make money out of the same markets as the banks' trading desks. Most of all, they compete for staff; a lot of hedge fund managers were former investment bank traders.

Regulators can find the prime brokers quite useful as a means of keeping tabs on the hedge funds. If the hedge funds are taking too many risks, then the prime brokers, as their main lenders, should notice. But the risk works both ways. When hedge funds borrow money from a bank, they are obliged to put up assets as collateral for the loans. When worries surfaced about Bear Stearns in March 2008, hedge funds worried about the safety of their collateral; so they cut positions with the bank, weakening its capital position. One can see it as sweet revenge for the way that banks, by trading against its positions, brought down LTCM. The credit crunch caused a shrinking of the hedge fund industry, with nearly 15 per cent of all funds closing during 2008. The industry's assets dropped from $1.9 trillion to $1.4 trillion.

TYPES OF HEDGE FUNDS

As of mid-2014, there were more than 6,000 hedge funds with around $2.7 trillion of assets, according to BarclayHedge. Some were of the basic Winslow Jones model – being long and short of individual shares in the hope that their stock-picking skills would prove superior.

But others were much more sophisticated. One group, known as arbitrage funds, tried to profit from price discrepancies in particular parts of the market, such as convertible bonds. Others, so-called distressed debt funds, specialized in the bonds issued by struggling companies. A third group used powerful computers to try to spot patterns in the market.

So one needs to beware of newspaper stories that say 'hedge funds are buying this asset' or that stock. The funds are so ubiquitous these days that they are probably on both sides of most trades.

The diversity of these strategies is part of the hedge funds' appeal to clients. The idea is that when they invest in the sector they get a different kind of return, one that is not dependent on the stock market. Indeed, the hedge funds claim they are focused on 'absolute return', producing a positive outcome regardless of market returns. Until 2008 the worst year for the hedge fund index was 2002, when the average fund lost just 1.5 per cent. The industry's near 20 per cent losses in 2008 dented its reputation.

Hedge funds can use a lot of leverage, which makes them risky at the individual level. So investors need to own shares in a bunch of them to get the potential benefits. Furthermore, the best hedge funds are often closed to new investors, because the managers worry that having too big a fund will reduce performance. The new investors may end up choosing between smaller managers without a long track record.

The biggest problem of all may be the costs. The managers claim superior skills, so they charge higher fees: 2 per cent annually and a fifth (20 per cent) of all returns. Those that want a diversified portfolio of managers may opt for a fund-of-hedge-funds, which will charge another 1 per cent annually (and 10 per cent of performance) on top. That is a big hurdle to overcome.

Worse still, the high performance fees may encourage hedge fund managers to take risks. After all, it is the performance fees that have turned some managers into billionaires; if you manage $10 billion of money, and the fund returns 20 per cent in a year, that is a performance fee of $400 million. If the fund subsequently collapses, the managers don't have to pay the performance fee back.

Clients have some protection against these problems. Performance fees are only paid if a 'high water mark' is passed, representing the previous peak in the fund's asset value; otherwise, a client could be paying twice for the same return. And managers often keep the bulk of their investments in their own funds; so they will lose if the clients do.

Nevertheless, the size of the fees is causing many people to look for alternatives. One possibility is to use computers to mimic hedge fund returns, at much lower costs. These 'replicators' or 'clones' may prove a threat to the long-term growth of the industry. The idea behind the clones is that hedge fund returns are driven by a few factors, such as movements in the US stock market or corporate bond yields. Mix the factors together in the right proportions and, in theory, you can get the same returns. Whether this will work as well in practice remains to be seen.

PRIVATE EQUITY FUNDS

The private equity industry is smaller than the hedge fund sector but equally controversial. Its critics argue that the industry makes itself rich by taking over firms and sacking workers, that it consists of asset-strippers who damage the long-term health of the economy. Its supporters claim that private equity represents a superior model for doing business, in which the interests of managers and shareholders are much better aligned than in the traditional quoted company sector.

The debate is muddied by the fact that many people confuse private equity with venture capital. The latter also invests in unquoted businesses, but at a much earlier stage. Venture capitalists are trying to find the companies that will be the Microsofts and the Apples of the future. They tend to have many more failures than successes but they hope that the gains on the latter will outweigh their losses on the former. Since innovation and small businesses are undoubtedly good things for the economy, it is rather unfair that venture capital gets dragged into the private equity debate.

Private equity, by contrast, invests in existing companies. Normally, funds will take over the entire company, attempt to improve its performance, and then sell it, either to the stock market or to a corporate buyer, a few years later. They will usually fund this purchase with a lot of debt, hence the original name for private equity funds was leveraged buyout funds. Often, the management of the company will be incentivized with equity stakes, which will make them rich if the value of the company rises sharply.

Loading up a company with debt is risky; if the business is unable to meet the interest payments, it will go bust. So private equity groups tend to look to buy companies with two characteristics: strong cash flow and a lot of assets. The cash flow can be used to meet the interest payments and surplus assets sold to pay down some of the debt. The theory is that the need to pay off the debt will concentrate the managers' minds and lead them to control costs and avoid wasteful projects. One way of controlling costs, however, is to sack workers; another is to limit spending on research and development. Hence the criticism that private equity groups run businesses for the short, not the long, term.

The industry has argued that, on the contrary, it is interested in growing the businesses it buys, since eventually it has to sell them again. A slash-and-burn policy would thus be counterproductive.

Various academic studies have looked into the issue (some funded by the private equity industry) with mixed results. One of the most authoritative, prepared for the World Economic Forum in 2008, cleared the industry on the issue of stifling innovation, on the basis of patent records. It did find the industry partially guilty in terms of job destruction, saying that more jobs were lost (compared with similar businesses) in the first two years.

Critics of the industry also focus on two other issues. The first is the lack of transparency. Because businesses owned by private equity groups are not publicly quoted, they do not receive the same level of scrutiny from outside investors or from the media. However, the industry would argue that being out of the limelight allows the businesses to make better decisions, without the pressure to meet short-term profit targets.

The second issue is tax. Debt is tax-deductible in both the UK and US systems. This can mean that a highly indebted business can end up paying no corporation tax. As more and more businesses move into the private sector, this could erode the tax base.

In an ideal world, the tax system would be neutral so it would not matter if a company funded itself with equity or with debt. But removing the tax deductibility of interest would penalize public as well as private companies, and might send the weakest companies to the wall.

A more telling criticism was that the partners in private equity companies were allowed to class most of their profits as capital gains rather than as income. For a while, the lowest rate of capital gains tax was 10 per cent. This meant, as Nicholas Ferguson, a private equity veteran, confessed, that he was paying a lower rate of tax than his cleaner. This remark seems to have inspired the move by Alistair Darling, the Chancellor, to raise the minimum capital gains tax rate, from 10 per cent to 18 per cent, in 2008. However, the move caused much resentment, as it penalized small businesses as much as private equity bosses.

Like other fund managers, private equity groups have a portfolio of investments made up of the companies they backed. The managers of private equity groups are called general partners; the investors in the fund are known as limited partners. The latter will normally agree to invest a set amount in the fund and to tie up the capital for several years; this gives the general partners the freedom to dispose of the underlying businesses when conditions suit. When they arrange a leveraged buyout, the private equity funds will use the capital subscribed by the limited partners as the equity capital for the deal, and then raise the rest of their money (in the form of debt) from the banking sector.

Like the hedge fund industry, private equity groups are motivated with performance fees, usually a fifth of all returns. Annual management fees of between 1 and 2 per cent will also be charged. But the managers claim that their high returns justify the payment of such high fees.

This is another subject of much debate. It is possible to show that private equity funds have beaten the stock market over extended periods. But the funds use a lot more borrowed money and, as a result, are more risky. Academic studies suggest that, once this risk is controlled for, private equity funds perform no better than the market. One quirk of the figures, however, is that the best-performing funds are consistently ahead of the pack (something which does not seem to be the case with unit trusts).

That raises a couple of questions. The first is, if it is possible to identify the best-performing private equity funds, why does anyone give money to the below-average performers? The most likely answer is that the best managers limit the size of the funds, so that not all investors can get a slice of the action. They end up taking a punt that some less renowned manager can achieve similar returns.

The second question is: what drives the returns of the exceptional managers? One reason was cited earlier in the book: lesser liquidity demands greater reward. Because investors are locked in to private equity funds for a period of years, they demand high returns to compensate.

Another potential explanation is that private equity investors have superior skills in selecting the right companies to back, and are better at motivating the managers they employ. A further possibility is that this is a financing trick, driven partly by the tax break given to interest payments (see above) and partly by a long period of low and falling interest rates since the 1980s.

In the early 1990s, when the UK did slip into recession, private equity funds suffered a very difficult period as buyouts of retail outfits like Magnet and MFI got into trouble. In the US, the best-known deal of the era, the takeover of tobacco-and-food group RJR Nabisco, delivered very poor returns for its backer KKR.

That episode reveals another potential problem for private equity funds – the feast-or-famine problem. When the asset class is popular, the funds have lots of money to invest. But when those conditions occur, the funds end up bidding against each other for control of attractive groups. That forces prices higher and future returns down. Conversely, when economic times are hard and share valuations lower, investors are less enthusiastic about giving money to private equity managers.

10 **Shares**

It is easy to get confused by financial jargon, and the stock market is no exception. Although people use the terms 'stocks and shares' as synonyms, there used to be a distinction, with stocks referring only to fixed interest instruments.

Shares are quite distinct from loans and bonds. Whereas someone who lends money to a company or buys its bonds is a creditor of a company, a shareholder is the owner of the company. A share, or equity, represents a share in the assets and profits that the company produces.

Unlike loans or bonds, a shareholder cannot count on ever being repaid by the company itself. If a shareholder wants to realize his money, he must sell the shares in the open market. Furthermore, the return available to lenders or bondholders is normally fixed in advance; the return to shareholders is infinitely variable. Once a business's costs (including interest payments) have been met, all the excess belongs to the shareholders. However, if the business goes bust, the shareholders are at the back of the queue for repayment.

Shares and shareholders are unique to the capitalist system. Under a communist system, bonds are issued but never shares, since ownership of virtually all commerce is in the hands of the state. It is not exaggerating the case, therefore, to say that shares are at the heart of capitalism. They have traditionally been the investment most likely to get people rich quickly and also to reduce them to poverty (remember the Great Crash of 1929).

OWNERSHIP AND CONTROL

Shares also provide the means through which ownership of industry can be divorced from control. Death and taxes have gradually weakened the grip of the founders of old family-run businesses. Few individuals now have the capital to finance a large firm's expansion. Modern industrial giants are run by boards of directors, who in turn appoint salaried managers to administer the day-to-day business of the company. Some managers sit on the board and have shares of their own but, except in a few special cases, managers rarely own a significant proportion of the company's equity.

An attempt has been made in the last twenty-five years to reverse this trend by giving managers share options, which allow them to buy shares at a set price. The theory is that this will ensure that the interests of investors and managers are aligned, since both will benefit from a rising share price.

In practice, the system has certainly made many managers rich. But it was something of a one-way bet while the stock market was rising for much of the 1980s and 1990s; managers were able to earn huge sums just for being reasonably competent.

The richest managers of all were those who took part in leveraged buyouts (see Chapter 9), in which the executives, aided by some private equity groups, made takeover bids for companies and removed them from the stock market. These deals tend to leave the managers with a big proportion of the equity but land the company with a big burden of debt; if things go well, the managers will earn a fortune, but if things go badly, the managers will lose their jobs and their shareholdings will be worthless.

THE RIGHTS OF SHAREHOLDERS

What rights do shares confer? The most common form of share is the *ordinary share*: it gives the owner the right to vote (although there are non-voting ordinary shares), the right to appoint and remove directors and, most importantly, the right to receive dividends, if and when declared. Remember that the dividend is to the shareholder what the coupon is to the bondholder (i.e. an opportunity to receive income rather than capital appreciation).

Most companies pay a dividend every six month, although some (particularly the multinational groups) now pay out every quarter. The first appears with the half-yearly results and is known as the *interim dividend* and the end year dividend is known as the *final*.

Because shareholders stand at the end of the creditors' queue if a company fails, shares are on the riskiest end of the risk–reward scale and can therefore attract the highest return. Like bonds, shares can increase in price but the potential for share price increases vastly exceeds that for bonds. Although dividends add to the attractiveness of shares, it is this chance of a sharp rise in price that makes shares such an exciting investment. An investor who placed £1,000 in Polly Peck shares at the start of the 1980s would have seen his sum grow to £1.28 million by the end of July 1989. But a year later, the shares were effectively worthless.

Just as individual companies can go bust, the whole market can experience sharp declines. The 23 per cent fall in the Dow Jones Industrial Average on 19 October 1987 was only one illustration of how quickly and dramatically share prices can take a turn for the worse. Between January 2000 and March 2003, the FTSE 100 Index more than halved. History is littered with stock market crashes and with companies that have gone bust. The ordinary shareholders are usually the losers from such failures.

OTHER TYPES OF SHARE

In order to attract investors who are wary of the risks of ordinary share ownership, companies have devised other forms of shares which are slightly less risky. *Preference shares* are different from ordinary shares in that they give the holder a first claim on dividends and on the company's assets, if and when it is liquidated. The amount of dividend attached to a preference share is fixed. If it is not paid, it is a sign that the company is in severe financial trouble. The lesser risk attached to holding preference shares means that the return in good years is less than that of ordinary shares. In addition, the voting rights of preference shareholders are normally restricted.

Cumulative preference shares entitle the holder to be paid in arrears if the dividend is not paid one year. Since they are slightly less risky than ordinary preference shares, the yield on cumulative preference shares is marginally lower. *Redeemable preference shares* will be repaid at a future date; they closely resemble bonds and must offer a similar return to be attractive to investors. *Participating preference shares* offer a lower basic rate of return but allow for a bonus rate if the ordinary dividend is high. *Convertible preference shares* can be converted into ordinary shares at a certain price – they closely resemble convertible bonds (see Chapter 11). Again, the investor is compensated for the lower initial rate of return by the chance of future gains.

As a group, preference shares resemble fixed-rate bonds; indeed, the yield from such shares tends to be compared by investors with the yield on long-dated gilts. However, unlike bonds, companies which issue preference shares cannot offset the dividend against tax. This made them increasingly unpopular in the bull market when it was cheaper to issue ordinary shares to a seemingly insatiable investing public.

OPTIONS

Options differ from other types of equity investment because they are not issued by the companies concerned. Instead, they are instruments traded on stock exchanges designed to give investors greater leverage and to act as hedging vehicles for those investors worried about future share price movements.

Options grant the buyer the right to buy (a *call* option) or to sell (a *put* option) a set number of shares at a fixed price. The option buyer is not obliged to buy or sell at that price if it is not advantageous to do so. In return for granting the option, the option seller receives a non-returnable premium.

An example will help explain the principles involved. Suppose an investor has bought British Telecom (BT) shares at £1.50. Their price moves to £1.70 each. The investor wants to make sure that he retains some of his gain, but does not want to miss out on the chance of seeing the price rise still further. So he buys a put option at £1.70 – giving him the right to sell his shares at £1.70 if he so wishes. In return, he pays a premium of five pence a share. If the share price falls to £1.50, the investor exercises the option and sells the shares at £1.70. Taking away the cost of the premium, he has retained a profit of fifteen pence. If the share price rises to £2.00 the investor simply lets the option lapse. He has paid five pence a share but has a profit of forty-five pence a share over his original purchase.

More speculative investors may try to use options for their leverage potential. Suppose an investor has no shares in British Telecom at all but merely believes their price will rise. In the above situation (BT shares at £1.70), he could buy a £1.70 call option for a premium of five pence a share (on 100 shares, that would cost him £5). If the price rises to £2.00, then the option will be worth at least thirty pence on the traded market, because he could buy his shares at £1.70 through the option and then sell them at £2.00 at the Stock Exchange. Rather than exercise his option, the investor would sell the option and receive £30, or a 500 per cent profit on his original investment. An ordinary shareholder, buying at £1.70 and selling at £2.00, would have made a profit of only 17.65 per cent.

Another way for investors to speculate on share price movements is via *contracts for difference*. These are agreements between two parties that one will pay the other the difference between the current price of a share and its value at some future date. To go back to the BT example, an enthusiast for the company might agree on a CFD based on the £1.70 price. If the price then moves to £2.00, the enthusiast will earn 30p per share; if it falls to £1.50, he will have to hand over 20p per share.

The attraction in CFDs for speculators is that shares can be bought on margin, that is, without putting up a lot of capital. This margin can vary widely but let us assume it is 10 per cent. To buy 10,000 BT shares in our example, the investor would have to pay £17,000; with a 10 per cent margin, he only has to hand over £1,700. The risk, of course, is that only a small market movement can wipe out a large part of his capital. In addition, in the UK, buyers of CFDs are exempt from the 0.5 per cent stamp duty charge. As a result, CFDs are often used by hedge funds as a way of getting exposure to a share; a process that can also protect the privacy of the hedge fund trying to build up a position.

A related way of speculating on shares is spread betting. Readers may be familiar with the concept from sport, where gamblers bet on such statistics as the number of wides in the cricket World Cup or the time of the first goal in the FA Cup final. A spread bet requires the gambler to bet that a given number will be higher or lower than the specified range; it does not really matter to the bookmaker what the subject of the gamble is. If the range is 100–105, it could be the number of rainy days in the year or the number of goals scored by Manchester United in a season.

How does it work for shares? Let us go back to our BT example and say the spread is 168–173p. Someone who believed that BT shares would rise would go high and bet, say, £100 a point. In other words, for every penny that BT traded above 173p, he would make £100. If the share price reached 200p, he would gain £2,700. However, the converse is also true. For every penny below 173p, the gamble will lose £100. So a fall to £1.50 would cost £2,300. This is a much riskier gamble than a fiver on the Grand National.

Spread bets have a defined period but the bet can be closed before that date by making an equal gamble in the opposite direction. Indeed, the bookmaker may force the gambler to take his losses (or put up extra money) if the gamble goes sufficiently wrong. The good news is that any profits are not subject to capital gains tax; the bad news is that the Treasury does not charge CGT because it reckons there will be more losers than winners. (Provided the bookmaker can run a matched book, the spread should be pure profit.)

NEW ISSUES

New issues are one of the most exciting parts of the stock market. Not only do they allow investors to spot the successes of the future at a relatively early stage, they are also a direct means of providing capital for industry. Obviously, the daily buying and selling of shares – known as the secondary market – is extremely important. Without the knowledge that their shares could easily be sold, investors would not subscribe for new issues. But it is new issues – and the subsequent capital-raising exercises for expansions and acquisitions – which provide the main economic argument for the Stock Exchange's existence.

Companies have a choice as to which market they can list on these days. The main market of the London Stock Exchange is designed for well-established companies; the Alternative Investment Market (AIM) is designed for younger companies and has fewer rules for qualification. Nowadays, it is quite possible for UK companies to list on overseas markets as well as, or instead of, London and indeed many overseas companies choose to list here rather than in their own country.

AIM is the successor to the unlisted securities market, an earlier attempt designed to attract young and growing companies. The rules for floating on AIM are much less stringent than for the main market, and depend heavily on the advisers, or sponsors, who bring the company to the market. After some early disasters, a review of sponsors led to some leaving the market.

The name of the sponsoring house may be very important in ensuring investors' confidence in the issue. The sponsor will also advise on the timing and the terms of the issue. After Black Monday in 1987, for example, several companies withdrew their issues, on advice from their banks or brokers, until the stock market was more settled. When they returned, they were able to raise less money than they had originally planned.

There are a variety of methods by which a company can join the market. If the company is particularly large – like British Telecom or Eurotunnel – it will make an *offer for sale*. This is the most expensive method of making a new issue since it requires a large amount of publicity and also the *underwriting* of the offer by investment banks and institutions.

Once the underwriting is arranged, a company will issue a prospectus setting out in very detailed form its structure, trading record and prospects. Investors are then invited to apply for shares by a certain day. On the day that applications close, the sponsor counts up all the offers and then announces whether the issue is *over-* or *under*subscribed. If oversubscribed, this means that investors have applied for more shares than there are on offer; either their applications will be scaled down or there will be a ballot, in which only a few will get shares. If the issue is undersubscribed, the underwriters will have to buy the remaining shares at the offer price.

In a conventional offer, investors are told the share price in advance; in a *tender* offer, they pick the price themselves (although a minimum price is usually set). When all the tenders are in, the highest will be awarded shares, then the next highest and so on down until all the shares are allocated.

Tenders are unpopular with institutional investors, since they reduce the chance of an increase in price (*premium*) when the shares start trading. Private investors also are not inclined to apply for tender offers. As a result, tenders are comparatively rare and only tend to be used when an issue looks certain to be popular.

A *placing* is by far the most common, and also the most prosaic, means by which a company joins the stock market. The sponsoring bank or broker contacts key investment institutions and asks them to take some shares; individual investors are unlikely to be approached. The placing method is cheaper than an offer for sale and tends to ensure that the shares are held in the hands of a few supportive institutions.

The success of all these new issue methods depends on setting the right price for the shares. The higher the price, the more money flows into the company. But the sponsor will not want to set the price too high, for fear that it will fall when dealings commence. The ideal is a modest price rise on the first day. That reflects well on the company and pleases the shareholders – in the long run that will be better for the company than squeezing the last penny out of the issue price. The sponsor's problems in setting the price will be exacerbated by the presence of stock market investors called *stags*, who are eager to make a profit out of new listings when the price is set too low.

Stags are one species of the financial menagerie which commentators use to describe different types of investor. Essentially, stags are speculators who believe that a new issue has been priced too low, and who therefore attempt to purchase as many shares as possible. If they have correctly assessed that the issue is underpriced, the shares will immediately rise in value when the issue is made. The stags can then resell the shares and make a quick profit.

Stags only really emerge for offers for sale; placings and tenders give them little chance for profit. Another mechanism has made the life of a stag more difficult: the so-called grey market for shares. This market, often supervised by the spread betting companies, allows investors to speculate on the likely issue price (or first trading price) of flotations. But it also allows the sponsors of the deal to assess the likely market reaction to an issue. As a result, they may move up their expected offer price. This happened during the dotcom boom with the travel company Lastminute.com. When this happens, stags find their opportunity for profit has been sharply curtailed.

RIGHTS ISSUES

A new issue normally takes place in the early years of a company's existence. As companies attempt to expand, however, they need more funds than were provided by the original sources. There are many avenues open to raise funds in the form of debt. However, too much debt makes a company unbalanced. At some point, the company will need further equity capital.

The traditional means of raising new equity is a *rights issue*. Shares are offered to existing shareholders in proportion to their holdings – a typical offer might be one share for every four owned. The shareholder may then take up the rights and pay for the new shares or sell his rights to do so to another investor.

Rights issues are a fairly expensive way of raising new money. They have to be underwritten and the shares usually have to be offered at a substantial discount to the market price. Such are the costs that some companies have tried to find alternatives to the rights offer. But the institutions have stood firm in defence of their rights. It is a general principle of UK companies' legislation that existing shareholders should have a pre-emptive right to subscribe to any new shares on offer. Without that right, the original shareholders' stake in the company would be eroded. So except for quite small issues, UK companies can still only place shares with new investors if the existing shareholders agree.

Some companies make so many acquisitions, using shares as their means of payment, that constant rights issues are out of the question. A compromise method is called a 'vendor placing with clawback'. It works like this. Company A wants to buy Company B and would rather pay in shares than in cash. But Company B's shareholders want cash rather than shares. So Company A issues shares to Company B and then immediately arranges for the shares to be placed with outside investors, thereby getting Company B its cash. To protect the rights of Company A's shareholders, they are given the entitlement to apply for (to 'claw back') any or all of the placed shares.

When considering a rights issue, the main questions facing the company and the bank or broker advising it are when to make the issue and at what price. The shares will normally have to be offered at a discount to the market price for the company's existing shares, otherwise those shareholders who want more shares will simply buy existing ones on the market. The bigger the proportion of new shares on offer (say, one to four), the heavier the discount will have to be, in order to attract the amount of funds needed.

The company will also have to allow a grace period, usually five to seven weeks, to allow shareholders time to decide whether or not to take up their rights. This is a weakness in the process since it leaves the company vulnerable to bad news, or a change in the fortunes of the stock market. If the price of the existing shares falls too far during that period, it can ruin the prospects of the issue; the discount offered may have to be substantial in order to avoid that risk. Sometimes the discount is not enough. In 2008 Bradford & Bingley decided to reprice its rights issue, following a profits warning; the decision saved the banks that underwrote its issue many millions of pounds. In the end, the bank had to be rescued by the government.

Timing the issue is very important – if the stock market is strong, then a company can raise a lot of money by issuing fewer new shares. However, shareholders may be unwilling to take up new shares which are highly priced. If the share market is weak and a company's share price is low, then a rights issue to raise a large amount will involve issuing a large number of shares. This can dilute the control of its shareholders.

The proportion of a company's total profits, dividends and assets held by existing shareholders is unaffected by the *price* at which new shares are issued under a rights issue or the *number* of shares issued – it is the proportion of equity raised which is important. A *one-for-four issue* will create 25 per cent more shares, in other words there will be five shares in issue for every four that existed before. If existing shareholders do not take up their rights, they will own four-fifths of the enlarged company, regardless of whether the shares were issued at 50 pence or £2 each. The important question for existing shareholders to decide is whether to exercise their rights to the issue or whether to sell them to a more willing buyer. That decision may depend on whether or not they have the cash available to pay for the new shares, whether they have an interest in controlling the company and what they see as its future prospects.

How much would their rights be worth? Assume that the company offered one million shares at £2 each and that its 4 million existing shares were trading at £2.50 (a one-for-four issue). The theoretical value of the rights can be calculated as follows:

4 million existing shares at 250 pence	£10 million
1 million new shares at 200 pence	£2 million
5 million shares in total	£12 million

Dividing the total value of the company by the number of shares, £12 million ÷ 5 million = £2.40. Subtracting the rights issue price of £2.00 gives a theoretical price for the rights of 40 pence. In fact, this theoretical value is rarely attained exactly but it is a rough guide for investors.

BONUS ISSUES

Capitalization issues, sometimes known as *scrip* or *bonus issues*, create more shares but without a resulting cashflow to the company. Each shareholder is given extra shares in proportion to his or her current holdings. These issues are essentially accounting operations, transforming retained earnings into shareholders' capital. Sometimes, they are undertaken to reduce the price of shares since it is usually believed that high-priced shares are unpopular with individual investors.

Although the price of a company's shares should theoretically fall in proportion to the size of the capitalization issue (since the number of shares has increased while the nominal value of the company has remained constant) this does not always happen. Capitalization issues normally take place during periods of high company profits, and shareholders may be encouraged by news of such an issue to improve their view of the company's prospects and thus bid up its share price. This effect is likely to be only temporary, however, if investors are rational. Just because a pizza is sliced into eight pieces rather than four doesn't mean that any more food is on offer.

SHARE BUY-BACKS

As well as using the stock market to raise new capital, companies can also return cash to shareholders. In the past, companies tended to hang on to spare cash, on the 'rainy day' principle. But financial theory suggests they should not do so. If companies have no profitable projects in which to invest, they should give the money back to shareholders so they can make use of it.

Under a share buy-back, a company simply goes into the market and buys its own shares. Not only will this help boost the share price, it will enhance one measure of a company's performance called the *earnings per share.*

Provided the company is earning a decent return on its business, then profits should not be dented much by the cost of share buy-back. But the number of shares in issue will fall, so the profits per shareholder, or earnings per share, will rise.

It may even pay for companies to borrow money to buy back shares since corporate finance theory shows that debt financing, which is tax-deductible, is cheaper than equity. Share prices may also be preferred to dividends by some shareholders if the tax rate on capital gains (when they sell their shares) is lower than the tax on income. But buy-backs can make companies look very silly. Banks, in particular, bought back shares in 2006 and 2007 and then had to issue more shares, at much lower prices, in 2008. They bought high and sold low.

THE STOCK EXCHANGE

The London Stock Exchange is the traditional arena where existing securities are traded. It has long been seen as one of the symbols of both the City and the British economy. The daily fluctuations in its index are seen as reflections of the nation's economic health.

An exchange has two main functions. First, it is a place for companies to list and to raise new capital. It therefore needs a set of rules. Companies are required to have a history of public accounts, to announce all major developments promptly, to treat shareholders fairly and so on. Second, it is a place for shares to be traded. You can't have the first without the second; who would want to buy shares without knowing that they could be sold? But the main economic rationale for an exchange is that it is a place where industry can raise the long-term finance it needs.

The Exchange's origins lay in the seventeenth century, when merchants clubbed together to form joint-stock companies, like the East India Company, to conduct foreign trade. After a time, some merchants sold their holdings to others, and in the process there developed a secondary market for shares in the joint-stock companies. At first, the shares were traded in the coffee houses which were then fashionable, but in 1773 the different sites for trading were centralized for the first time. By 1801, the Stock Exchange was established in roughly its modern form.

Exchange members built up some of the country's most colourful traditions. Legend has it that if a member spotted an outsider on the Exchange floor, he would shout, 'Fourteen hundred!' (for a time, there were 1,399 members), and the offending individual would be ejected into the street, minus his trousers. Another tradition which has vanished is that of 'hammering', the term used to describe the financial failure of a member firm. The term arose because in the old days failure would be announced after an official had interrupted proceedings by hammering on a rostrum.

Times change, and the old gentlemanly agreements have given way to the age of the computer. The Big Bang, back in 1986, saw the end of the old trading floor. Instead of being marked up by hand, prices were displayed on electronic screens, via the Topic system. Traders then contacted each other by telephone to do the deal. This allowed traders a fair degree of leeway; on 19 October 1987 when US shares fell 23 per cent, those who called the leading traders in the hope of dealing found the phones were never answered.

As prices went electronic, so did company announcements, which were broadcast through the Topic news service. And electronics led to the slow demise of the share certificate, now largely confined to private investors. Details of share ownership are now held electronically and many investors hold their shares in nominee form, with a stockbroker standing between them and the company. The result has been a bit of a disconnect between companies and private shareholders, who may no longer receive annual reports from the business whose shares they hold or attend annual meetings.

In the 1990s and 2000s, the system gradually changed again. Rather than conduct deals by phone, it became possible to do deals electronically, simply by pushing the right button or clicking on the right area of the screen. Large hedge funds and so-called quantitative investors often used computers to search the market for pricing anomalies and do deals automatically when they found them.

Investors sought ways of conducting trades without moving market prices against them. (If other people know you have a big position to sell, they will cut their buying prices.) Techniques called algorithmic trading and smart order routing emerged that were designed to trade as efficiently as possible. Some of these traders aimed to do deals in fractions of a second.

THE INTERNATIONAL CHALLENGE

In this new world, the whole idea of national stock exchanges seems a bit anachronistic. Some of the biggest companies on the London stock market have their origins in other countries – BHP Billiton or Anglo-American, for example. Others like BP may have British origins but are clearly global businesses with only a tenuous link to the UK economy.

Investors who want an exposure to the oil sector are as likely to choose ExxonMobil in the US or Petrobras in Brazil as BP. And they probably do not care whether they buy those stocks in London, New York or Frankfurt – tax and costs are the main consideration.

Indeed, why do they want to buy the shares on an exchange at all? For regulatory reasons, exchanges like to publish the details of their transactions, so a false market is not created. But if you are a big investor with 20 million shares in BP, you probably do not want other investors to know you are selling part of your stake. They may anticipate the sale of the rest of your stake and drive the price down against you.

So there are rivals to the established exchanges. One format is crossing networks, where sellers and buyers are matched to save costs. The seller of BP shares simply waits until a buyer is found. Another format is dark pools; here both buyers and sellers are anonymous. The aim is to prevent deals from having an impact on market pricing.

In a sense, the existence of these networks reveals the conflict between the aims of transparency and liquidity. It is nice to know what everybody in the market is doing but not so nice for those who are participating. It is a bit like having your poker hand revealed. An EU regime called MiFID (Markets in Financial Instruments Directive) came into place in 2007 and required the details of all trades to be published, regardless of where they were conducted.

Another big issue is the role of high-frequency traders (HFTs). These use computer programmes to trade on a host of other markets, hoping to exploit small differences in prices and dealing in milliseconds, faster than the blink of an eye. Supporters claim they add liquidity to the markets; detractors, including the author Michael Lewis, claim they exploit other investors through their time advantage. An insurance company seeking to sell 1 million shares may find that prices move against it, as the HFTs see it coming and adjust prices accordingly.

With investors going global and competition emerging from new kinds of network, the London Stock Exchange can no longer rely on its national monopoly. Indeed, it is possible to imagine that one day all shares will be traded on a global electronic exchange. At the very least, there might be just one exchange for Europe, to go alongside New York and Tokyo.

For a long time the London market was the biggest in Europe, but the others have been catching up. The LSE recognized the problem by agreeing terms for a merger with the Frankfurt exchange in the late 1990s, but the deal fell through. That was when London was operating from a position of strength. But as European exchanges merged, London seemed to be left behind. A particularly strong competitor was Euronext, the exchange created by the merger of the Amsterdam, Brussels and Paris markets. The shift in power was neatly illustrated in 2002 when Euronext bought LIFFE, London's futures market, from under the London Stock Exchange's nose. Euronext merged with the New York Stock Exchange in late 2006.

In 2004, London was on the receiving end of a bid from the Frankfurt exchange, with the implication that London would be the junior partner. That bid was only defeated by the actions of shareholders in the Deutsche Börse. Such a bid was only possible because the London Stock Exchange demutualized, after a vote of members in 2000, and became a public company. It floated on itself in 2001.

The long-term future of the London Stock Exchange is still open to question. NASDAQ, the US electronic exchange, made a bid in 2006 but eventually lost interest. The LSE's own imperial ambitions have been limited to a merger with Borsa Italiana, the Italian exchange in 2007 but further consolidation seems likely. A deal with TMX, the owners of the Toronto Stock Exchange, was announced and then abandoned in 2011.

The LSE has not stood idly by. It has used the more flexible rules of AIM to attract foreign companies to list (the number of overseas groups rose from 4 in 1998 to 220 in 2005). This attracted some criticism that its rules were too lax but it did allow the market to steal a march on its US rivals.

HOW INVESTORS VALUE COMPANIES

Why do share prices move up and down? What makes some companies into poor investments and others into the equivalent of pools winners? In the end, the price of a share should be equal to the value of all future cash flows that the investors will receive, discounted to allow for the time value of money. But it is very difficult to agree on the right discount rate and even more difficult to estimate all the future cash flows. So investors have to find some short cuts.

One obvious step is to look at profits. But what is profit? It is not quite as simple as deducting a company's costs from its revenues. A charge must also be made for the gradual fall in the value of a company's fixed assets. This charge is known as *depreciation*. It is a useful concept, since it prevents accounting blips (such as a sudden drop in profits because a firm needs a new boiler). Allowances for depreciation make it easier to judge the trends in a company's profits performance.

Since tax rates can vary substantially because of the proportion of profits made overseas and because of accumulated losses in the past, it is the pre-tax profit figure which is most often chosen for analysis. If a newspaper headline talks of a company's profits being up 25 per cent, then it will be the pre-tax figure that is being referred to.

But profits cannot be the only measure of corporate performance. It is easy for companies to improve their profits by buying their competition in return for shares. Shareholders will not necessarily benefit – they could end up with 5 per cent of a company earning £20 million instead of 20 per cent of a company earning £10 million. So an important way of valuing a company is to look at its *earnings per share* (i.e. the base profits of a group divided by the number of shares in issue). That calculation is made after tax has been deducted.

Calculating earnings per share is one step on the road towards the comparison of different companies. The next step is to divide the share price by the earnings per share; the result is the price/earnings (P/E) ratio, perhaps the most popular way of valuing shares. It gives an immediate rough guide to the time needed for the investor's initial stake to be paid back in full. If the P/E ratio is 15, then it will take fifteen years (on current earnings) to pay back the shareholder's investment. If the P/E ratio is 2, then it should take only two years. Of course, for the P/E ratio to be a perfect guide to the payback period, the firm would have to keep its profits constant and distribute all of them in the form of dividends. Both events are extremely unlikely, but the P/E ratio is still an important measure of a group's worth.

One might assume that the lower a company's P/E ratio (and therefore the shorter the payback period), the better the shares are as an investment. This is far from being the case. Since all investors would prefer to have their stake repaid in two years rather than in fifteen, if they thought that the prospect was feasible they would flock to buy the shares of the company with the P/E ratio of 2. As a result, the price of that company's shares would rise, and so consequently would its P/E ratio. Other investors would sell the shares of companies with *high* P/E ratios and those companies would see their share price (and therefore their P/E ratio) fall.

The P/E ratio thus reflects investors' *expectations* of a company's earnings power. If the ratio is *low*, it indicates that investors expect the company's earnings to fall or stagnate. If the ratio is *high*, it normally means that investors expect the company's earnings to rise extremely quickly.

Another frequently consulted index of a company's performance is the *yield*, calculated by dividing the dividend by the prevailing share price. This calculation differs from the P/E because not all of a company's post-tax profits are paid out to shareholders. Sometimes the dividend can be a tiny fraction of the profits. The rest of the company's earnings will be retained by the company to finance its investment.

Yield figures and P/E ratios are given in the *Financial Times* every day for most of the shares traded on the Stock Exchange. An important point to note is that share prices fall just before the company issues its dividend and the shares are sold 'ex-dividend'. The person selling the shares will receive the dividend rather than the person receiving them and the fall in price will reflect the likely dividend payment. Shares become cum-dividend shortly afterwards and for a few days it is possible to choose whether to buy shares ex- or cum-dividend.

There are other valuation methods. One is to calculate the value of the company's assets and then, after deducting the value of its debts, calculate a net asset value per share. If the company's share price is lower than its net asset value per share, then, in theory, it would be possible to buy the company, sell off all the assets and make a profit.

Asset value is a quite useful valuation method for some companies but in modern industry, when many businesses are service companies with very few tangible assets, it has a limited application.

In the late 1990s, investors started to use other valuation measures to assess shares. In some cases, these were designed to overcome the problem of companies that had no profits or dividends, mainly in the internet sector. In other cases, the aim was to produce something more sophisticated than earnings per share, a figure that can be easily manipulated. The most popular new measure was EBITDA (earnings before interest, tax, depreciation and amortization), a figure which aimed to show the cash flow of the company. Another measure was free cash flow, the cash left over after the company had paid its working costs and any necessary capital expenditure.

TAKEOVERS

Although corporate profitability is very important to share prices – and a sudden move into losses or extra-high profits can have a dramatic impact on a particular share – it is the prospect of a takeover that really gets investors excited.

Takeovers have been the basis for many scandals in the City, and they can also arouse much passion as the managers and the workers in the target company unite to fight off the unwanted predator. The concept is quite simple – one company buys up the majority of the share capital of another. Usually, for tax and other reasons, the predator will buy all the share capital but it is not inevitable. A simple majority will give the owner control but 75 per cent may be needed to force through key decisions about a company's future. More than 90 per cent is needed if the predator wants to eliminate all minority shareholders; beyond that level, the buyer has the right to compulsorily acquire the remaining shares.

Occasionally, takeovers are dignified by the name mergers and the talk is of a partnership between equals. There may even be co-chairmen and the lead management positions are shared out between the two sets of executives. However, in the vast majority of cases, one party has the upper hand. Genuine mergers are quite rare.

What motivates the company making a takeover? Normally, it is the belief that it can run the target company better than the existing management. This might be because the incumbent management is particularly incompetent; it might be because combining two businesses can bring cost savings; it might be because the target company has moved into industrial sectors which it does not understand. In some cases, predators may simply believe that the shares in the target company are cheap. It may be possible, once the target has been acquired, to sell off the various parts of the company for more than the whole – a process which used to be known as 'asset-stripping'.

Most takeovers involve private companies (i.e. those not quoted on the stock market). Normally private companies are owned by one individual, or a group of individuals, and the predator cannot gain control without their agreement. Why do companies agree to be taken over? There are lots of potential reasons. If you own 80 per cent of a thriving private company, you are in theory wealthy but your money is locked up. Only by selling your shares can you get hold of the capital to buy your dream house, luxury yacht, or whatever. Since your shares are not quoted on the Stock Exchange, few people will want to buy them. In most instances, the only practical way to realize your cash is to agree to a takeover. Another reason for a private company agreeing to be taken over is to obtain funds for expansion. A big, publicly quoted company finds it easier to pay for a new factory or set of computers.

When a predator wants to take over a quoted company, a whole set of complex rules and customs have to be followed. The Takeover Code is voluntary but, in practice, City firms have to follow its rules if they want to keep their reputation. (Or at least, they have to avoid *being caught* breaking the rules.)

It is a general principle that all shareholders must be treated equally, and many of the rules are designed to ensure this happens. For example, it is obviously in the interests of the predator to ensure that his intentions are kept as secret as possible. As soon as news of a bid leaks out, the share price of the target company will rise substantially. Thus the greater the secrecy, the more shares the bidder can acquire at lower prices. However, the proportion of shares that a predator can acquire without revealing its stake is just 3 per cent. Once that level is reached, a buyer must reveal the amount of shares he owns and any further purchases. Otherwise, other shareholders might sell their stakes at 'artificially low' prices, only to see the price rise when the bid is announced. Another rule is that a bidder cannot buy more than 30 per cent of a company, without offering to buy the rest of the equity. Again the principle of equal treatment applies. If the rule did not exist, a bidder could buy just 50.1 per cent of the equity at a high price; the owners of the other 49.9 per cent would then miss out.

So what happens when a bid is launched? Usually, a predator will try to win the consent of the board of the target company. That board has a duty to recommend the bid, if it thinks it is in the best interest of shareholders. Sometimes, the price offered is so high or the advantages of combining the businesses are so obvious that the board will agree to the offer. In such instances, bids are nearly always successful.

It is when a bid is rejected that the fun starts. Each side will hire one, and sometimes two, banks to advise them on tactics; each will have a public relations firm putting its case to the press. On the day the predator launches its offer, it will outline the logic of combining the two businesses and describe its offer as extremely generous. The target will come back quickly with a statement proclaiming its desire for independence and dismissing the offer as 'derisory' and 'opportunistic'.

The whole process takes up to eighty-one days. It is up to the predator to convince shareholders in the target company that the price offered is fair and the logic of a combination sound. If the predator is offering its own shares in exchange for those in the target, it will have to show that there is a prospect of long-term growth in its own profits.

The process is kept to a short timetable. After announcing its intention of making a bid, the predator has twenty-one days to send an offer document to shareholders in the target company. Then the predator has sixty days in which to win the argument; if it has failed to get the majority of shares by then, it must give up the bid.

Normally, companies are only bid for if their profits record has been disappointing. So, they are in the difficult position of arguing, 'We've been bad before, but we'll be good in the future.' Target companies will usually put some flesh on the bones of their promises with a profits forecast. They will also attack the record of their opponent. If such tactics appear to be having little success, they may be forced to call on a 'white knight' – a third company which will outbid the unwanted predator. The target company will have lost its independence but it will at least have deprived the enemy of total success.

Most shareholders wait until the last minute before deciding, in case a higher bid is put on the table. The final count can be agonizingly close – bids have been disallowed because the vital acceptances were delivered just a few minutes after the final deadline. These days hedge funds may often be involved. Some may follow a strategy known as merger arbitrage in which they buy the shares of the target and sell short (bet on a decline in) the shares of the predator. Others may be activist funds that buy stakes and try to force a company's managers to increase the share price by seeking a bid.

Takeovers tend to be terribly acrimonious, although the kind of high-profile advertising that characterized the takeover battles of the early 1980s has been discouraged. They are also very lucrative for the banks, lawyers, accountants and public relations advisers involved. The costs of a substantial bid, successful or not, will run into many millions of pounds.

It is unsurprising, in the circumstances, that banks are eager to get work as bid advisers. Some of the big commercial banks have tried to make inroads in the market by financing, as well as advising on, the bid. This can leave the banks rather exposed if things go wrong.

There is plenty of controversy over whether takeovers are actually good for industry. Academic studies have been written arguing that the larger businesses created are rarely more efficient than the old. Some believe that the fear of a takeover restricts the managers of companies – they tend to worry about short-term results rather than investing for the long-term good of the firm. It is certainly true that some companies are more famous for their takeovers than for actually running the businesses they own. The stock market history books are littered with the names of whizz-kids who built up vast empires through a series of acquisitions, only to see the whole edifice crumble in disaster.

But it is hard to see how shareholders would ever rid themselves of incompetent managements without the prospect of a takeover. It is possible that if taking companies over was made more difficult, control of industry might be seized by less open means – boardroom coups, for example. At least, under the current system, the arguments are made public.

TAKEOVERS AND FRAUD

Since so many of the City's scandals are tied up with takeover battles, it is worth explaining the practices that incur such disgust. The first is *insider dealing*. This is not an offence confined to takeovers, although bids offer most of the best opportunities. All it involves is someone – the chairman's brother, the stockbroker, the lawyer – buying or selling shares in advance of some piece of important corporate news. Say that Acme Inc. is about to bid for Dullsville. Acme employs the First National Bank of Wigan as its adviser. A young broker at the First National learns of the bid and buys a large slug of Dullsville shares just before the bid is announced. He makes a substantial profit *but* he is an insider dealer.

Not everyone thinks that insider dealing is wrong. Some think that it makes the markets more efficient, since it is a way of ensuring that all the information about a company is in its share price. It is, such people say, a victimless crime. And insider dealing is very hard to define as an offence. There have been some scandals which involved people learning of the shares that newspapers were about to tip in their columns and then buying accordingly. But you could argue that the only people to suffer were those foolish enough to buy on the back of a newspaper tip. Then there is the question of how you obtain the information. Supposing you overhear two men in a bar saying that they think Barclays is about to be taken over. The chances are very high that the two men do not know what they are talking about. If you buy Barclays shares, you may actually lose money. But if, by chance, the men were right, does that make you a criminal?

The second sort of scandal involves the tactics used in the bid. Since many offers are made using the shares of the predator company as payment for those in the target company, it is obvious that the higher the price of the predator's shares, the better the chances of the bid. Thus, there is an incentive for the predator to try to manipulate its share price, perhaps by bribing others to buy its shares. Such schemes are now against the law, but they can be difficult to prove. Similarly, if a few shareholders have large stakes in the target company, the predator may try to bribe them to accept its offer, perhaps in return for some commercial deal after the bid is successful. Again such arrangements can be difficult to prove.

THE FTSE INDEX

Every day, on the television news, some reference will be made to the performance of the FTSE Index – the so-called barometer of industry's health. If the FTSE Index goes up, that in itself is regarded as 'good' news. If it goes down and keeps falling, talk of a national crisis begins.

There are several indices in use, but the one most commonly referred to is the FTSE 100, which stands for the Financial Times Stock Exchange 100 Index. The hundred firms involved are some of the biggest in the country – the so-called 'blue chips'.

The idea is to select companies of such size and range that they reflect both the industrial diversity of Britain and the shares involved in the market. Every time a company is taken over or falls on bad times, the index must be changed.

In earlier times, the main index that was followed was the FT-30, which as its name suggests covers just 30 companies. But that index is now felt to be too narrow a base since a large move in the price of just one firm can affect the whole index. An even wider index than the FTSE 100 is the FTSE All-Share Index. The latter, despite its name, does not include all the shares traded on the Stock Exchange but it does include all those (around 700) in which there is a significant market. Indices have also been developed to cover medium- and small-sized companies. There are equivalent indices in other markets. The US uses the Dow Jones Industrial Average and the S&P 500 index, Tokyo the Nikkei 225 average and Frankfurt the DAX.

Does it really matter if the FTSE Index falls or rises? The answer is not clear-cut. Day-to-day shifts are of little importance. They may result from a chance remark of a government minister, from an unexpected set of economic statistics or because investors expect any or all of these things to be good or bad. What actually happens to the economy or to the government is usually not as important as the *expectations* of investors about what might happen.

Remember that the vast majority of shares are held by investing institutions. They must not only judge the prospects of individual companies but also the prospects of the share market as a whole. If they think that, say, interest rates are about to fall, they might shift their portfolios into bond investments because the prices of bonds will rise as rates fall. However, they might feel that a drop in rates will reduce the costs of industrial companies and cause share prices to rise. Either line of reasoning would have logic behind it. The net result will be that some investors will sell shares and some will buy, moving the index up or down depending on where the balance lies.

Such day-to-day shifts are what statisticians call noise and have little effect on the performance of business, although they may be costly for shareholders who buy or sell at the wrong time. Obviously a disastrous day like 19 October 1987 ('Black Monday'), when the Dow Jones Industrial Average fell 508 points, has an enormous impact. But such earth-shattering days are fortunately few in number. It is long-term shifts in the index which are important.

There is little doubt, for example, that the Wall Street Crash of 1929 contributed to the depths of the 1930s depression. In the UK, share prices bounced back in the late 1970s from their lows of January 1975 as the economy recovered from the three-day week, the miners' strike and hyperinflation. Some thought at the time that Black Monday signalled a repeat of the 1930s. Although the 1990s recession was bad, it did not plumb the depths of that earlier era.

Through the auspices of the London International Financial Futures Exchange (see Chapter 13), it is possible to buy futures based on the FTSE 100 Index. If the index rises, the price of the futures will also rise. Under the system through which futures are traded, a rise in the futures price benefits futures buyers and a fall benefits the sellers. That allows institutional investors to sell futures to protect their shareholdings against a general fall in prices by selling index futures. For those who do not fancy the intricacies of the futures market, several bookmakers offer simple bets on whether the index will fall or rise.

Bulls are investors who believe that share prices are about to rise, and rise substantially. They may even borrow money to invest in shares, in order to get the maximum possible benefit from any increase. *Bears*, in contrast, believe that share prices are set to fall. They will try to sell now and buy back later at a lower price. As we saw in the chapter on hedge funds, they may even sell shares they do not own, a practice known as *going short*, to try to exploit the price fall. In accordance with the risk/reward rules, aggressive bulls and bears take great risks, in the hope of making their fortunes. Anyone who went bearish before the crash of 1987 could have made a lot of money from that otherwise disastrous event.

The growth of the international capital markets is probably the single most important development in the international financial markets since the Second World War, because it has created a market in which borrowers and lenders can borrow and invest funds, virtually untouched by the wishes of nation states.

For many years, this international market was known as the Euromarket after so-called 'Eurodollars' – dollars that were held outside the United States. Other currencies held outside their country of origin were known as Eurocurrencies.

Some people believe that this market had its origin in the unwillingness of the Soviet Union to hold dollars in New York for fear that the US government might freeze its deposits at times of political tension. However, the Russians still needed dollars to be able to conduct international trade, and they began to borrow in Europe through a Russian-owned bank, Banque Commerciale pour l'Europe du Nord, whose telex code was Eurobank.

Where did the dollars that the Russians borrowed come from? From the late 1950s onwards there were plenty of dollars around outside the United States because of the current-account deficits run up by the Americans. If a country has a current-account deficit, it pays out more of its own currency than it receives in foreign currency. Dollars were therefore flowing out of the country into the hands of foreign exporters. At the same time the US Treasury imposed Regulation Q, which set upper limits on the level of interest rates that US banks could offer to domestic and foreign investors. Those people who held dollars outside the United States and wanted to invest them found that non-US banks were able to offer more attractive rates than their US counterparts. Thus the Eurodollar market was born.

As more currencies became convertible (readily exchangeable) following the dismantling of post-war controls, the market grew. There was a range of major convertible currencies by the late 1950s. Investors were able to put their money into Eurodollar deposits in the knowledge that they would be able to convert their holdings into their domestic currencies if they wished.

A liquid market for these deposits quickly developed, and banks began to quote interest rates for dollar loans up to a year. After a short while London became the centre of the market, restoring to the City a position which it had begun to lose to New York. This was an immensely important development: the City's financial pre-eminence, formerly a concomitant of sterling's role in world trade, had been eroded by the UK's economic problems. By comparison with its rivals, London had a distinct advantage – its position in the middle of the time zones between Tokyo and New York, which allowed London-based dealers to talk to those in other centres in the course of the working day.

Those American banks which had been precluded by Regulation Q from attracting foreign investors' deposits began to set up branches in London, enabling them to compete with the European banks in the Eurodollar market. In addition to its time-zone position, London had the extra advantage of speaking the same language as the Americans, thus making it easier for bankers to live and work in Britain.

The market has a great importance in the world economy, since it provides a mechanism by which funds can flow quickly between one currency and another. As the market is largely outside governmental control, it can prove a potent weapon for destabilizing a currency.

SYNDICATED LOANS

Having begun with short-term deposits, the Euromarket was quickly adapted to serve the needs of longer-term borrowers by the development of the syndicated loan. This is merely a large, long-term bank loan which a syndicate of banks club together to provide because no one bank wants to commit that much capital to any one borrower. Usually, these loans carry interest rates at a margin relating to LIBOR or EURIBOR, the equivalent measure for the Eurozone. Companies, countries or institutions with a good credit rating can sometimes borrow below LIBOR or even the London Interbank Bid Rate (LIBID), but borrowers whose financial position is not so healthy can expect to pay a considerable margin over LIBOR.

The syndicated loan market gives borrowers access to large sources of long-term funds (loans can extend to billions of dollars) in a short space of time. Another advantage for borrowers is that, having got the loan commitment, they do not need to borrow it all. The overall limit on the loan may be $1 billion, but borrowers pay interest only on the amount outstanding at any time. (This compares favourably with a bond issue, interest on the full amount of which must be paid until the bond is repaid.) Syndicated loans have been particularly attractive to nation states which wish to raise large amounts of money in a single borrowing. The advantage to banks of such loans is that they can lend long term at rates above their normal costs of funds without committing too much capital to any one borrower.

In the early 1980s the syndicated loan market was badly hit by the number of government loans which were rescheduled or deferred by the international debt crisis. The banks were faced with bad debts which cut their profits and reduced their credit ratings. Banks became unwilling to tie up their money in syndicated loans and started to lend money in more liquid forms or even to act as arrangers rather than providers of borrowings.

However, corporations and supranational institutions continued to borrow in syndicated loan form and the market continued, if not quite in the lavish style of the 1970s.

LEVERAGED LOANS

The international loan market has been transformed in recent years by the growth of leveraged loans. These are loans used by private equity groups (see Chapter 9) to finance their takeovers of companies.

The term leveraged is used because the companies concerned take on a lot more debt than would normally be considered prudent. As a result, leveraged loans pay much higher interest rates than conventional syndicated loans. But this makes them attractive to a certain type of investor, particularly hedge funds who are aiming to achieve outsize returns.

The hope is that the private equity groups will be skilful enough to cut the costs and improve the cash flow of the companies they buy, so that it is easy for them to pay the interest on the loans and, in relatively short order, repay the debt. But the danger is that if such companies hit recessionary conditions, the burden of repaying the debt will prove insuperable. Some investors diversify their risk in the leveraged loan market by putting their money into portfolios of loans known as collateralized loan obligations, or CLOs. But the CLO market dried up in the wake of the credit crunch.

THE EUROBOND MARKET

In parallel with the growth of the syndicated loan market in the 1960s and 1970s, borrowers issued long-term tradeable instruments – Eurobonds. A bond, as seen in the Introduction, is merely a piece of paper which promises, in return for an immediate loan, to pay the holder interest until the loan is repaid. Since the original purchaser can (and usually does) sell the bond, repayment will be made to whoever ends up holding the bond (the bearer) on maturity. Attached to each Eurobond are coupons which the bearer can tear off in order to claim the interest payment. Normally the maturity of the bond will be at least two years; the maximum maturity is around thirty years, although some bonds have been issued on the express condition that they will never be repaid.

The borrower can arrange to pay back the debt by setting aside a certain amount each year during the life of the bond through a sinking fund or by waiting until the end (a so-called 'bullet maturity'). Bonds can be repaid early if a borrower buys back the debt in the traded market or if it incorporates a call option at the time of the issue, allowing it to repay a certain amount of bonds each year. The effect of all these strategies is to minimize the impact of repayment on the borrower's cashflow.

There are bond markets in most parts of the world. Traditionally borrowers raised money only in their domestic bond markets. Formerly issues in foreign markets were the exception rather than the rule. As a consequence a bond issued by a foreign institution became known as a *bulldog* in the UK, a *Yankee bond* in the US, a *samurai bond* in Japan and so on (these terms are rarely used these days).

As we saw in Chapter 7, in the sterling market the main issuer of bonds (in the form of gilts) is the government. In the Eurobond market a whole range of borrowers issue bonds, such as corporations, banks, governments and supranational institutions like the World Bank.

Some companies, governments and banks have borrowing requirements which are so large that their domestic market cannot accommodate them. It is possible for them to borrow at a much better rate abroad. Domestic investors may have already bought large numbers of their bonds and no longer wish to buy the bonds of that institution unless they are guaranteed a high rate of interest. Foreign bond issues give borrowers access to other countries' investors: Eurobond issues grant access to international investors.

How did the Eurobond market develop? In 1963 the USA imposed an Interest Equalization Tax (IET) to discourage foreign borrowers from raising capital in the US market. President Kennedy was worried about continuing US current-account deficits; he considered that these were encouraged by US investment overseas. The IET was imposed, at a rate ranging from 2.75 per cent to 15 per cent, on the purchase value of foreign bonds bought by US citizens, thus making it considerably more expensive for foreign institutions to borrow money in the US (since they had to offer higher yields to compensate investors for the tax disadvantages). Non-US borrowers were still keen to borrow dollars, however, and therefore began to look for investors outside the US who had dollars to lend.

Although this is the subject of debate, some people regard the first Eurobond as a $15 million issue of Autostrade, the Italian motorway company. As we have seen, a Eurodollar is merely a dollar held outside the US: a Eurobond is a bond sold outside the country of the denominating currency. The vast majority of the early Eurobond issues were denominated in dollars – a reflection of the dominant role played by the dollar in international trade.

European bankers, especially those based in London, realized that the IET had created an opportunity which they could exploit. Traditionally dollar-denominated bonds were managed by US banks, which pocketed the substantial fees involved (0.5 per cent was then standard, and on a $50 million issue that would mean $250,000). The US banks also acted as underwriters for the issues – that is, they agreed to buy any bonds which failed to be sold to outside investors. The fee for underwriting was often as much as 1 per cent. European bankers seized a portion of this lucrative business and created a London-based market to bring together international borrowers and investors.

To whom did the banks sell Eurobonds? In the markets the legend was that the typical Eurobond buyer was the Belgian dentist, the middle-class professional attempting to avoid the stringent tax laws of the Benelux countries. Indeed, an important reason for the success of the Eurobond market was the fact that bonds are denominated in bearer form, allowing the investor almost complete anonymity. Whoever presents the coupon to the bank for interest, or the bond itself for repayment, will receive payment. There is no register of owners; accordingly, they cannot be traced by regulatory authorities. As a result investors who hold bonds outside their own countries are normally able to escape tax. Anyone who enjoyed the thriller *Die Hard* will recall that the aim of Alan Rickman's group of terrorists was to rob the office building of a vast sum in bearer bonds. In fact Eurobond investors include banks, investment management firms, pension funds and insurance companies all over the world as well as wealthy individuals like the Belgian dentists.

Nowadays, the term Eurobond market is falling out of use because the market is so international in scope, with debt issued by US manufacturers being bought by Chinese banks, an unimaginable concept in the 1970s. Bonds are issued in a wide range of currencies, including sterling, Canadian dollars, Japanese yen and even the Kuwaiti dinar. Borrowers are not limited to issues denominated in their domestic currency. With the help of swaps (see Chapter 13), they can issue in one currency and end up with cheap funding in another.

The arranging bank must set the bond's yield at a level that will be attractive to investors but will be the lowest rate possible for the borrower. At one time, the banks were paid their fees in the form of a discount to the issue price, which led to losses if the bond was mispriced. That changed from 1990 onwards, when the fixed price re-offer system started to be used. Under this system, the banks involved agree to sell the bonds at a fixed price for a set period; their fees (usually between 0.25 and 0.3 per cent) are paid quite separately.

GROWTH IN THE MARKET

The advantages of the international bond market – the degree to which it is unfettered by regulation and the size of the investor base – have resulted in its truly phenomenal growth since that first Eurobond issue in 1963. In that year the volume of Eurobond issues was just over $100 million. In 2013, total debt issuance reached $5.6 trillion, according to Thomson Reuters.

Once a bond has been issued, it moves into the secondary market. A primary market is one in which bonds are sold for the first time; a secondary market is one in which existing bonds are traded. Traders sit in vast dealing rooms, surrounded by electronic screens displaying the current prices of bond issues, the latest moves in interest rates and the trends in the economy. They look for bond yields which have moved out of line with the rest of the market and can therefore be bought or sold for profit. They also try to anticipate whether interest rates will fall (and bond prices will rise) or rise (and bond prices will fall). If they make the right decision, they can earn their companies a lot of money; in consequence, they are some of the most highly paid men and women in the country.

Trading is now incredibly sophisticated. Investors will be looking to bet on whether issues of one particular maturity (say, ten years) will outperform those of shorter or longer duration. They will bet on whether riskier bonds will outperform safe bonds. They will separate the interest payments of bonds from the capital. They will speculate that one type of debt issued by a company will deliver higher returns than another (because, for example, that class of debt has better rights in case of bankruptcy). They will separate the interest-rate risk of the bond from the prospects of default.

London is the centre of this market. The Americans have tried, without much success, to switch the market to New York by setting up international banking facilities, which allow banks to treat some of their New York offices as being off the US mainland. The UK government has also managed to see off the idea of a European withholding tax, which would deduct tax at source for bond payments. Since one key appeal of the market is the fact that payments are made gross (leaving it up to the investor whether to declare the income to the tax authorities), such a tax might drive the market to, say, Switzerland.

The location of the market may still be London, but it is the American rather than the British banks who now have the lion's share of the business of Eurobond arranging. The early lead of the European bankers evaporated when US banks set up London-based subsidiaries to recapture their hold over the dollar bond market. And the market is now highly sophisticated, with debt being issued in a wide variety of forms.

FLOATING-RATE NOTES

Most people are aware of the concept of floating-rate debt. After all, nearly all mortgages are a form of floating-rate debt: a building society can (and does) frequently change the interest rate to be paid on the amount borrowed. The same is true for most people's savings. The interest paid to a lender is subject to change, largely at the whim of the deposit-taking institution.

Floating-rate bonds (more often called floating-rate notes or FRNs) have been a major part of the market only since 1970. One reason was that traditionally many UK borrowers, particularly companies, preferred the idea of fixed-rate debt because they could calculate their costs in advance. (Floating-rate debt was more common in the USA.)

When interest rates are high, borrowers become reluctant to borrow long-term at fixed rates because they would then find themselves saddled with a very expensive debt obligation should interest rates subsequently fall. The interest payments on an FRN, however, rise and fall with the level of rates in the market. This is particularly attractive to banks. Most of the money they invest (lend) is lent at floating rates, so borrowing through FRNs allows them to be sure of a constant relationship between the return on their investments and the cost of their funds.

Investors tend to be especially interested in buying FRNs at times when the yield curve is inverted – that is, when short-term interest rates are above long-term rates. Since the return on FRNs is linked to a short-term rate, they provide a higher income than equivalent fixed-rate bonds at such times. Booms in FRN issues have therefore taken place when high interest rates (which make borrowers want to issue FRNs) have occurred simultaneously with an inverted yield curve (which makes investors want to buy FRNs). Such conditions existed in 1970, 1974 and again in 1984–5.

Typically, FRNs are linked to six-month LIBOR (the rate which banks charge other major banks for six-month loans) and are reset every six months. Most borrowers pay a margin over LIBOR that is related to their creditworthiness. The first issue was made by the Italian public utility Enel, which paid a margin of 0.75 per cent over the mean between LIBOR and LIBID, the rate which banks are prepared to pay in order to borrow.

What about the secondary market in FRNs? As we saw in Chapter 2, the level of interest rates has a major effect on the market price of fixed-rate bonds. Because they are closely linked to the prevailing level of interest rates, one might expect FRNs to stick fairly close to their issuing price. However, this does not always happen. Although the interest rate on FRNs changes, it does so only once every six months. In the intervening period the general level of interest rates can rise and fall, affecting the price of FRNs.

If interest rates rise, investors will receive a return on the FRNs which, because it is set by an out-of-date benchmark rate, is unattractive. They will sell their FRNs, causing their prices to fall, until the yields come back into line. If rates fall, FRNs will be offering a higher return than the market rate and their prices will rise. However, because the FRN rate is changed every six months, these fluctuations are nowhere near as substantial as those on fixed-rate bonds: most FRNs trade in a range of 96–104 per cent of their issuing price.

'BELLS AND WHISTLES'

Banks have developed other variations on bonds, so-called 'bells and whistles', which are designed to attract investors and thereby help the issuer to achieve a lower interest rate than would be possible with a conventional issue.

One of the most prominent 'variations' is the zero-coupon bond, which, as its name suggests, pays no interest at all. Instead it is issued at a discount to its face value. Say it is issued with a face value of £100; its selling price may then be £50. When the bond matures in five years' time, the borrower will repay the full £100. The investor has effectively received all the interest in a lump, rather than spread out over the years. This can be particularly attractive to investors in countries which have tax regimes that differentiate between income and capital gains. The difference between the prices at which the bond is bought and sold is treated by some tax systems as a capital gain; capital gains taxes are normally below the highest rates of income tax. If the investor is going to pay less tax on a zero-coupon bond, he will be willing to accept an interest rate effectively rather lower than that on a straight bond. Both investor and borrower thus benefit.

It is possible to calculate the 'interest' on a zero-coupon bond, though this sounds an odd concept. Assume that the bond has a one-year maturity and a face value of £100, and that it is sold for £80. An investor who buys the bond on issue will make a £20 gain if he holds it until maturity. A profit of £20 on an investment of £80 is a return of 25 per cent per annum. If the bond had a two-year maturity, an issue price of £64 would achieve the same return (25 per cent of £64 is £16, which, added on to £64, makes £80).

Another variation is the partly paid bond. This allows investors to pay only a proportion of the bond's face value when the bond is issued and to pay the rest later on. This gives them an opportunity for 'leverage'. Suppose a bond is issued at a yield of 10 per cent and the investor is asked to pay only £50 on a bond with a face value of £100. If, because of a change in the market level of interest rates, the price of 10 per cent bonds rises from £100 to £110, then the price of the partly paid bond will rise to £60. The partly paid investor will make a gain of 20 per cent on his initial stake, whereas a conventional bond in the same conditions would have earned him only 10 per cent. Of course, had conventional bonds fallen from £100 to £90, partly paid bonds would have fallen from £50 to £40, a drop of 25 per cent as against 10 per cent (the risk/reward trade-off again).

A further potential advantage to buyers of partly paid bonds is the scope for currency speculation. Investors can buy a partly paid bond in another currency, believing that the foreign currency will fall against their own. If it does, they will have to pay less for the second part of the bond.

The problem of currency risk affects all investors who buy bonds denominated in foreign currencies. A US investor who buys an issue denominated in sterling will want sterling to appreciate against the dollar during the lifetime of the bond. Suppose the bond is worth £1 million when it is bought and the exchange rate is $1 = £1. If, when the investor redeems the bond, the sterling exchange rate has risen to $2 = £1, then the investor will receive $2 million (double the original investment). However, if the pound has fallen against the dollar, the investor will receive less than his original investment.

Dual-currency bonds fix the exchange rate at which the investor is paid. The investor pays for the bond in one currency but will be repaid in another at a pre-arranged exchange rate. The borrower will protect this rate through the forward foreign-exchange markets (see Chapter 14).

Just as exchange-rate movements can adversely affect the investor, so can changes in the level of interest rates. Bonds have been devised to combat this risk with fixed and floating characteristics. Among the special features on offer from issuers have been the warrant and capped and collared floaters.

The warrant. This is similar in principle to an option. Warrants are normally sold separately from the original issue and give the investor the right to purchase a new bond, bearing a fixed rate of interest. The borrower gets additional and immediate cash from the sale of the warrants but incurs the risk of being forced to issue extra debt at above-market rates. The investor enjoys the prospect of profiting if interest rates fall but faces the risk that the warrants will be worthless when they expire because interest rates have stayed above the level available for the warrants.

Capped and *collared floaters.* These are FRNs where the rate can fluctuate but cannot rise above a certain level – 'the cap' – or fall below a different level – 'the collar'.

One of the problems with the bells and whistles described above is that they can be briefly fashionable, then go out of favour with the market. That can be bad news for investors who bought the bonds when they were first issued. However, one type of bond which has been a constant feature of the markets has been the equity convertible.

CONVERTIBLE BONDS

Convertible bonds, as their name suggests, are bond issues which can be converted into shares of the issuing company. The company issues a (normally fixed-rate) bond. The investor may exchange each bond into a given number of shares, which becomes advantageous when the shares reach a price on the stock market which is usually 20–25 per cent above their current value. The investor has two ways of profiting from a convertible issue: through the interest rate and possible capital appreciation of the bond, and through conversion into shares, which permits him or her to earn dividends and a possible further increase in the share price. The borrower will be able to offer a reduced coupon on the original bond issue because of the potential benefits to the investor of conversion. If the investor converts, the company will increase its equity base but will dilute the value of its shares.

Another means of achieving a similar effect is to issue a bond with equity warrants attached which grant the investor the right to buy the company's shares at a set price. The difference between the two methods is that with a straight convertible the borrower gets the benefit of a reduced cost of borrowing because of the lower coupon, and with a warrant the borrower receives the benefit in the form of additional cash from the sale of the warrant.

One problem with equity convertibles occurs when the share price of the issuing company falls sharply. This is bad news for bondholders, since they will be left with a low-yielding bond in a company with diminished prospects. It is also bad news for the issuer. Instead of acquiring a new bunch of shareholders on conversion, they will have to find the money to repay the bond on maturity.

This was a particular problem in the late 1980s. Companies issued convertible bonds in the bull market of 1987 when share prices were rising rapidly; after the Crash, it became clear in 1988 and 1989 that the bonds would never be converted into shares.

In the wake of the financial crisis of 2008, a new element was added to the market in the form of contingent convertibles, or coco bonds, issued by banks. The crisis had revealed that the banks had too little equity capital and were too reliant on short-term funding, which would quickly be withdrawn at the first hint of trouble. Some banks lost 6–8 per cent of their assets in the crisis but had equity cushions of as little as 2 per cent. Ideally, some of the losses could have been borne by bondholders, but the regulators were reluctant to insist on this, since a loss of capital by bondholders at one bank might cause a sell-off in the bonds of all banks. As a result, governments felt obliged to step in and rescue the banks themselves.

Cocos are designed to get round this problem. When bank capital falls below a certain level, cocos will be converted into shares and will thus boost the capital ratio. Whether this will work in practice remains to be seen; there could be a mass stampede out of cocos if conversion seems imminent.

GETTING A BOND RATING

It is almost impossible for investors around the world to be aware of the strengths and weaknesses of the multitude of borrowers who issue bonds. Largely for this reason, rating agencies have assumed an important and unusual place in the financial hierarchy. The market is dominated by three agencies – Standard and Poor's, Moody's and Fitch. Before most bond issues, the borrowing institution will pay one of the rating agencies to rate the issue. Standard and Poor's ratings range from AAA (the ability to repay principal is very strong indeed) to D (the bond is in default and payment of interest or repayment of principal is in arrears). Only bonds rated BBB or above are regarded as being of investment grade and eligible for investment by the more cautious institutions.

The criteria which Standard and Poor's use for rating issues made by governments are quite interesting and give an insight into the minds of international investors. The first is political risk. The agency makes an assessment of the country's underlying political and social stability: it sees the most important factors as 'the degree of political participation, the orderliness of successions in government, the extent of governmental control and the general flexibility and responsiveness of the system'. Standard and Poor's add: 'Signals of high political risk include such events as periodic social disorder and rioting, military coups or radical ideological shifts within the government.'

Among the social factors that the agency examines are the rate of population growth, its location and its ethnic mix. The more fast-growing, concentrated and racially diverse the population, the greater the social risk. Further factors are the degree of the country's integration into the Western political system and the extent of its participation in international organizations. The more the country is enmeshed in the Western system, so the reasoning runs, the less likely it is to repudiate its debt and therefore the better its credit rating.

An economic analysis of a country's prospects is undertaken by comparing the total of the country's debts with its foreign-exchange reserves and its balance-of-payments position. This last factor is seen by the agency as one of the most important of the economic criteria, since most debt defaults have occurred when countries have incurred persistent trade deficits. However, the standard of living of the inhabitants is also considered – the higher it is, the more able a government will be to cut down demand if it is faced with a trade deficit. A good economic growth rate also helps: the agency feels that 'A high rate of growth in total output and especially exports suggests a better ability to meet future debt obligations.'

Rating governments can occasionally get the agencies into trouble if a political administration dislikes the result. The agencies can also have problems rating companies. If they assign too low a grade, the companies may complain; a reputation for being too strict may send issuers elsewhere. This is important because it is the issuer, not the investor, that pays the agency their fee. But if the agency is seen as too lax, then investors will complain. The collapses of Enron and Worldcom in 2002 brought criticism that the agencies only acted after a company's finances had deteriorated, not before.

But the greatest flak came with the boom in structured products, the repackaged asset-backed loans (particularly linked to subprime mortgages) that were described in Chapter 3. The growth of this market caused a huge boom in the profits of the agencies and led to criticism that the lure of fees was warping their judgement. When the market collapsed, the agencies did admit to a few mistakes.

One problem was that the new products were so complicated that it was harder to predict their behaviour; another was that the agencies based their ratings on the likelihood of default, not on the risk of sharp price falls. But investors were understandably taken aback when AAA-rated debt, the safest in the market, fell to 90 per cent of face value or below. That would not happen with a conventional issue, unless the bonds had been downgraded. The net result was that the reputation of the agencies undoubtedly suffered; perhaps they should have been more cautious in handing out their highest mark of approval.

JUNK BONDS

Bonds are generally seen as a conservative investment. They offer more security than equities, but a lower return. For much of the 1980s, however, a US phenomenon made the bond market seem positively exciting (in financial terms, at least); this was the enthusiasm for junk bonds.

The term initially referred to bonds which had collapsed in price, normally because the company which issued them had become mired in financial difficulties. The market marked down the price of the bond because it feared the company would be unable to repay the capital, or even maintain the interest payments. In the language of the rating agencies (referred to above), the bonds would be 'below investment grade' with a rating below BBB.

A smart trader called Michael Milken, who worked for a US banking group called Drexel Burnham Lambert, saw the opportunity for profit in junk bonds. Say a bond was issued with a coupon of 10 per cent, but the company gets into difficulty and its price falls to 50 (compared with a face value of 100). If the company just pays the interest, the investor will earn a running yield of 20 per cent (10/50). And if the company repays the bond in full, the investor will double his capital.

Obviously, there is a strong chance that the company will go bust. But Milken worked out that if the investor bought a large enough portfolio of these bonds, enough of them would earn high returns to wipe out the effect of those which went wrong. His early clients who followed his advice made large amounts of money.

Later on, Milken played a key role in the takeover boom of the 1980s, financing predators with newly created 'junk bonds'. These would trade at, or near, face value, but would offer much higher yields than other bonds in the market (to reflect the higher risk). The term junk bonds extended to cover all high-yielding bonds of this type.

Milken fell from grace and was eventually jailed, and many investors who bought junk bonds at the peak of the market lost money. As with other financial theories, by attempting to exploit it so heavily, Milken and his followers altered the rules. If there was any merit to the junk bond theory, it was because few people bothered to follow the market and it was therefore possible to find bargains. Once everyone started to get interested, the bargains disappeared and investors started to forget the heavy risks involved.

Nevertheless, the junk bond market eventually recovered and has gone from strength to strength ever since. Nowadays, it tends to be known by the more enticing term, 'high yield market'. Some $462 billion of high-yield debt was issued in 2013, according to Thomson Reuters; such bonds were particularly appealing at a time when savings accounts in much of the developed world were yielding less than 1 per cent.

The problems faced by banks in the aftermath of the financial crisis resulted in a decline in corporate lending; many companies have turned to the bond market instead. Companies also tend to have more debt than they used to, not least because interest payments are tax-deductible; 71 per cent of all issues were rated B (and thus junk) in 2013 by Standard and Poor's.

LOAN FACILITIES

Companies may not want to raise money via a bond issue, on which they have to pay interest throughout its life. In the 1980s, it was quite common for companies to borrow via loan facilities, which allowed them to draw down money when they wanted it. In return, they would pay a commitment fee to a panel of banks, for agreeing to lend the money at any time.

These facilities were known by a variety of acronyms, such as RUFs and NIFs. In the late 1980s, the most common was the MOF or Multi-Option Facility which allowed the borrower to borrow money in a variety of forms, such as in different currencies or over different periods.

The 1990s recession caused so many bad debt problems that banks began to regret having committed themselves to so many facilities, often at very low spreads. Many overseas banks decided to withdraw from the UK lending market. This caused immense problems for companies trying to renegotiate their facilities; they had to deal with a large number of banks, some of whom were unwilling lenders.

The early 1990s saw a shift to so-called 'bilateral lending', as companies decided to opt for a series of loans from individual banks, rather than group all the banks together in a complex facility.

Almost everyone in the country has insurance of one form or another, whether it is for their house, their car or their life. Most have insured all three and more besides. Companies need insurance as much as individuals – for damage to factory buildings or equipment, and even against claims for damages from aggrieved customers. The result is a multi-billion-dollar industry represented by insurance institutions which, as we saw in Chapter 8, play a vital part in the financial system and in the economy, because of their role as investors in industry.

The insurance sector has, since the Second World War, been one of the country's biggest foreign-exchange earners. It plays a vital role in assuming part of the risk involved in industry. Without insurance, a severe fire, for example, might render a department store bankrupt. With insurance, the company can concentrate on the *commercial* risks it faces (i.e. whether it can attract enough customers). In return for assuming an insurance risk, insurers charge a premium. They hope that their premium income will exceed the money they have to pay to those with legitimate insurance claims. If an insurance company feels that the risks it runs are too great, it can pass some of them on to a second company, the process known as *reinsurance*.

Financial institutions, by providing this service, oil the wheels of the economy just as they do by giving savers a home for their funds and by lending the proceeds to industry for investment. And providing protection against the risk of fire or theft is little different in theory from protecting against a rise in interest rates or a fall in sterling. It is just a question of calculating the risks and setting the premiums accordingly.

But the business is a highly volatile one. The UK consumer market can be highly competitive as new companies move into the business, driving down premium rates.

The last twenty years have seen the emergence of direct insurers, which sell policies over the phone on via the internet, rather than through insurance brokers or salesmen, and also the arrival of comparison websites like Moneysupermarket and Confused, which allow consumers to find the cheapest deal. The business has become highly competitive.

Insurers have also faced the risks associated with global warming, which seems to have led to more extreme weather and flood damage, and a blizzard of motor claims associated with whiplash injuries, an area where fraud seems to be prevalent.

The insurance industry has responded with a series of mergers, both in the high-risk end of reinsurance and in the consumer sector, where savings can be made in the back office. Regulators have also been extremely keen to ensure that insurers have enough capital to meet claims, putting some pressure on their balance sheets.

LLOYD'S

The changes in the insurance market have had a particular impact on London's most famous insurance market, Lloyd's. A series of scandals and financial problems have significantly reduced the market's importance and prompted substantial changes in the way the market operates.

Lloyd's of London developed from a coffee house opened by one Edward Lloyd just before 1687. Gentlemen from the City used to meet there and discuss insurance over their beverages. By the middle of the eighteenth century they decided that they might as well make it their main place of business.

From the beginning, the speciality of Lloyd's was marine insurance, helped by the fact that England has traditionally been a great naval power. Like underwriters in the other financial fields we have looked at (bonds and shares), Lloyd's underwriters accept a payment (in this case called a premium) in return for providing against an unfortunate eventuality. In the case of underwriters of financial instruments, they guarantee to buy the bonds if no one else will, in return for a premium. Early Lloyd's underwriters agreed to pay shipowners for the damage to, or loss of, their ships and cargo. For a long time, Lloyd's had the best intelligence on the movements of foreign shipping. Perhaps the most famous occupant of Lloyd's is the Lutine Bell, which is rung when important news is about to be announced (one ring for bad news, two rings for good).

THE LLOYD'S STRUCTURE

An elaborate structure was built on the flimsy edifice of a coffee house. First and foremost, there are the *clients*. Merchant shipping has long since passed its peak and Lloyd's now provides insurance for a wide variety of customers and products, including film stars' legs, potential kidnap victims and space satellites. Sometimes the clients may be other insurance companies and markets for whom Lloyd's provides reinsurance.

The second tier in the structure are the *brokers*. They link client with underwriter in return for a commission. Their business is rather less risky than the underwriters', since they are not liable to pay out for any claims. But with Lloyd's challenged by other insurance markets around the world, Lloyd's brokers have been forced to travel far and wide to drum up business. Not all of it goes to Lloyd's; indeed the bulk goes to outside insurance companies. However, Lloyd's still retains the flexibility that encourages brokers to place with it substantial or unusual risks. Brokers provide a service which goes beyond merely broking: they advise clients on the best kind of insurance protection for their needs and they act for clients by administering their insurance business and by collecting any legitimate claims they may have. The big broking firms have gradually come to dominate the market, in the process buying many underwriting agencies. As we shall see, this has led to many problems.

The next tier up are the *managing agents*, who run syndicates on behalf of investors in the market. The agents decide whether to underwrite the risk, hence their traditional title of underwriters. In 2008, there were eighty syndicates run by fifty-one managing agents, some of which are in speciality areas such as marine, aviation, professional indemnity and motor.

To bring in the capital to allow the market to work efficiently, Lloyd's has to attract outsiders. Hence the need to bring in outside investors – private individuals and companies – and members' agents (to service these investors).

The private individuals were traditionally known as *names*. Being a name was standard practice for wealthy and upper-class individuals for much of the twentieth century. There were tax advantages, income was steady, and disastrous years were few. That was until the mid-1980s, when losses started to pile up and many names were ruined.

The problem was the principle of unlimited liability which underpinned the market. If you invest money in Marks & Spencer and the company goes bust, you have lost your stake and that is it. Under unlimited liability, the market can come for the rest of your savings or your home in order to meet the losses.

The individuals concerned were horrified when the full extent of their losses became clear. Many claimed they had been misled about the risks; some said they had been defrauded and placed in syndicates which bore the heaviest losses. A sizeable number said they could not, or would not, pay, which led to lengthy court cases and negotiations about a settlement.

The only answer for Lloyd's was to bring in new capital to strengthen the market. A series of corporate vehicles were established, which had the crucial advantage of limited liability; investors' losses were limited to the amount of their stake. This corporate capital quickly came to dominate the market; by 2014, there were only 447 active names, compared with 1,686 active corporate members.

The *members' agents* act as a sort of dating agency: they earn a fee in return for introducing private individuals to Lloyd's and for placing them on profitable syndicates.

In theory, underwriting can be immensely profitable. The capital employed by the underwriter can be invested so that it earns interest. (Or invested in equities. This is the secret of how Warren Buffett made his fortune. He applied his immense skill to investing the capital of an insurance company.) The premium income that results from assuming risk can also be invested; the key is that the premiums are received long before any claims have to be paid out. If premiums exceed claims, there is also a profit. An underwriter's money is thus working several times over. In addition, Lloyd's has certain tax privileges. Underwriters can carry forward losses in order to offset them against underwriting profits for tax purposes in future years.

The effect of investment earnings means that underwriters can afford to pay out slightly more in claims than they receive in premiums and still make a profit. However, if the deficit between claims and premiums becomes large, the arithmetic begins to look less healthy.

REGULATING LLOYD'S

A series of scandals in the late 1970s cast doubt over Lloyd's ability to regulate itself and led to the passing of the Lloyd's Act in 1982. A new committee was appointed on which representatives from outside the market were introduced and a chief executive brought in from the Bank of England.

But the reforms were unsuccessful in assuaging the market's critics and self-regulation was condemned by a parliamentary committee report in 1995. Eventually, the market itself accepted that the system would have to change and the market is now regulated by the Financial Services Authority (see Chapter 16).

Meanwhile, the shift from names to corporate capital might have helped protect the long-term future of the market but did nothing to deal with the past losses. That problem was dealt with by the creation of a new company called Equitas, which reinsured more than £8 billion of the market's old liabilities. As part of this process, a settlement was reached with the loss-making names and most (but not all) of the legal cases were dropped.

There have been bad years, such as 2011, when the market faced the cost of hurricanes in the US, an earthquake in Japan and floods in Thailand and Australia. But in 2013, Lloyd's earned a profit of £3.2 billion as a 52 per cent fall in catastrophe claims offset a fall in investment income.

INSURANCE COMPANIES

The insurance companies that most people deal with are not members of Lloyd's. Many of the companies are no longer involved in general insurance (cars and homes) at all but focus on savings products, with a bit of life insurance thrown in. Between them, these companies represent a substantial category of the institutional investor sector, whose characteristics we examined in Chapter 8.

Most of the big companies are *proprietary* companies (i.e. owned by shareholders in the same way as a normal business). Some, however, are mutual companies which are owned by the policyholders in the same way as building societies are owned by their depositors.

In the case of both life and general insurance, the approach to risk is broadly the same. Companies can look at their past experience and estimate how many claims will be made in a given period; how many people will die, houses will be burgled, cars will crash and so on. The life business is somewhat more predictable, however. Insurance companies also have the advantage that they receive the premiums upfront but the claims come in much later; they thus have a pile of cash, or float, on which they can earn income. This investment income can cushion the effect of losses from underwriting.

Those insurance companies that sell savings products have a more stable business; essentially they earn a proportion of the money they manage on behalf of others. There has been a good degree of change in the types of products that they sell; with profits policies, that tried to smooth investment returns, are much less important than they used to be, thanks to an investor revolt over high charges and disappointing returns. But the insurance companies have adapted quite well and still sell a lot of products, particularly in the area of pensions.

Perhaps the biggest problem facing insurers in recent decades has been the litigious nature of modern societies, a development fuelled by the emergence of 'no win, no fee' legal firms. In the past, people who tripped on a paving stone or slipped on a wet floor might be inclined to put the experience down to bad luck; now they are more ready to sue. At the same time, risks have emerged that might not have been anticipated when policies were written; the health implications of using asbestos, for example. And the growth of mankind's population means that when disasters strike, be they earthquakes, hurricanes or floods, they tend to hit more heavily populated areas, creating bigger bills.

Science has also created other dilemmas. Genetic testing now means that it may be possible to know the probability that an individual will develop a disease later in life; is it right that this risk should be reflected in a higher premium? The courts have tended to look askance at such discrimination, ruling (for example) that insurance companies cannot pay lower annuity rates to women even though they live longer.

This runs counter to a general principle of insurance and indeed of finance; greater risk demands greater reward. Insurers always face a problem of moral hazard; those who are most likely to claim on their policies are most likely to take out insurance. Taken to extremes, this would make insurance prohibitively expensive for most people. One answer, which is the basis for the US health system known as Obamacare, is to make it compulsory for people to take out insurance. Another answer, which is how the UK has dealt with flood claims, is to guarantee low premiums for those in affected areas. These claims will be met by a special scheme, which is funded by a levy on the entire industry.

It seems certain that these issues will crop up more regularly, especially as insurers learn to exploit 'big data' which can reveal more and more about the factors that make claims more likely. Insurance forms are now much more complex than they used to be, asking questions about locks, the extent to which houses are unoccupied and so on; it turns out that houses have an optimal distance from the road which affects the likelihood of being burgled (too close and opportunist thieves are more likely to strike; too isolated and neighbours might not notice suspicious characters).

In the savings market, insurers have huge opportunities, particularly as people are now more responsible for financing their old age. In 2014, the government announced that it was abolishing the requirement for retirees to use pension pots to buy annuities (which guarantee an income for the rest of their lives). That will hit one segment of the insurance market, but companies will doubtless come up with new products, as retirees will still need an income.

And the big insurance companies are very excited about the commercial opportunities in Asia, where populations and wealth are growing fast, and which have much less sophisticated markets. Many have made acquisitions, or partnered local companies, with the view of taking advantage of the Asian market.

Risk Management

COPING WITH FINANCIAL RISK

It is tough running a business. You have to make a product that customers like. You have to find offices or factory space, reliable suppliers, employees that will be productive at a reasonable wage; cope with value added and corporation tax; have a bank that will lend you money and so on.

Even if you overcome all those hurdles, you face issues that may be beyond your control. Your cost of borrowing may rise because the Bank of England raises interest rates. The pound may rise sharply, making your exports uncompetitive in Europe or the US, or fall sharply, raising the cost of the spare parts you import. Oil prices may rise, increasing the cost of running your lorries or aeroplanes.

A whole host of financial products have been created to try to help companies manage these risks. They are known as derivatives, because their price is derived from those of other assets. Inevitably, derivatives also create opportunities for speculators, which make them controversial. But without speculators, the markets would not function and companies would find it much harder to protect themselves. One could argue that regular insurance companies are speculating that the premiums they charge for fire and theft will bring in more money than the claims they pay out.

INTEREST RATES

A problem that faces all borrowers and investors is the possibility that future interest-rate movements will leave them at a disadvantage. A company can choose either to fix its borrowing rate or to let the rate follow the trends in the market. Each decision has its potential disadvantages. A company which borrows at a fixed rate when market rates are 10 per cent will find itself regretting the decision if rates fall to 5 per cent. Similarly, borrowing at a floating rate may ensure that the company's borrowing costs are in line with those in the market, but if rates rise during the life-time of the loan, the borrower may regret not having fixed the rate.

In each of the above cases investors are exposed to the opposite out-come. If they have lent at a fixed rate, they hope that interest rates will fall rather than rise. If they have lent at a floating rate, their returns will always stay in line with the market. However, if market rates fall, they will regret not having fixed the rate on the loan at the prevailing levels.

Institutions which have borrowed large amounts will try to ensure that they are not overexposed to interest-rate movements. They will accord-ingly aim to strike a balance between the proportion of their debt which has a fixed interest rate and the proportion which is floating. Fixed-rate funding is normally available only long term, and UK companies have been notoriously unwilling to borrow on a long-term basis. As a result they are extremely vulnerable to interest-rate increases – a fact proved by the sharp falls in profits and the job losses throughout much of the British manufacturing industry during the early 1990s.

It is important to strike a balance between short- and long-term debt. Too much short-term debt means that the company is very vulnerable to sudden interest-rate rises; too much long-term debt means that the company may find itself with higher than average borrowing costs because, as we saw in Chapter 2, long-term rates are often above short-term rates. It is also essential for companies to structure the maturity dates of their debt very carefully. If too much debt matures (and is therefore due for repayment) in any one year, the company may find itself short of funds with which to repay the debt. Companies aim, therefore, to structure their debts so that the amounts due to be repaid do not fluctuate violently from one year to the next.

The ideal debt portfolio would have a mixture of fixed- and floating-rate debt and would have as wide a range of maturities as possible.

However, such ideals are hard to attain, and most companies find themselves with portfolios that are extremely vulnerable to a rise in interest rates. When that happens the financial markets offer a range of instruments as protection, including the forward-rate agreement, the financial future, the interest-rate option and the swap. These instruments (futures, options and swaps) can also be used to hedge other risks, such as exchange-rate movements (see next chapter).

FORWARD AGREEMENTS

A forward/forward, or forward agreement, is simply an arrangement between two institutions to lend or borrow a set amount at a set rate for a set period which will not begin for some months. Suppose, for example, a company knows that it wants to borrow £1 million for a six-month period commencing in six months' time. Rather than wait six months and accept whatever interest rate is then applicable, the company decides to fix the rate in advance and arranges with a bank a forward agreement.

If six-month interest rates are 10 per cent and twelve-month interest rates are 10 per cent, what rate should a bank charge for a six-month loan, beginning six months from now? Surprisingly, the answer is not 10 per cent.

Suppose the amount to be borrowed is £100. If the bank agrees to lend under a forward agreement, it will set aside that £100 for six months until the agreement begins by investing it in a six-month deposit. At the end of six months it will have accumulated £105 (£100 + £5 interest). The bank can now compare its return with the return it would have received had it invested the original deposit for a year, which would have been £110 in total. Under the forward agreement it has £105 after six months and need only charge 9.52 per cent for the second six months to achieve a total return of £110. The rate which the bank will charge for the forward agreement will therefore be slightly over 9.52 per cent (assuming that the bank has no strong view about the direction of future interest-rate movements).

Why does the bank not just avoid all the complex calculations and charge 10 per cent? Competition means that other banks can make all the same calculations and offer borrowers a better rate.

The problem with forward agreements is that they involve the actual borrowing of a sum. If a borrower is seeking to cover existing debt, the effect is to double his credit lines. As a consequence, less cumbersome instruments have been developed which do not involve the principal sums.

Forward-*rate* agreements (FRAs) establish interest rates for borrowers, for lenders or for a set period in advance. When that period is due to begin the parties settle the difference between the prevailing level of interest rates and the rate agreed under the FRA.

Suppose a company has a long-term bank loan on which it pays interest at a floating rate that is reset every six months. At the start of the year the company may decide that it does not want to pay more than 10 per cent interest on the loan during the second half of the year. So the company takes out an FRA with a bank (this can, but need not, be the same bank as the one with which the company has the loan). When 1 July arrives the six-month market interest rate is 11 per cent, 1 per cent more than the company has agreed to pay under the FRA. So the bank pays the company 1 per cent to bring its borrowing costs down to 10 per cent. Had interest rates been 9 per cent on 1 July, the company would have paid the bank 1 per cent.

Unlike in the forward/forward market, no principal sum is transferred. Notional principals agreed which matches the size of the loan so that the FRA covers the company's risk. The important part of an FRA, though, is the *rate* at which it is arranged.

FINANCIAL FUTURES

Financial futures are among the biggest growth areas in the world of finance. Their origin lies in the world's commodity markets. In the twentieth century Chicago traders, aware of their vulnerability to sharp swings in agricultural prices, began to quote prices for the delivery of produce many months in advance. Soon trading in wheat, pork belly and coffee 'futures' (as they became known) became as vigorous as trading in the commodity itself. Precious and industrial metals, like gold, silver and copper, soon developed their own futures markets.

Trading on the futures exchanges was traditionally conducted by open outcry (the less polite term for it is 'shouting') in floor areas called *pits*. The London International Financial Futures Exchange used to be a riot of colour with each firm's traders wearing different, brightly coloured jackets. If prices are moving fast, a futures exchange can seem like Bedlam as traders desperately seek others who are ready to buy or sell contracts. (A good example of futures trading appears in the film *Trading Places*.) Outside clients can deal with floor traders only through brokers and therefore have to pay their commissions.

In the late 1990s, however, LIFFE abandoned trading in the face of competition from the German futures market. Trading moved to a screen-based system, which was designed to be cheaper for investors. However, Chicago, the world's biggest futures market, retains the pits and coloured jackets.

With the advent of floating exchange rates (see Chapter 14), it occurred to Chicago traders that there might well be a market for trading in currency futures, since exchange rates seemed to be exhibiting the same volatility as commodity prices. Currency futures quickly became a success; some experts now estimate that 10 per cent of all US foreign-exchange transactions take place on the Chicago futures floor. After the late 1970s and early 1980s had seen equally sharp moves in interest rates the Chicago traders developed interest-rate futures.

How are interest-rate futures used? Essentially, if an institution is worried about the effect of a rise or fall in the level of interest rates, it should buy or sell interest-rate futures to the extent that any movement in interest rates will be cancelled out by a change in the value of the future. The price of an interest-rate future is determined by subtracting the implied interest rate from 100. Thus a futures price of 88 would imply an interest rate of 12 per cent. When interest rates fall, the price of interest-rate futures rises. A cut in rates of 2 per cent will normally push up the price of the future by 2 points; conversely, a rise in interest rates will cause the futures price to fall.

Futures are especially useful as a mechanism for protecting against interest-rate risk because only a small proportion of the nominal value of the future (the margin) is required to be deposited. That margin is adjusted as the price of the future rises or falls. Since both sellers and buyers must deposit the margin, it is possible to use futures to cover the risk both of an interest-rate rise and (if you are an investor) of an interest-rate fall.

To see precisely how a future works, suppose that a UK company knows in September that it will need to borrow £1 million for three months in the following December. The company might worry that interest rates could rise in the interim from the September level of 10 per cent.

As the company fears an interest-rate rise, it sells futures (remember, a rise in rates leads to a fall in the price of futures).

On LIFFE the nominal size of the sterling interest-rate contract is £500,000. To cover its £1 million risk the company therefore sells two sterling contracts. Each contract carries a margin (set by LIFFE) of £1,500, so both buyer and seller deposit £3,000 with LIFFE's clearing house.

By November interest rates have risen to 12 per cent, the very event that the UK company feared. The futures price has duly fallen from 90 to 88. This means that the position of the futures buyer has deteriorated, since he or she has bought for 90 something which has now fallen to 88. The position of the seller (the company) has improved. The clearing house accordingly credits the account of the seller and debits the account of the buyer. Each full point that a futures price moves is worth £1,250. So the company's position has improved by £2,500 per contract, or £5,000 on its whole position. The futures buyer, however, is £5,000 worse off, and the clearing house accordingly asks the buyer to pay additional margin to bring his or her net position back up to £3,000.

Shortly before the contract is due to expire the buyer and seller agree to close out the futures position without actually exchanging the £1 million. (Most financial futures contracts end without the nominal contract being exchanged.) The clearing house then gives the seller the original £3,000 margin plus the £5,000 payment to reflect the improvement in the company's position. The buyer also receives back the £3,000 margin, but since he or she has paid £8,000, in all the net position is a loss of £5,000.

How has the futures transaction helped the company that was worried about the interest-rate rise? Remember that it was due to borrow £1 million for three months. Had interest rates been 10 per cent, the cost of borrowing £1 million for three months would have been £25,000. However, interest rates rose to 12 per cent in November, and the company's borrowing cost became £30,000, an increase of £5,000. The profit from the futures transaction therefore met the extra cost of the borrowing exactly. The company was able to protect itself against the rise in interest rates. Had interest rates dropped, the company would have lost on its futures position but had lower borrowing costs.

The most frequent users of interest-rate futures are not companies but banks and institutional fund managers. Many company treasurers have been unwilling to accept the work needed to keep up with the margin payments involved. Banks use futures to cover their open positions when they have failed to match their investments with their liabilities. The fund managers use futures to ensure that a fall in interest rates does not reduce the return on their investments. To do so they *buy* rather than *sell* futures. A fall in interest rates will lead to a rise in the futures price which will off-set the losses on investors' portfolios.

In all futures markets, speculators are needed to maintain liquidity. In Chicago, these speculators are affectionately known as locals. Although futures are useful for those who are concerned about existing loans or assets, they also offer a means of reaping substantial profits from a small initial position, the process known as *leverage*. As we saw in the example above, an initial deposit of £3,000 gave both buyer and seller an interest in £1 million. The company achieved a profit of £5,000 on an initial deposit of £3,000, a promising return for a three months' investment. It is this sort of opportunity for profit that the Chicago locals hope to exploit. Leverage, however, works both ways – the futures buyer in the example lost £5,000 – so locals can as easily be ruined as they can be made millionaires. However, by seeking to take advantage of these speculative opportunities, locals provide the liquidity that helps the banks, fund managers and companies to use the markets effectively.

LIFFE never had the local interest that made Chicago such a success but it was very successful after a slow start in 1982. It suffered from one weakness in that the UK markets, where it had a natural advantage, were not that interesting to international investors.

While LIFFE compensated very well for a while by dominating the business in German government bond futures, it gradually lost that mar-ket to its natural home in Frankfurt. In late 2001, LIFFE agreed to be taken over by the European exchange Euronext. In subsequent deals, Euronext was taken over by the New York Stock Exchange and the com-bined company by the International Exchange or ICE. LIFFE now has a healthy business trading interest-rate derivatives.

INTEREST-RATE OPTIONS

Under the interest-rate option, which is in some ways a refinement of the forward-rate agreement, an option buyer purchases the right (but not the obligation) to lend or borrow at a guaranteed interest rate. In return the option seller receives a payment known as a *premium*, generally paid at the time the option is sold. On the day the option expires it is up to the option buyer to exercise the option and to lend or borrow at the guaranteed rate if it is possible to do so. However, if the option buyer can achieve a better rate of borrowing or lending in the money markets, he or she will let the option lapse. The maximum loss to the option buyer is therefore the cost of the premium. The size of that premium depends on three factors: the relationship between the interest rate guaranteed under the option and the interest rate in the money markets; the time left before the option is due to expire; and the option seller's assessment of whether interest rates are likely to move quickly.

If, for example, a company wanted to buy an option to borrow at 8 per cent at a time when interest rates were 10 per cent, there would be automatic potential for profiting from the option. As a result, the premium for the option would be at least 2 per cent and would be much larger than the premium for an option to borrow at 12 per cent in the same circumstances. An option to lend at, say, 12 per cent when interest rates were 10 per cent would carry a large premium, however, since it would have built-in profit potential.

Options which run for longer periods will also carry larger premiums. This is because the probability is greater that, over a long period, rates will move in such a way that the option will become more profitable to exercise. The option seller will charge a larger premium to reflect this extra risk.

How quickly interest rates will move is the hardest of the three elements for the option seller to assess. If the rate has shown a tendency to fluctuate violently in the past, it will obviously carry a higher premium than a rate which has shown a tendency to be stable.

An example will help to clarify the point. A company buys a three-month option to borrow at 10 per cent for three months, based on a nominal principal sum of £1 million. At the time the option is sold, interest rates are 10 per cent and the option seller charges a premium of 1 per cent (£2,500).

Outcome 1 At the end of the three-month period interest rates are 12 per cent. The company exercises the option, thus borrowing at a rate 2 per cent cheaper than if it had not bought the option (this is equivalent to a saving of £5,000). However, the premium cost 1 per cent (£2,500), and the savings that the company makes (compared with its borrowing costs if it had not bought the option) are £2,500.

Outcome 2 At the end of the three-month period interest rates are 8 per cent. The company lets the option lapse but is free to borrow at the cheaper rate available. Its extra costs are £2,500, the cost of the premium, but its borrowing costs are £5,000 less than it might have expected at the time when it bought the option.

SWAPS

Swaps were once seen as exclusive products which were tailor-made to suit the few sophisticated borrowers who could understand them. Nowadays they are a huge global market, with many simple, standardized products.

The basic concept behind the interest-rate swap is that two borrowers raise money separately and then agree to service each other's interest payments. However, many swap deals are much more complicated and can involve several currencies and half a dozen borrowers, with only the bank in the middle aware of all the details.

Why should two borrowers want to pay each other's interest? There are two main reasons. The first concerns the different perceptions of different markets. Investors in one country may be prepared to lend to a US borrower at an advantageous rate but will ask for a higher rate from a UK borrower. In another country it may be the UK borrower who receives the better rate. In those circumstances it can benefit both borrowers to raise funds in the market where their credit is best and then swap the funds.

An example of an early swap deal may help to explain. The World Bank and IBM both wanted to raise funds, the World Bank in Swiss francs and IBM in dollars. Swiss investors had already accepted a good deal of World Bank debt and would accept more only if it were offered at a higher rate. They were keen, however, to invest in a top US corporation like IBM. In the US the World Bank's credit was perceived as being better than IBM's. So the World Bank borrowed in dollars and IBM in Swiss francs. They then arranged a swap, so that IBM got its dollars and the World Bank its Swiss francs. Each ended up paying less than if they had borrowed separately. Such are the opportunities for borrowing at advantageous rates through swaps that in some years 80 per cent of Eurobond issues have been swap-linked.

The second reason for arranging swaps concerns the different perceptions of *borrowers* as to the likely direction of future interest-rate movements. As we have seen, borrowers can choose to borrow either at a fixed or at a floating rate. If they think interest rates will rise, they should borrow fixed; if they think interest rates will fall, they should borrow floating. However, they may subsequently decide that they have made the wrong decision. A swap allows borrowers to manage their existing debt. They can choose to swap not only from fixed to floating or vice versa but also from one currency to another.

Now that there is a secondary market in swaps, borrowers can reverse their swap decisions if they wish. Say a borrower had swapped from borrowing fixed to borrowing floating when interest rates were 12 per cent and that rates subsequently dropped to 8 per cent. That swap would now have a value because the borrower is receiving 12 per cent from its counterparty but paying only 8 per cent. The first borrower could sell the swap or arrange another swap by which it would agree to pay a fixed rate of 8 per cent and receive a floating rate. Its floating-rate payment under the first swap would be cancelled out by the second swap. However, it would have cut its fixed-rate payments from 12 to 8 per cent.

How are banks involved in swap deals? Some act as swap principals, agreeing to switch into fixed or floating debt or into another currency as the borrower requires. Normally, such banks have a 'book' of swaps, and they may find that their positions over a number of different swap deals balance each other out. Other banks act purely as swap arrangers, bringing together two different companies with corresponding needs: they earn fees in the process. A third set of banks follows a compromise strategy, acting as principals in a deal until they can find a matching borrower.

Swaps are off-balance-sheet transactions – they are not regarded as assets, and banks are currently not obliged to take precautions against the possibility of default. However, regulatory authorities have shown their concern about the growth of the market. Many poor credits are involved, since swaps give them the opportunity to reduce the cost of borrowing. If swap parties do default, banks may be faced with the payment of above-market interest rates.

What swaps have done is to open up the world's capital markets to a wide range of borrowers. It is now possible for a UK borrower, say, to pick a particular world market where borrowing seems cheap, borrow there and still, through a swap, end up with the sterling debt it really wants.

CREDIT DEFAULT SWAPS

For investors, interest-rate risk is not the only danger they face. There is also the possibility that the borrower will not repay the loan or bond. In the old days, there was not much that the investor could do about this. Bond investors could at least sell their holdings if they felt bad news was due; loan investors were usually stuck. The best protection was to have a diversified portfolio of bonds or loans and hope that the good payers outweighed the defaulters.

But the financial markets are remarkably ingenious at finding ways to insure against risk. The credit default swap is their latest wheeze. It is like an insurance policy against default. One party pays a premium to another; in return, the seller agrees to pay up if the borrower defaults. The higher the premium, the riskier the company.

This small idea created a market with some $62 trillion of outstanding contracts by the end of 2007. The phenomenal growth of the market was due to the great scope it created for both investors and speculators. Traditionally, there was not much they could do if they believed the outlook for corporate bonds and loans was deteriorating. But now they can buy credit default swaps; if it looks likely that more borrowers will default, premiums will rise. That will push the speculators into profit. Similarly, those who believe the corporate bond market will do well can take the other side of the deal. If premiums fall, they will profit. The scope for big gains would be much greater than could be achieved by just holding the bonds themselves.

Some people worry that the credit default swap market could lead to a crisis in the event of a lot of corporate failures. In some cases, the value of outstanding swaps is much greater than the value of bonds in issuance. One of the reasons for the collapse of the insurance group AIG was its huge exposure to credit default swaps. In 2009, attempts were made to improve the market by introducing a clearing mechanism, so that dealers would not be so exposed to the collapse of a counterparty.

The swap is such an incredibly versatile instrument that it is used in many other areas. For example, investors and banks can agree to a *total return swap*. The investor agrees to pay the bank an interest-rate-linked return; the bank agrees to pay the investor a return based on a particular market, such as commodity prices. At the end of the agreed period, the two payments are netted out. If commodities have returned more than the investor's borrowing costs, he is in profit. This may be a quicker and cheaper way of betting on commodities than buying them directly. Total return swaps are now widely used as a cheap way for investors to get exposure to a whole range of asset classes.

SPECIAL BOND ISSUES

Another way for investors to protect themselves against interest-rate movements is to buy special types of bonds (some of which are described in Chapter 11).

One type of bond issue deserves treatment here because it closely resembles a swap. The *capped floater* offers investors a floating rate set at a margin above LIBOR. However, if LIBOR rates go above a certain level, the bond rates do not follow. A 'cap' is set, which is the maximum rate the issuer will pay. The investor is compensated for the cap because the bond pays a higher than usual margin over LIBOR.

The issuer sells the cap to another borrower which wishes to lock in a maximum cost for its borrowings. The bond issuer can invest the money received from the sale of the cap, so that it receives a stream of payments which it can offset against the higher than usual margin over LIBOR that it is paying on the bond issue. This effectively can bring the cost of the issue to below LIBOR. So the issuer ends up paying less than LIBOR; the investor receives a higher than usual margin *above* LIBOR; and the cap buyer receives protection against a rise in interest rates.

After an initial surge the number of capped floaters declined. Instead banks now sell a product known as a 'cap' separately from specific bond issues. Such caps are effectively long-term interest-rate options and give the buyer the right to borrow at a specific rate. The bond market is forever ingenious, however, and it is safe to predict that issues will be designed with a similar clever mix of fixed and floating payments in the future.

All the above instruments deal with interest-rate risk. However, the risk that currencies will move is important to both borrowers and investors and also to businesses which export and import. It is that risk we shall examine in the next chapter.

In foreign-exchange markets, billions of pounds change hands every minute and nations can be humiliated by the actions of a few hedge fund managers. Currency volatility affects everyone, from the biggest multinational to the humblest tourist. Every overseas trade deal involves foreign-exchange decisions. First the people involved must agree which currency should be used to settle the deal. If one party is from Japan and the other from Switzerland, should the transaction take place in yen, Swiss francs or some other currency such as the US dollar? Equally important, when should the currency be delivered? Just as the price of the goods being sold is central to the transaction, so the exchange rate (which is the price of one currency in terms of another) can determine whether the parties make a profit or a loss.

BRETTON WOODS AND AFTER: THE ROLE OF FORECASTING TODAY

The post-war system of fixed exchange rates was set up in 1944 at an international conference held in Bretton Woods, New Hampshire. The system pegged the world's major currencies at fixed rates to the dollar. In turn the dollar was given the strength to act as the linchpin of the world's financial system because of its 'convertibility', at a set rate, into gold.

Gradually the system broke down as the American economy ran into trouble because of President Johnson's attempts to finance the Vietnam War and his 'Great Society' reforms at the same time. By 1971 the dollar lacked the strength to support the system, and President Nixon announced the suspension of the dollar's convertibility into gold. A series of attempts to shore up Bretton Woods failed; eventually it proved impossible to fix the value of the major currencies against the dollar.

The assumption that lay behind the fixed-rate system was that if one country had an excessive current-account deficit, it would alter its domestic economic policies until balance was restored. The system was capable of surviving the occasional hiccup, such as the sterling devaluation in 1967. However, since the system hinged on the dollar, a US balance-of-payments crisis was a potentially mortal wound.

Thanks to President Johnson's attempt to pay for both guns and butter, the US developed enormous current-account deficits which it proved unable to rectify. As a result, the foreign-exchange markets were overloaded with dollars ($1 billion a day flowed into the Bundesbank in May 1971). Speculators had a one-way bet. If they sold dollars and bought a strong currency such as the Deutschmark, they were highly unlikely to lose money, but if the dollar devalued, they would make substantial gains.

The enormous scale of international capital flows today means that no central bank has the reserves to defend its currency against market speculation indefinitely. Economists like Milton Friedman hoped that efficient markets would ensure that currencies traded in line with fundamentals once they were floating; in fact there have been very sharp swings in the dollar against sterling, the yen and the euro.

Why have exchange rates been so unstable since the collapse of the Bretton Woods system? Many theories have been developed to explain why exchange rates change, but none has so far explained their movements in such a way that future exchange-rate moves can then be predicted with any degree of accuracy.

Economic theories attempt to explain exchange-rate moves in the long run. Foreign-exchange dealers have to predict exchange rates in the very short run indeed – a day or two at the most. Companies whose profits are hurt or boosted by currency movements often need to know about the medium term – between two months and a year or so. When they turn to currency forecasters they are often disappointed. Surveys of foreign-exchange analysts regularly come to the conclusion that the forecasters are right in less than half of their predictions – a record worse than might be expected from tossing a coin.

There are two schools of currency forecasters – the economists and the technical analysts – and their methods are radically different. The economists have academic respectability and intellectual recognition. Sometimes, however, the technical analysts have the greater influence in the market.

THE ECONOMISTS

Because the system of fixed exchange rates survived for so long, economic theories about exchange rates have been developed from earlier studies about the way in which the balance of payments changes.

The most important initial distinction to make is that between the current and capital accounts of the balance of payments. The *current account* broadly covers trade payments, although it also includes tourist expenditure and, most important, interest payments and dividends. The *capital account* is concerned largely with purchases of assets – foreign securities such as German bonds, Japanese shares or physical assets like a factory in the Philippines. Note that purchase of a foreign bond counts as a debit on the capital account, but interest on the bond will be shown as a credit on the current account. The notion of a balance of payments is that a surplus or deficit on a current account will be balanced by a deficit or surplus on the capital account.

If, under the Bretton Woods system, a country was in current-account deficit, then to pay for the excess goods and services that it received from abroad it would have to act to correct the deficit. Trade barriers were ruled out under the General Agreement on Tariffs and Trade (GATT), so the country would be obliged to run down its foreign physical and financial assets or to borrow abroad in order to pay for its imports. In either case the inflow would be recorded as a capital-account surplus that matched the current-account deficit.

In the long term a deficit government was expected to curb demand in the economy, so that domestic consumers cut back their expenditure on both domestic and foreign goods. The price of domestically produced goods would fall in response to this drop in demand, making them more attractive to foreign consumers and pushing up the country's exports. Since imports would fall (because domestic consumers could not afford to buy them), the net effect would be to restore the balance-of-payments equilibrium. According to this model, devaluation would occur only when a country had run down its reserves so far that it was unable to restore current-account balance at the prevailing exchange rate.

The above example assumes that the capital account is not an independent variable but responds only to changes in the current account. In fact, the international flows of capital mean that the capital account is very much at the mercy of investor demand for foreign and domestic securities. As we saw, this was one of the reasons why the fixed exchange-rate system did not survive.

In the era of floating rates, economists have attempted to study how the exchange rate affects, and is affected by, both the current and the capital account. Their study has centred on two factors, the level of prices and the level of interest rates.

The study of the effect of prices on exchange rates has focused on the purchasing power parity (PPP) theory. At its simplest the theory argues that exchange rates will tend towards the point at which international purchasing power is equal. In other words, a hamburger would cost the same in any country, something *The Economist* highlights in its Big Mac index. In turn that means differential inflation rates are the most important driving factor behind exchange-rate movements.

Inflation matters because high prices make a country's goods uncompetitive. If the UK's inflation is 10 per cent per annum while the US's is zero, British goods will be 10 per cent more expensive than American goods after a year has elapsed. Unless British productivity outpaces that of the US by 10 per cent, UK sales abroad will fall as customers find it cheaper to buy American or other alternatives, and UK imports will increase as domestic consumers prefer US goods to their own. Hence the current account will deteriorate.

This sorry picture, PPP theorists claim, is redeemed by the exchange rate. If the pound falls by 10 per cent against the dollar in the above example, the cost to the US customer of UK goods (in dollars) stays the same. Similarly, the dollar has risen by 10 per cent, and therefore the cost to the UK customer of American goods (in pounds) stays the same. So the exchange rate has acted to restore the balance.

Monetarists adopted and modified this theory. They believe that price increases are caused by an excess money supply. Thus, since the markets know that nations with slack monetary regimes will suffer inflation, they will sell the currency of that country and buy the currency of countries with stricter monetary control. The resulting exchange-rate depreciation will in the long run match the differential in money-supply growth between the two countries. Unless money-supply growth is checked, the process of inflation-provoked devaluation will continue.

The concept of an equilibrium level for exchange rates has given PPP theorists a lot of trouble. There is no point of zero inflation and equilibrium currency rates from which subsequent exchange-rate movements can be measured. A base year must therefore be chosen, and the choice of base year often determines whether an exchange rate appears under- or overvalued.

Another major difficulty with the PPP theory is deciding what is defined by inflation. If the price of hairdressing is included in the consumer price index (CPI), will that make the index a reasonable measure of UK competitiveness? How many Americans will cross the Atlantic to get a cheaper perm? More seriously, an important component of any CPI is housing costs, which are irrelevant to consideration of export competitiveness. Even wholesale prices cover items that are not internationally traded. The most popular measure of competitiveness has therefore been unit wage costs – that is, the amount paid to workers per unit of output.

The PPP theory held very well for many Third World countries in the 1980s, in particular Latin American nations where exchange-rate depreciation against the dollar tended to follow the inflation rate quite closely. When it comes to predicting and explaining the exchange-rate movements of the currencies of the major industrialized countries, however, it has been far less successful.

If PPP theory is correct, real exchange rates (nominal exchange rates adjusted for inflation) should stay fairly stable. In fact, research has demonstrated that real rates show considerable volatility and exhibit little sign of returning to any equilibrium level. Some explain this by the concept of 'overshooting', in which, because of market inefficiencies, exchange rates over-adjust in response to inflationary differentials. If they do, that makes it all the more difficult to use PPP theory as an exchange-rate predictor.

The level of interest rates is clearly a major factor in the strength or weakness of a currency. This is even more the case after the wave of financial deregulation which we noted in Chapter 1. The world is now virtually a single capital market, in which vast quantities of money shift from one country to another in search of short-term gains.

The influence of interest rates is not as easy to assess as might first be thought. To begin with, are investors attracted by the nominal rate or the real rate (the nominal rate adjusted for inflation)? Second, are high interest rates a sign of a healthy or of an ailing economy?

For a long time foreign-exchange speculators perceived currencies in high-interest economies as weak and currencies in low-interest economies as strong. If a currency were weak, the argument went, few people would want to hold it or lend it, since currency depreciation would soon reduce its value. Debtors would want their borrowings denominated in a weak currency, however, since currency depreciation would reduce their debt burden. As a result there would be few lenders and many borrowers in that currency. In other words, demand for borrowings would exceed the supply and thus force the interest rate up.

The converse would apply to strong currencies. Many people would want to hold or lend them, since, added to the interest received would be the extra value gained from the currency's appreciation. On the other hand, few would want their debts denominated in a strong currency, since currency appreciation would keep increasing the effective total of their debt. In a strong currency, therefore, there would be many lenders and few borrowers. The supply of borrowings would exceed demand, forcing the interest rate down.

The position is complicated further by the willingness of governments to push their interest rates up in order to defend their currencies. Take the desperate attempts of the UK to prop up the pound in September 1992. The then Chancellor Norman Lamont was forced to increase interest rates twice in one day from 10 to 12 per cent, and then to 15 per cent, in an attempt to keep sterling within its Exchange Rate Mechanism band. But high interest rates impose a heavy burden on the economy, in terms of lost jobs and output, and few traders believed the UK government would sustain rates at that level. The pound fell anyway, and the UK was forced out of the ERM.

Oddly enough, ever since the UK was forced out of the ERM, currency markets have shifted again in their view of the influence of interest rates. High rates have generally boosted a currency's value. This seems to be due to the 'carry trade' which sees speculators borrow money in a low-yielding currency and then invest the proceeds in a higher-yielding one. One popular trade, for example, was to borrow yen and to buy Australian or New Zealand dollars. Such a tactic would earn a positive 'carry', the difference between rates in the two countries, of several percentage points.

In theory, these speculators should worry that the risk of devaluation should at least equal the higher interest rates on offer. In practice, the carry trade has been profitable most of the time.

The carry trade is thus an example of how investment decisions, as much as trade in goods, affect exchange rates. Accordingly, another theory of exchange-rate movements is the portfolio balance model. Proponents of this theory argue that exchange rates are effectively the relative prices of international financial assets (e.g. bonds and shares). Expectations of the likely risk and return of financial assets determine exchange-rate movements as investors shift their portfolios from one country to another.

The portfolio balance theory is persuasive partly because capital flows are far larger than trade flows. Another reason is that major economic or political events have an effect on the financial markets much more quickly than they do on the prices of goods. Bond prices move almost constantly, thanks to the electronic communications systems; the prices of goods change more slowly and depend on many factors. The combination of trade and capital flows results in the erratic paths of exchange rates as the two factors act sometimes in the same direction and sometimes in opposite directions.

Currency movements thus seem to depend to a large extent on the subjective views of those involved in the international capital markets. This concentration on expectation has given a great boost to the other strand of currency forecasters – the technical analysts.

TECHNICAL ANALYSIS

Technical analysts, or 'chartists' as they are often known, believe that all the factors which the economist studies – inflation, the balance of payments, interest rates, etc. – are already known by the market and are thus reflected in the prices of goods and commodities. This is as true of pork bellies and oil as it is of currencies. The chartists, as their name suggests, study charts which represent the price movements of a particular commodity. Over long periods certain price patterns emerge, which cause the analysts to claim that further developments in the price pattern can be predicted.

Economists have a tendency to reject the chartist theories out of hand. However, many traders in the foreign-exchange markets follow the chartists' predictions. To some extent such predictions can become self-fulfilling if enough people believe them. The markets react when a certain point of the chart is reached.

The underlying rationale behind chart analysis is that the key to price movements is human reaction, and that human nature does not change markedly in response to similar events. Among the main patterns that chartists see are the following.

Head and shoulders. This pattern is made up of a major rise in price (the head) separating two smaller rises (the shoulders). If this pattern is established, the price should fall by the same amount as the distance between the head and a line connecting the bottom of the two shoulders.

Broadening top. This pattern has three price peaks at successively higher levels and, between them, two bottoms with the second one lower than the first. If, after the third peak, the price falls below the level of the second bottom, this indicates a major reversal in the price trend.

Double bottoms/tops. A double bottom or top indicates a major reversal in the price trend. Both consist of two troughs (or peaks) separated by a price movement in the opposite direction.

Apart from pattern recognition, technical analysts also study *momentum* and *moving average* models. *Momentum* analysis studies the rate of change of prices rather than merely price levels. If the rate of change is increasing, that indicates that a trend will continue; if the rate of change is decreasing, that indicates that the trend is likely to be reversed. The concept behind the study of *moving averages* is that trends in price movements last long enough to allow shrewd investors to profit and that rules can be discovered which identify the most important of these trends. One of the most significant rules for technical analysts is that a major shift has occurred when a long-term moving average crosses a short-term moving average.

Although technical analysis has very little intellectual respectability in economists' circles, it has had a great impact on the foreign-exchange markets. Many believe it to be a useful forecasting tool in the short term. In the long term, despite some setbacks, economic analysis may yet prove a more successful forecasting technique.

THE EUROPEAN SINGLE CURRENCY

Since 1999, the foreign-exchange markets have witnessed one of the great economic experiments of all time – the creation of the European single currency, or euro.

European governments struggled for a long time with the breakup of the Bretton Woods system. By nature, they were less inclined to embrace floating exchange rates than the more laissez-faire economies of the UK and the US, and the subsequent twenty-five years saw a series of attempts to restrict currency movements.

The first attempt in the mid-1970s – the 'snake' – collapsed fairly quickly and the second attempt – the Exchange Rate Mechanism – was plagued by repeated crises between 1979 and 1983.

Change started to occur when the French government decided to aim for a strong currency, or *franc fort*. This made it easier for the franc to stabilize against the established currency of Europe, the Deutschmark, and removed some of the tensions within the system.

But in the early 1990s, the ERM broke down. The catalyst was the reunification of Germany which created inflationary pressures that the German central bank, the Bundesbank, decided to tackle by increasing interest rates. To maintain their parity against the Deutschmark, other currencies within the system had to increase their interest rates, driving some economies into recession.

Some countries, including Britain but also Italy, could not stand the strain. They eventually opted in 1992 for the less painful option of devaluation and interest-rate cuts. One year later, speculative attacks looked like forcing the French franc to devalue; in the event the ERM was changed to allow much wider trading bands, which were close enough to floating rates as to make no difference.

The breakup of the ERM created the impetus for the drive towards a single currency. The Maastricht Treaty (from which Britain had an opt-out) established the criteria which countries needed to meet including annual budget deficits less than 3 per cent of gross domestic product and inflation rates close to the European average.

The process for preparation went rather more smoothly than sceptics might have expected. There were no speculative attacks in the last days of the old system; interest rates and bond yields in the higher-risk countries, such as Italy and Spain, smoothly came down to German levels.

At the start of 1999, European exchange rates were 'locked in' at set levels against the euro and it became possible to use the currency for commercial transactions. Notes and coins duly arrived at the start of 2002, at which point the old currencies of the twelve member countries – Germany, France, Belgium, Luxembourg, the Netherlands, Ireland, Spain, Austria, Portugal, Finland, Italy and Greece – ceased to exist. By 2014, eighteen countries were members of the system with Cyprus, Estonia, Latvia, Malta, Slovakia and Slovenia all joining. Those countries that join the EU are expected to sign up for the Euro in due course.

A single currency brings a number of advantages. First it removes a level of uncertainty when European companies do business with each other; they no longer have to worry that exchange-rate movements will eat into their profits.

Second, it reduces the costs of doing business within the continent. Every time money is converted from one currency into another, there are commission and dealing costs to be paid.

Third, it should make markets more efficient. It is now easier for Europeans to compare prices in different countries and to buy from the cheapest supplier. (Although there are still some tax and regulatory barriers that make this difficult.)

Against all this is the lack of flexibility which has resulted. One currency means one interest rate for the whole continent, no matter what the economic conditions in each country. In the early years of the euro, Germany had rather higher interest rates than its economy probably deserved, which meant a long period of sluggish economic growth. From 2003 to 2007, Ireland and Spain, with fast-growing economies, had interest rates that were too low, leading to booming housing markets and rising inflation rates.

Of course, the US is a big country, with one currency and interest rate. But it has a fairly mobile population; if one region is depressed, workers can quickly move to another. Language makes that option a lot harder for Europeans.

These weaknesses were thrown into stark relief by the crisis that began in 2010 when Greece revealed that its budget deficit was much higher than previously thought. All of a sudden, investors began to doubt whether Greece could meet its debts and stay in the euro. That prompted them to sell Greek debt, pushing bond yields higher. That raised the cost of Greek borrowing and made it even harder for Greece to pay its way. Other countries – Ireland and Spain (whose banks were crippled by the collapse of housing bubbles), Portugal (sluggish growth and an uncompetitive economy) and Italy (high government debt and one of the slowest-growing economies in the world) – were drawn into the net.

Low interest rates in the euro zone during the first decade of the twenty-first century had encouraged speculative booms in some countries and made it easier for the likes of Greece and Italy to service their debts. Over time, however, these countries had become less competitive with their wage costs rising faster than Germany's; trade deficits had been the result. Under a floating-rate system, their currencies would have depreciated to keep their exports competitive; under the ERM, a one-off devaluation would have achieved the same effect. But the single currency made that impossible.

The only answer was to cut wages and prices in the countries concerned. But that was both deeply unpopular and made it harder for companies and individuals to service their debts. Hence the crisis. For a while, it looked like the euro might break up. Endless crisis meetings cobbled the system together. The richer nations set up a fund to lend money to the banks of the debtor nations; the European Central Bank backed up the weak banking system and bought government bonds; some Greek debt was written off. But as of 2014, the system still looked fragile, with restive voters who were backing parties of the far right and left and ageing populations that were likely to ensure sluggish growth over the long term. The euro's long-term survival is still not assured.

EMERGING MARKET CURRENCIES

The problems of dealing with floating exchange rates have not been confined to the countries of Europe. The so-called emerging markets, the developing nations of Asia, Latin America and eastern Europe, have also grappled with the issue.

Economic problems have a habit of showing up in exchange-rate movements. In Latin America, historically high inflation rates caused massive depreciations of currencies against the dollar, particularly in the

1980s. Then in 1994, the Mexican government was prompted into devaluing the peso in the face of a massive trade deficit.

Asian countries had traditionally produced much better economic performances than Latin America and their currencies had traditionally been stronger. But then in 1997, Thailand suddenly devalued its currency, the baht, triggering a wave of devaluations round the region.

Asia's apparent strength had hidden some underlying weaknesses. Many countries had linked their currencies, formally and informally, to the dollar, encouraging many companies to take out US dollar loans because of the lower interest rates in America. Furthermore, their reputations as fast-growing economies had resulted in a massive influx of capital, much of which had been invested at economically unfeasible rates. In short, a speculative bubble had been created.

When sentiment turned, the bubble burst very quickly. The hot money that had flowed into the Asian countries flowed out again; as the currencies depreciated, the burden of meeting the corporate system's dollar debts became oppressive. Asian banks, which had lent heavily to the corporate sector, saw their finances deteriorate in the face of bad debts.

Many south-east Asian economies plunged into recession; the IMF was called in to provide rescue financing packages. The whole issue cast doubt on the 'Asian economic miracle' and prompted a lot of debate about free-market regimes.

Some countries and commentators argued that the system showed the instability of global capitalism, and the need for controls; Malaysia duly imposed capital controls in 1998. Free-market enthusiasts argued that it was the attempts of governments to track the dollar and their interference in the free running of their economies which caused the problem.

The reaction of the Asian countries to this debacle set up a new phase in the currency markets. They decided that they must cease being dependent on foreign capital. That required them to build up trade surpluses, an economic policy that used to be dubbed mercantilism.

They were very successful at this, with China building up surpluses of several hundred billions a year. Russia, a basket case in 1998, is now a surplus nation thanks to its oil and has reserves. Countries with current-account surpluses normally see their currencies appreciate. But most Asian nations opted to control their currency movements, for fear that too rapid a rise in their exchange rates would reduce the competitiveness of their exports.

A country with a surplus, however, accumulates a lot of foreign-exchange reserves. These tend to be held in the form of government bonds. Those government bonds, in turn, tend to be issued by countries with current-account deficits.

Thus developed a system that has been dubbed Bretton Woods II. China supplies America with cheap goods. In return, America supplies China with IOUs in dollar form. China is willing to accept the deal because the export boom provides employment for its vast population, which is steadily moving from the countryside to the cities. America accepts the deal because it keeps inflation and interest rates down, allowing its consumers to keep spending with apparent impunity.

Lots of people, however, doubt whether the deal is sustainable in the long term. Eventually, China will get fed up with owning dollar bonds, especially as the US currency is likely to depreciate. Holding its currency (the yuan) down means that Chinese inflation is likely to accelerate.

America is fed up with the loss of manufacturing jobs to China and some politicians have muttered about trade barriers. In addition, China, Russia and others are diversifying their reserves away from government bonds and have set up sovereign wealth funds that invest in shares and property. That has led to fears in the West; big companies are being bought by funds controlled by our geopolitical rivals. The contrast with how Russia treats overseas investors (often forcing them out through legal and tax moves) is striking.

THE FOREIGN-EXCHANGE MARKET

Participants in the foreign-exchange market include everyone from the governor of the Bank of England to tourists when they buy foreign currency for a holiday. Tourist purchases are, in fact, among the few foreign-exchange transactions in which notes and coins actually change hands. The vast majority of deals take place electronically or over the telephone.

At the core of the market are the banks. Most commercial banks have their own foreign-exchange room. Although banks could not deal if they were not providing a service for their corporate clients who need foreign exchange as part of their everyday business, the majority of any bank's deals are done with other banks. One bank has estimated that 95 per cent of its foreign-exchange business is done with other banks and only 5 per cent with outside customers.

There are three major dealing time zones, all of which have more than one centre. London was considered the most important centre, although New York has now probably taken over that role. The market begins each day at 1 a.m. Greenwich Mean Time (GMT), when Tokyo opens. The Far Eastern time zone holds sway until 9 a.m. GMT, by which time London, Frankfurt, Paris and Zurich have begun the European time-zone trading. By 2 p.m. GMT, New York has opened trading in the American time zone. The market does not close in New York until 10 p.m. GMT. Those dealers who are still awake can trade in San Francisco and Los Angeles until Tokyo opens the next day.

With so many markets to keep track of, the pace of a dealer's life is often frenetic. Most are young, and some are burnt out by their middle thirties. How do they operate?

Suppose a dealer gets a commercial request to buy or sell a large volume of currency. He has several choices. He can satisfy the request himself or ask one of his colleagues to do so. If his colleague cannot, he can ring up a dealer in another bank and hope that he will be able to sell the currency to the rival bank. But this can be time-consuming. His alternative is to contact a foreign-exchange broker, whose job is to find a willing counterparty to the deal. In return for this service, the broker charges a commission, which can be as small as one-hundredth of 1 per cent. However, one-hundredth of 1 per cent of deals worth £10 million a time can quickly add up to a lot of money.

The broker will always attempt to cover his position; in other words, he will ensure that he is selling and buying the same amount of currency, so that he is safeguarded against fluctuation. Dealers will usually do the same, although they are allowed, within limits, to leave surplus funds in currencies which they believe will appreciate.

An exchange of currencies for immediate delivery is conducted at the *spot* rate. Dealers will quote two exchange rates for each currency, one at which they will buy the currency and one at which they will sell. The difference between the two is one way in which a bank makes money and is called the *spread*. So if you wanted to buy dollars in exchange for sterling, the bank might offer $1.4850/£1. If you had wanted to buy sterling in exchange for dollars, the rate would have been $1.4870/£1. (For brevity the sterling/dollar rate would be given by a dealer as 50/70.) The 0.2 cent difference between the two rates is the spread. These rates are displayed and continually updated throughout the day in foreign-exchange dealing rooms and on Reuters screens, and they appear every day in the *Financial Times*. The faster an exchange rate is moving, the wider the spread, since the dealer will not want to be committed to dealing at an unfavourable rate.

Tourists buying foreign currencies will find that the spread is very wide, often several percentage points. Banks can afford to charge each other a narrow spread because the deals are large and frequent and because the competition is intense. The tourist, by comparison, has little bargaining power, and the bank's costs in supplying the small amounts of currencies involved are proportionately higher.

THE FORWARD RATE

Banks will quote a price for a currency which is not wanted for immediate delivery. If a UK company knows that it is going to receive goods from Switzerland in three months' time, for which it will have to pay Swiss francs, it can fix its exchange rate in advance by locking in a forward rate with a bank. If the spot rate is Sfr 2.2568/72 per £1, the bank might offer a three-month forward rate of Sfr 2.2291/97 per £1. Once again the bank is taking a spread – notice that the spread for the three-month forward rate is larger than for the spot rate. On screen the bank will in fact show only the differential between the spot and forward rates. So in this case the screen would show:

RATES AGAINST THE £

	Spot	Forward
Swiss franc	2.2568/72	277/275

Currencies that are more expensive to obtain at the forward rate than at the spot rate are described as being at a *premium*, and those that are cheaper on the forward than on the spot market are at a *discount*. In this case, the Swiss franc is at a premium to the pound and the pound is at a discount to the Swiss franc. On a dealer's screen the distinction is shown by the ordering of the forward's spread. As the Swiss franc is at a premium to the pound, the largest figure appears first in the forward column. If the Swiss franc were at a discount, the forward column would read 275/277.

Forward rates are determined largely by interest differentials. Imagine that Swiss interest rates were 10 per cent and UK rates were 5 per cent and that the spot and the twelve-month forward rates for Swiss francs against sterling were the same. A UK investor would then be able to buy Swiss francs at the spot rate and invest the money in Switzerland to earn the higher interest rate. At the same time the investor could take out a forward contract with a bank to buy back sterling in exchange for Swiss francs in a year's time. No money would be lost as a result of currency movements, since the investor has guaranteed the same Swiss franc/sterling rate as when the investment was made. So the investor could benefit from higher Swiss interest rates without risk. This method of profiting from inconsistencies between markets is known as *arbitrage*.

Attractive though it may seem, the above example could not happen in the real world. Every investor would be anxious to profit from the trade. The result would be: (a) increased demand from UK investors for Swiss francs at the spot rate, driving the Swiss franc up against sterling; (b) increased demand for Swiss and reduced demand for UK assets, driving Swiss interest rates down and UK rates up; (c) increased demand for twelve-month sterling, driving the twelve-month Swiss franc rate down and thus opening up a differential with the spot rate, which would be pushed in the opposite direction. All these factors combined would quickly eliminate the investment opportunity described.

Although arbitrage possibilities do sometimes exist and some speculators make a living out of exploiting them, the speed of the markets means that inconsistencies do not last very long. A country which has higher interest rates than those in the UK will have a currency at a discount to the pound on the forward market, so that investors would lose on the currency what they would gain on the interest-rate differential. By contrast, countries with lower interest rates than the UK's will have currencies at a premium to sterling.

THE COMPANY'S DILEMMA

Any company involved in overseas trade has to face the problems described in the introductory paragraphs of this chapter. Which currency should it choose to pay or be paid in, and when should it arrange for that currency to be delivered?

The volatility of the foreign-exchange market is such that currency moves can wipe out profit margins and render companies bankrupt. Suppose a US company had made a five-year investment denominated in sterling in 1981, when the dollar/sterling rate was $2.40/£1. By early 1985 the rate had fallen to $1.10/£1. The investment would have had to double in value to eliminate the currency-depreciation effect.

To counter these problems many companies have a set policy for choosing the denominating currency for their transactions. Often this policy will be to trade always in the currency of the country in which the firm is based, in an attempt to eliminate currency risk altogether. This policy works very well until the company attempts to deal with another firm with the same policy but in a different country. It is also very unlikely that a UK company would accept payment in, say, Venezuelan bolivars, because of the difficulty of converting the currency when delivered.

For these reasons the majority of international trade is denominated in dollars. Not only is the US unit freely convertible but it is also used by many governments as a reserve currency. Since such a large proportion of their business is done in dollars, companies can match up their payments and receipts to reduce their foreign-exchange risk, using the dollars received from sales to pay for supplies.

If a company cannot arrange to pay or be paid either in dollars or in its native currency, its best option is to ask to be paid in some other strong currency. The euro may yet develop to challenge the dollar as the currency of choice. Multinational companies, which usually have to cope with a wide variety of currencies, will attempt to match their payments and receipts in all of the units in which they have transactions in order to keep their total exchange risk to a minimum.

Once a transaction in a particular currency has been arranged, how does a company cope with the foreign-exchange risk involved? Most companies think that their business is trading and not currency speculation, so they will try to avoid risk as much as possible. Suppose a UK company is due to receive dollars three months ahead. It has a number of choices.

First, it could wait for three months, receive the dollars and exchange them for sterling on the spot market. If, in the meantime, the dollar has appreciated against the pound, the company has made money; if the dollar has fallen, the company has lost money.

Second, it could arrange a forward transaction with a bank to sell dollars three months ahead or to buy a dollar-denominated deposit which matures in three months' time. The company's treasurer can sleep at night; the firm is protected against a dollar collapse. But if the dollar rises, the firm will find itself getting a great deal less for its dollars than it might have done.

Third, a middle position: the company could assess which way it thinks the dollar will move. Say it feels there is a 50 per cent chance that it will get a better dollar rate three months ahead than by using the forward market. It therefore sells enough dollars forward to cover 50 per cent of its total position and waits to buy the rest on the spot market. Total disaster has been avoided, and there is the chance of profiting if the dollar rises.

In recent years more and more companies have shown a preference for taking a fourth possible course of action – buying a currency option.

CURRENCY OPTIONS

Currency options are similar to the interest-rate options described in Chapter 13. They give the buyer the right, but not the obligation, to buy foreign currency at a specified rate. Thus the buyer is protected against an adverse exchange-rate movement but retains the potential to take advantage of any favourable movement.

Suppose that a UK company is committed to paying US dollars for oil in three months' time. It is worried that sterling will fall during that period, thus forcing up the cost of the oil. Sterling is at that moment $1.20 on the spot market. So the company buys a three-month sterling put option (the right to sell sterling in exchange for dollars) at a strike price of $1.20. If, during the life of the option, sterling falls to $1.10, the company exercises its option and sells sterling at the more favourable rate of $1.20. However, if sterling rises to $1.30, then the company allows the option to lapse and sells sterling (and buys dollars) on the spot market.

The catch is the cost. The option buyer must pay the seller a premium when the option is purchased. That premium is non-returnable and is considerably larger than the cost of using the forward market. The option seller charges more than for forward cover because of the higher risk involved. An option can be exercised at any time before its expiry date, and that means that the seller must be constantly prepared to exchange currency at an unfavourable rate. In the forward market, however, the day and the rate at which currencies will be exchanged are known in advance.

Although the option buyer pays more, it is for a better product than forward cover. If the UK company in the example above had covered its risk by buying a three-month forward contract at $1.21, it would have been unable to benefit from a move in the spot rate to $1.30 and might well have ended up paying more for its oil than its competitors. It is also important to remember that the premium represents the maximum possible cost to the option buyer.

Let us take another example. An American company wishes to buy Swiss goods. The company negotiates a price of Sfr 1,250,000, which it must pay in three months' time. The spot rate is $0.73 per Sfr. The forward rate is 0.74 per Sfr. The premium of a $0.73 option is $0.015 per Sfr.

SCENARIO A

The spot rate moves to Sfr 0.76.
If the company does nothing, the cost of goods is:
Sfr 1,250,000 × 0.7600 = $950,000.
If the company buys forward, the cost of goods is:
Sfr 1,250,000 × 0.74 = $925,000.
If the company buys an option and exercises it, the cost of goods is:
Sfr 1,250,000 × 0.73 = $912,500,
plus cost of premium
Sfr 1,250,000 × 0.015 = $18,750.
Total = $931,250.

SCENARIO B

The spot price moves to Sfr 0.70.
If the company does nothing, the cost of goods is:
Sfr 1,250,000 × 0.70 = $875,000.
If the company buys forward, the cost of goods is:
Sfr 1,250,000 × 0.74 = $925,000.
If the company buys an option and does not exercise it, the cost of goods is:
Sfr 1,250,000 × 0.70 = $875,000,
plus cost of premium
Sfr 1,250,000 × 0.015 = $18,750.
Total = $893,750.

In both scenarios the option outperforms the worst strategy but does not perform as well as the best strategy. This makes options very attractive to many companies, which see them as a form of insurance covering foreign risk rather than fire or theft.

Most companies buy options direct from banks (over-the-counter options – OTCs). However, it is also possible to buy and sell options on futures exchanges such as the LIFFE (the London International Financial Futures Exchange). Traded options are for standardized amounts and time periods and are available only in a limited number of currencies. However, the premiums are generally cheaper than those of OTC options.

CURRENCY FUTURES

Currency futures are priced in dollars per foreign currency unit. (For example, a sterling contract on a Chicago futures exchange might be priced at $1.10 per £1.) Contract sizes are quite small to accommodate the small speculators who give futures exchanges their liquidity.

Those who use currency futures can be divided into two groups: *speculators* and *hedgers*. *Speculators* act on a hunch that currencies are moving in a particular direction. If they believe that the dollar is going to fall against sterling, then they buy sterling futures in the hope that the value of these will appreciate. *Hedgers* will already be committed to a foreign-exchange position and will buy or sell enough futures contracts to ensure that their initial position is cancelled out.

Suppose a US company is due to pay out £100,000 in three months' time. Its worry is that sterling may rise against the dollar over that period. So it buys four sterling futures contracts, each worth £25,000. The prevailing sterling exchange rate is $1.10. If sterling rises to $1.25, the company will find itself paying out $115,000 – $5,000 more than it would have paid if the exchange rate had stayed the same. But the futures contracts will have increased in value by the same amount. The company will have covered its losses.

As explained in Chapter 13, the system of margin payments allows users of futures contracts to insure against the risks of currency movements without actually exchanging the nominal amount of the contract.

15 Personal Finance

Individuals have a wide range of options when considering savings and investments and the thorough reader should seek professional advice before investing a large sum. There is rarely a perfect answer to an individual's investment requirements. It is wise to remember that even professional advisers make investment mistakes, and they have a lot of time and resources with which to investigate and analyse the market. All this chapter can do is indicate the range of investments on offer to the individual and their advantages and disadvantages.

The rules which govern the finances of individuals are not much different from the ones that govern the finances of institutions. There is still a trade-off between liquidity and reward. The deposit account which gives the customer the best interest rate may impose penalties for early withdrawals of money. Those investments which offer the best return – shares, options, etc. – also involve the possibility of loss. The safest investments offer a steady but unspectacular return.

Investments can also appear safe when they are not. Those who invested money with the fraudster Bernie Madoff thought, erroneously, that they were opting for a conservatively run portfolio. They learnt that the choice of investment manager can be just as important as the choice of investment.

So before investors sign away their hard-earned savings, they should consider carefully what they expect from their investments. Might they want to withdraw their money early to pay for a car or a holiday? What is their attitude towards risk (how would they feel if their investment fell 40 per cent)? Would they rather forgo the chance of capital gain in order to avoid the possibility of capital loss? Have they a lump sum to invest or a small amount each month? Do they pay income tax and, if so, at what rate? When they have the answer to those questions, investors can examine the merits of the various investments on offer more efficiently.

At the risk of sounding very banal, there are also some very simple steps which can be as effective as months of analysis of new forms of savings accounts. A wise rule, for example, for a credit card holder is to pay off the balance at the end of every month. It is very rare for an individual to be able to earn more from his investments than he pays on his borrowings. So it is better to take money out of the building society to pay off debt.

PROPERTY

Most people make their life's main investment in property. Taking out a mortgage is a different form of investment from the others discussed in this chapter since it is an investment financed by borrowing. The other schemes discussed involve the use of money saved from income. Historically, one great advantage of investing in a house was that the interest cost was tax-deductible. But successive governments whittled away the benefit, abolishing it entirely in the 1999 Budget. At least the profit made on the sale of a homeowner's main residence is still free of capital gains tax.

Although the attractions of home ownership seem obvious, it is well to remember that house buyers are, in fact, making a complex calculation. The alternative to house buying is, of course, renting. Depending on the size of the deposit, mortgage repayments can be considerably more expensive than rents, and other items such as buildings insurance and maintenance can add to the bill. However, mortgage payments go up and down with the rate of interest and not, like rents, with the rate of inflation. So over the long term, rental payments should grow by more than the monthly mortgage.

In the past, most people saw the benefits of property investment in terms of the increase in house prices. However, as one house's price is increasing, so are the prices of all the others. When the house is sold, the next house may be even more expensive. The costs of moving are also high. Estate agents normally take 2 per cent of the price, legal costs can easily reach 1 per cent and stamp duty up to 4 per cent more, making up to 7 per cent in all. On top of those costs are the charges of removal men and the inconvenience involved.

But these difficulties were dwarfed in the early 1990s and then again in 2007–8 by the problem of negative equity. Most homeowners (particularly first-time buyers) own only a small proportion of their house. The rest is covered by the mortgage. The mortgage lender does not care whether the house rises or falls in price; it wants the amount of the loan to be repaid in full.

Supposing a homeowner buys a house for £100,000 with a deposit of 5 per cent and borrowing the remaining 95 per cent from a building society. If the house falls 10 per cent in value (to £90,000), the homeowner still owes the building society £95,000. But he cannot sell the house to repay the debt since he would not raise enough money. He is trapped in 'negative equity'.

The 1980s boom in prices was repeated in the early years of the twenty-first century. Since it was accompanied by a bear market in equities, many people decided that property was the only safe home for their nest egg. There was a boom in 'buy-to-letting' where investors bought houses to rent to tenants, and the TV networks were replete with property shows. Buying-to-let is a rather different bet from owning the home you live in. There is no exemption from capital gains tax for profits. Tenants may default on their rent, damage the property and at some times it may not be possible to find any tenants at all. The rent may not be sufficient to meet the mortgage payments, particularly after letting agents and maintenance costs have been paid.

By 2005–6, rental yields (the rent as a proportion of the property value) were below mortgage rates. That was bearable as long as house prices were rising. The market turned in 2007 and, as of mid-2008, was heading down quite sharply. But the market was rescued when the Bank of England cut interest rates to their lowest level in history.

As in previous cycles, there was some lax lending (see section on Northern Rock). It was possible to borrow up to five times an individual's income or more than the value of the house itself. This abruptly stopped in the second half of 2007 once banks started to worry about the potential for bad debts.

There are different types of mortgage agreement – the best-known being the *repayment mortgage*, under which the monthly payments are structured over the lifetime of the loan so that at the end of the period both interest and capital have been repaid. Over the first few years of the mortgage, very little of the capital is repaid. This can surprise home buyers who sell their houses after a few years.

An alternative to the repayment mortgage is the *endowment mortgage*. At the same time as the borrower takes out the mortgage, he or she takes out a life assurance policy with a monthly premium payment. At the time that the mortgage ends, the insurance policy matures and repays the full amount of the loan. In the meantime, the borrower has paid interest but not capital each month to the building society. There are two further advantages of endowment mortgages. One is that if the borrower dies, the loan will be repaid in full. The second is that the policy can be transferred from house to house as the borrower moves.

However, endowment mortgages have many disadvantages. The main one is that they are very inflexible. It is normally twenty-five years before the policy will be paid out in full. If the buyer abandons the policy in the first few years, he will probably get back less than he paid in. This is because the costs involved in setting up a policy are so heavy and are reclaimed from policyholders. It may be as long as ten years before a policyholder can get back his premiums in full.

Endowment mortgages were sold very heavily in the 1970s and 1980s, pushed by salesmen who earned substantial commissions for recommending them (they earned nothing for recommending repayment mortgages). But it has become clear in recent years that future investment returns will be poor and that many endowment policies will not grow sufficiently to repay the mortgage. This has severely dented the popularity of endowments.

Interest-only mortgages are also available in boom times, with the lender relying on the assumption that house prices will keep rising, allowing the borrower to repay the loan when he or she sells.

Borrowers also have a choice between borrowing at a fixed and at a variable rate. In each case, they take a risk. If they borrow at a variable rate, they risk that rates might rise; if they borrow at a fixed rate, the danger is that rates may fall and you will not see the benefit.

Fixed rates offer borrowers the certainty that they know what their payments will be and can budget for them. However, many lenders insist on extras, such as insurance policies, for those who take out fixed-rate deals; these can add substantially to the cost. Lenders also impose redemption penalties, equivalent to several months of mortgage payments, on fixed-rate deals, so it is very expensive to switch out of them.

A relatively recent addition to the list of deals is the capped mortgage. This sets a ceiling above which the rate cannot rise but allows the borrower to benefit if rates fall below that level. This deal offers the best of both worlds, protecting borrowers against a sudden surge in interest rates without locking them into an unattractive rate.

PENSIONS

The field of pensions is one of the most complex of all to cover. Everyone knows about the basic old-age pension, funded by National Insurance contributions. Few think it is adequate as a sole source of income. From the 1970s, governments offered a second pension called the State Earnings Related Pension Scheme or SERPS, for those not involved in company schemes; this will be abolished and replaced by a basic citizen's pension of around £144 a week.

Large companies have traditionally offered pensions to their workers, usually funded by the employers and employees combined. The traditional company pension scheme was known as a defined benefit plan. Such funds must be approved by the Inland Revenue and are set up as independent trusts. They provide a very good benefit for those who retire after a long period of service for one firm. The maximum benefit available is generally retirement on two-thirds of the final salary, and there are guaranteed benefits for widows or widowers (whether the staff member dies in or out of service). The majority of schemes allow employees to take part of the pensions as a tax-free lump sum. Contributions from both employers and employees are free of tax and the fund itself can accumulate tax-free.

However, defined benefit schemes represent a risk to the companies involved. They are obliged to offer a set level of pension but they have no guarantee that the pension fund will grow by enough to meet that liability. If investment returns are poor, then the employer will have to make up the shortfall. In addition, plans are obliged to link pensions to inflation, so employers face an ever-increasing liability. (The employee also faces a risk: that the company will go bust and be unable to pay the pension in full, or at all.) When the stock market fell between 2000 and 2002, many pension schemes dropped into deficit. Employers reacted by closing schemes to new members and (in some cases) existing ones. In some cases, employers have gone into liquidation without sufficient funds to cover the pension payments. To cover this risk, the government set up a Pension Protection Fund, a kind of insurance scheme. When a scheme fails, employers are entitled to 90 per cent of their projected benefits with a maximum limit of £32,761 (in the 2014–15 tax year). Those who have already retired will be paid in full.

Instead of a defined benefit plan, many employers now offer what are known as defined contribution plans (they are also known as money purchase plans). Under these, the employer does not guarantee the final payment. The employee puts money into the fund; his or her contributions are then matched by the employer. If investment returns are good, then the final pension will be high; if they are poor, then the pension will be low. This transfers the bulk of the risk from the employer to the employee.

However, defined contribution schemes may be a good deal for people who move jobs often, an increasing trend in recent years. And the fund is owned by them outright; there is no problem if the employer goes bust.

In the 1980s, the government introduced personal pensions, which were designed for frequent job movers and the self-employed. Like the defined contribution (DC) plans described above, personal pensions are invested in a fund; the eventual pension is entirely dependent on the performance of that fund. But the advantage is that employees can carry on making payments into the same fund, regardless of how often they change jobs.

In the past, employees had to use their pension pot to buy an annuity, an income that lasts for the rest of their lives. In effect, this was a quid pro quo for the tax breaks that pensions attract; the government did not want people to spend all their pension pots on a cruise and then become dependent on the state. But annuities were unpopular. The money could not be passed on to the worker's heirs; if they retired at 65 and died aged 66, all the money was gone.

Annuity rates also fell sharply in the 1990s and 2000s. This was for two good reasons; people were living longer and interest rates were much lower. As a result, a given pension pot bought a much lower income. The average pension pot is around £30,000; the best annuity rate for a male

aged 65 would turn that into £1,800 a year with no protection for inflation. If future inflation averaged 4 per cent a year, that would halve in
value in 18 years. But if the worker used the same pot to buy an inflation-
protected annuity, his starting income would be just £1,200 a year.

As of April 2015, there will be no need to buy an annuity. Retirees can
take the whole sum as cash (although there will be tax to pay when they
do). While this was greeted in the press as a blow for freedom, it may not
make pensioners any better off. First of all, a pot of £30,000 cannot guarantee a decent income, however it is invested. Secondly, workers may be
tempted to buy products that are more risky, and have higher charges,
than annuities. Thirdly, they may run though their pots too quickly and
end up with an impoverished old age.

A lot of people have been put off pensions by their complexity. Over
the years, there have been a variety of different schemes with slightly different rules govering things like the level of tax-free contribution.

The then Labour government tried to simplify the rules in 2006, introducing the self-invested personal pension (SIPP) for plans those who
wanted to handle their own money. Initially, this scheme had a very generous annual limit for contributions. But in effect that meant wealthy
people could shelter a lot of money from tax. Over time, then, governments placed a lifetime cap on both the size of pension pots and the
amount of annual contributions.

If you do take out a personal pension (or join a defined contribution
scheme), remember that the level of contributions is up to you. Money
cannot be created out of thin air. If you want a decent income in retirement, you will have to save a sizeable chunk of your current income. You
work for forty years or so, but you may be retired for thirty.

SIPPs are mainly used by wealthy investors. Indeed, there is a big pension gap between the better-off and ordinary workers, a good deal of
whom have no company pension at all. In part, this is because it can be
hard for a worker in their twenties to think forward forty years; they may
have a desperate need for cash today. So the government has introduced
auto-enrolment in pension schemes; instead of opting in to a pension
plan, workers must opt out. This takes advantage of a key psychological
trait – inertia. Many people will not be bothered to sign the forms to
opt out. The hope is that they will get used to saving for a pension and
build up a decent sum. The money will largely be invested in NEST, a
government-established scheme with low costs.

LIFE INSURANCE

Life assurance or insurance has traditionally been one of the biggest forms of personal savings. Until 1984, life assurance premium payments were tax-deductible. The combination of tax advantages and small regular payments made the schemes very popular. Many investors had endowment mortgages or other insurance-linked savings plans. Indeed, the 'man from the Pru' used to pop round and collect savings door-to-door.

Insurance plans were a fairly safe way for investors to save money in an earlier age. The sums were pooled and invested in a range of assets from shares through to government bonds to property. Often returns would be smoothed to prevent sudden changes in value.

But the model had its problems. One was high costs. Insurance agents are expensive to employ and even independent advisers need to be paid commissions to sell policies. These costs may not be too onerous if spread over a 20–25 year plan. But they take a big chunk out of returns when policyholders want to cash in early.

The plans are also opaque. They mix together life insurance with savings, when it might be more efficient to buy the products separately. The smoothing process can penalize one generation of savers to the benefit of another.

Worst of all, the plans suffered when interest rates fell in the 1990s. If they were sold on an assumption of a 9 per cent return, that was difficult to achieve when government bonds yielded 5 per cent. Some plans overcommitted to equities as a response and were badly hit when the stock market slumped between 2000 and 2002. Insurers had to impose market value adjustments on policies and send out red letters to say that plans would not be sufficient to repay mortgages.

None of the above should deter investors from buying *term policies* which provide insurance against death within a specified period of years. If the insured person lives through the period, no lump sum is paid. Premiums are consequently cheap since insurance companies can rely on the iron laws of probability to determine how likely it is that a given person of a given age will die.

Another option is *whole life policies*, which lack a specified term of benefit. Whenever the insured person dies, the insurers must pay (and so these policies cost more). However, the laws of probability still apply. The insurance company will be able to calculate when, on average, it will be required to pay.

DEPOSITS

Leaving aside the massive investment that many people make in property and pensions, the most common investment for the small investor is in deposit-based savings products of one kind or another. These fall into two main groups: those run by building societies or banks, and the government.

BUILDING SOCIETIES AND BANKS

The two institutions compete on a pretty level playing field these days, thanks to a host of mergers and the development of the internet. Anyone with access to a computer can find the best rates available through comparison websites such as moneysupermarket.com. For small sums, it is merely a matter of deciding whether you want a fixed-rate account and whether you are prepared to receive a little more interest in return for losing the benefit of instant access to your money. As of 2014, central bank policy was keeping rates so low that depositors were losing money after the effects of tax and inflation.

For larger sums, you need to worry about the health of the financial institution concerned, as the Northern Rock example showed. That saga led to the guaranteed amount per customer being raised to £35,000, followed by a further increase to £50,000 in October 2008 and to £85,000 at the end of 2010. Those with larger sums to invest may well choose to spread their money among several banks and to be aware that a high interest rate could well be a sign of higher risk. The collapse of the Icelandic banks showed a further problem. Savers were covered not by the British deposit guarantee but by Iceland's. The foreign government lacked the resources to pay: under pressure, Britain stepped in.

Banks and building societies can now pay interest without deducting tax but depositors must first fill in a form to prove they are non-taxpayers.

NATIONAL SAVINGS

An even safer investment than either the banks or the building societies is, of course, lending to the government. The main way that the government borrows from the mass of citizens is through the various National Savings schemes, which are operated through the post offices and over the internet. The government offers both taxed and untaxed schemes. The untaxed schemes are mainly in the form of certificates and bonds, which are issued in batches with each issue setting its own terms. Savings certificates offer a guaranteed (fixed) rate of interest if savers deposit money for a set term and there are penalties if money is withdrawn before the certificates expire. They are normally sold in £100 units and the maximum holding is £10,000.

To protect the saver against the effects of inflation, the government has introduced index-linked certificates, sometimes called 'granny bonds' because they were designed to appeal to old-age pensioners. The formula for calculating the yield on index-linked certificates is quite complicated but gives investors inflation protection, plus interest on top. Most issues offer not only indexation but a bonus interest rate for each successive year that the certificate is held.

National Savings products have tended to vary in their appeal in line with competition from the private sector and the government's needs for cash.

Premium bonds are another form of tax-free investment open to the individual investor but the chances of getting any return at all are fairly small. In early 1993, the government revamped the scheme, increasing the top prize to £1 million in an attempt to compete with the National Lottery. The yield on the fund varies with the level of interest rates.

The government also issues long-term bonds in large denominations, known as gilts. These can be bought through a stockbroker.

Unlike most of the other investments we have so far described, gilts offer the chance of capital gain. As we saw in Chapter 2, the prices of bonds move up and down in inverse fashion to the level of interest rates. So, it is possible to buy a gilt at £80 one year and sell it the next at £100 and earn interest in the process. It is also well to remember that gilts can fall in price as well as rise, so there is a risk which is not involved in holding a building society deposit. The best time to buy gilts is when you expect interest rates to fall. Note the distinction between the risk that the borrower will not repay, the *credit risk*, which for gilts is virtually nil, and the risk that the investment will not be profitable, the *market risk*.

Most gilts have a fixed interest rate, which varies per issue depending on the general level of rates at the time that they were issued. However, in parallel with the issue of index-linked savings certificates, the government also issues index-linked gilts, which carry a return at a certain level above the rate of inflation.

A new area of gilt investment has opened up with the creation of gilt strips. These, as described in Chapter 7, are essentially the component parts of a gilt issue: all the interest payments and the final repayment value. Each has a fixed value and repayment date and thus can be useful for financial planning. Each strip will trade at a discount to its repayment value; a long-term strip might trade at £20 to £30 per £100. The strip should gradually rise to that level (with some sharp fluctuations on the way).

Unfortunately, the tax treatment is not favourable; the annual gain on a strip is currently subject to income tax, although the investor has not received any income.

SHARES

In the 1960s and 1970s, the riskiness of share ownership and the distortions of the tax system contributed to a decline in the proportion of shares held by private individuals. Instead, investment institutions dominated the equity markets. In the 1980s and 1990s, privatizations, building society flotations and the ability to trade shares through the internet encouraged many individuals back into the stock market, albeit in a small way.

The main problem for individuals in equity investment is the risk. As the crash of 1987 amply illustrated, share prices can fall dramatically in a single day. Even if the market as a whole does not collapse, individual shares can fall very sharply and the smallest investors are usually the last to hear the news that sparks the drop. Many technology stocks fell by 90 per cent between March 2000 and September 2001, for example. It may be bad news about an individual company that causes its share price to plunge or bad news about a sector of the economy that causes a group of share prices (e.g. computer companies) to fail.

The best way of dealing with the risk of individual price falls is to spread shareholdings over a wide range of companies. This is a matter for careful judgement; obviously, buying five separate oil stocks will not protect you against a fall in the price of oil.

The problem is that the costs of dealing – the commission paid to stockbrokers, the stamp duty, and the spread between the buy and sell prices – mean that shares have to rise by several per cent just for the investor to break even. Of course, the wider the portfolio, the greater the costs. Since one should really have a portfolio of ten to twelve stocks, the investor ought to have at least £10,000 to £12,000 to spend. He or she should also be ready to invest long term. Also, individual sectors may be more risky than others. Investing in diamond mining may give you a chance to make your fortune but you are also far more likely to lose your stake than if you had bought shares in British Telecom.

Tips and rumours can be misleading. Many investors rashly seize on a newspaper report. A story about booming coffee prices in Brazil will have been known to others long before, and the share price of coffee producers will already reflect the news. The tips given by financial journalists are often useful but not, alas, always right. Internet bulletin boards offer a new forum for tipsters but there is no reason to assume that this information is reliable. Indeed, those who own a share have every incentive to sing its praises over the internet since an increase in the number of buyers will push up the price.

Privatizations did seem to offer easy profits for the small investor. Everyone who bought shares in British Telecom did well at first. Alas, there is little left to privatize. By no means all new issues are so successful, however; those who bought shares in the flotation of Lastminute.com were sitting on losses of 90 per cent eighteen months later. The investor should read the financial press carefully before such issues. If enough publicity is favourable, then it is likely that plenty of other investors will be willing to buy. That will mean that the issue will be oversubscribed and those investors who do not get the shares they want will try to buy the shares on the Stock Exchange, bidding up the price in the process.

Experts have an important rule of thumb – avoid trading too much. Investing in shares is for the long term; the most successful investor in the world, Warren Buffett, holds many shares first bought in the 1970s. Every time you trade, you incur costs and this reduces your return. This is why the idea of 'day trading', living off your profits from dealing over the computer screen, makes no sense. Studies in the US show that 70 per cent of day traders lose money.

HOW TO FOLLOW SHARE PRICES

Most serious investors should buy the *Financial Times*, which carries each day a host of information about companies and the financial markets. At the back of the paper, it prints the previous day's closing share prices. The listings of companies are separated into various groups, which can help the investor to narrow down his or her choice to a particular industry or field.

In the first column is the name of the company. Special symbols indicate factors about the company, such as the tradability of the shares. The price column shows the mid-price at the end of the previous day. This is not necessarily the price you will get if you buy or sell the shares. Traders quote different prices for buying and selling and make a profit on the spread between them.

So if a share is quoted at 100p, the price which you may have to pay to buy would be 102p, while the price you might get if you wanted to sell would be 98p.

The next column to the right shows the share price change on the day. Moving across we find the high and low for the year.

The next column is headed 'Yield' and shows the dividend return on the shares over the previous year. So if a share cost 100p and had a yield of 5 per cent, you would expect 5p of dividends in a year. This is not necessarily what you will receive, however. Dividends can be cut (and increased); and you may pay further tax on your dividend, depending on your income.

The next column, headed P/E, shows the price/earnings ratio (for a full explanation, see Chapter 10). The final column is headed Volume '000s. This shows the level of business conducted during the previous day. It can be a useful means of checking whether a share price fall or rise is 'serious', or simply the effect of a rogue trade. Heavy volume is an indication that something may be going on at the company – whether it is a takeover approach or a forthcoming profit warning.

A study of the figures of a particular company, Barclays, on a particular day, 25 July 2008, may help. Barclays is in the 'banks' sector. A symbol following its name shows that the earnings numbers (in the P/E ratio) are calculated on preliminary figures and not the annual report. The share price on that day was 348p, down 4p on the session, well down on the high for the year of 754.5p but above the low of 238.75p. Over 119 million shares had been traded, worth around £420 million. The shares yielded 9.8 per cent and had a price/earnings ratio of 5.5.

USING A STOCKBROKER

To buy and sell most shares you need to use a stockbroker. (The main exception is a new issue where you can apply for shares by filling in a coupon in a newspaper. Even then, you will eventually need the services of a stockbroker to sell your holding.)

Stockbroking services fall into three main categories.

Execution-only brokers will deal on your behalf but will not offer any advice on which shares to buy. The commissions they charge for buying and selling are usually lower than other brokers. A good example of an execution-only broker is T. D. Waterhouse, a Canadian-based group.

Many execution-only brokers now operate over the internet, which allows you to trade without ever speaking to an individual. This has lowered the costs of dealing but it has also increased the temptation to deal more often. It is worth remembering that investment is a very complex business that many professionals fail to master. If you are successful in your early trades, it is more likely to be due to luck rather than judgement.

Advisory brokers will, as their name suggests, give advice on the right shares to buy or sell; the ultimate decision still lies in your hands. Their commissions are normally higher than those of execution-only brokers, but they claim their advice and standard of service is worth it.

Discretionary brokers take complete control of your money. This type of broker is best suited to the better-off, with say £1 million to invest, and to those who do not feel expert enough to select their own shares. Such brokers may well charge a fee, based on a percentage of the amount of money invested.

Readers can search for registered stockbrokers via the Wealth Management Association's website at www.thewma.co.uk.

TAX AND STOCK MARKET INVESTING

Profits from investing in shares are taxed in two ways. First the dividends earned are subject to income tax. The system is rather complicated, but higher-rate taxpayers have to deduct tax while basic-rate payers do not. (They are effectively assumed to have paid tax already.)

If your shares rise in price, you may face a capital gains tax bill. The government regularly overhauls the capital gains tax system. The latest change abolished the taper relief that had applied in previous years (relief for inflation had applied before that). Most people will be lucky to make more than the tax-free allowance of £11,000 (in the 2014–15 tax year). If they make more than that, they would be wise to consult an expert.

PEPS AND ISAS

The Individual Savings Account, or ISA, is a government-devised shelter, designed to persuade UK citizens to save more money. It is the successor to personal equity plans, or PEPs, which were introduced by Margaret Thatcher's administration.

The basic idea of ISAs and PEPS is the same. Investors get an annual allowance (£15,000 in the 2014–15 tax year) which they can invest into a range of assets. Any returns are tax-free. Unlike pensions, investors do not get any tax relief on contributions. However, unlike pensions, all withdrawals are tax-free (and can be made at the investor's discretion).

ISAs allow a broad range of investments to be held in a tax-free form, including gilts, life insurance, national savings and long-term cash holdings. The old distinction between cash and equity ISAs has been abolished and investors can mix and match the assets how they like.

Old PEPs can continue, although they cannot receive any new money. The ISA has rather less generous tax breaks than the old PEP, thanks to the change in the taxation of dividends. Basic-rate taxpayers are no better off, from an income tax point of view, buying shares inside an ISA than outside. Higher-rate taxpayers do benefit from a tax break on their share income (a net dividend of £75 is grossed up to £100). Both avoid paying capital gains tax, no matter how well they do. And those that hold bonds or cash still benefit from the lack of tax on their interest income.

UNIT AND INVESTMENT TRUSTS

Picking the right share is a difficult business. Most private investors only have enough money to buy two or three shares, and are thus very exposed to the risk of one of those companies going bust.

Unit and investment trusts (explained in Chapter 8) offer a way round this problem. They each buy a widespread portfolio of shares – private investors then acquire units, or shares, in the trusts. Those with a small sum can thus enjoy the benefits of a diversified portfolio.

It is possible to buy units in trusts which specialize in certain geographical areas (such as the US, Japan or Europe) or in commodities like gold. However, the more narrow a trust's focus, the greater the risk.

Investment trusts have shares rather than units. These shares are not directly linked to the value of the fund, but rise and fall according to supply and demand. Say there are 100 million shares and the fund is worth £100 million. The shares might well trade at 90p, rather than at £1. In such a case, they would stand at a discount to net assets.

If this discount narrows, the investor will make a profit even though the value of the underlying portfolio is unchanged. If the discount widens, the investor will make a loss.

Another development in the 1980s and 1990s was the growth in split capital investment trusts. These have different classes of shares; a typical division is for one class to receive all the income of the trust, and the other all the capital growth. These structures can be very complex and risky, and many trusts got into difficulties in the face of falling stock markets in 2001. Anyone considering buying such shares should take expert advice.

The two sectors often argue among themselves about which is the better. Charges are certainly higher on unit trusts; but the existence of the discount adds an extra layer of risk for those buying shares in investment trusts. Both offer savings schemes, ways of investing on a monthly basis to smooth out some of the market peaks and troughs. If an investor can find a fund with a good performance record and a low-cost savings scheme, it probably does not matter whether it is a unit or investment trust.

INDEX FUNDS

One type of fund that has only become available to small investors in recent years is the index-tracker. Rather than research the market and look for attractive stocks, an index fund attempts to match the performance of a particular benchmark, such as the FTSE 100 Index. Investors can buy index-trackers in the form of a unit trust or as an exchange-traded fund (see Chapter 8).

The advantage of trackers is their lower costs. The components of an index change only rarely, so a fund manager who tracks the index faces few dealing costs. Active managers are forever turning over their portfolios in the effort to find the next winners; the costs incurred are passed to retail investors, reducing their long-term returns.

The second reason is called *efficient market theory*. In essence, the theory states that all the information about a share is already included in the price. So if you notice that everyone is using mobile phones and rush out to buy shares in a mobile phone company, you will be too late; other people will have noticed first and pushed the shares up to reflect the sector's improved prospects.

The only thing that will cause a share price to move is genuine 'news', which by definition cannot be known in advance.

Efficient market theory still prompts much debate among academics and is derided by many fund managers, but the fact is that only around 20 per cent of fund managers beat the index over the long run.

Index funds will almost never be the best performers but their low costs and broad spread mean that they will not be the worst. They are an attractive option for private investors. All the above funds, however, will fall in value when the general market drops, as it did in 2008. Buying any kind of equity-linked investment is only for the long term, i.e. several years.

The credit crunch caused politicians and regulators to rethink their approach to the financial sector completely. The hundreds of billions that had to be spent in rescuing the banks was understandably seen as a sign of the failure of the old system.

In a wide-ranging review of regulation, Lord Turner, the chairman of the Financial Services Authority, admitted that the old regime was based on a flawed intellectual approach. It was assumed that markets were self-correcting, with market discipline a more effective tool than regulation. It was also assumed that senior managers and boards of directors were better placed to assess business risk than regulators.

This led, Lord Turner argued, to a focus on individual businesses rather than on the system as a whole. The result was that regulators failed to spot that the banking industry was taking too many risks. Specifically, Turner admitted that the FSA 'was not in hindsight aggressive enough in demanding adjustments to business models which even at the level of the individual institution were excessively risky'. He added that, with Northern Rock, 'the FSA also fell short of high professional standards in the execution of its supervisory approach, with significant failures in basic management disciplines and procedures'.

Many people felt that the tripartite system of regulation, with the system watched over by the FSA, Bank of England and the Treasury, had proved to be flawed. Government ministers had boasted of Britain's 'light touch' approach, although Lord Turner claimed the FSA had never used that phrase.

But it was not just the British authorities that felt they had failed. In the US, Congress passed the Dodd–Frank Act, a mammoth law that ran to 848 pages, some of which merely required regulators to draw up more rules. The Volcker rule, designed to stop banks trading on their own account, comprised just eleven pages of the Act but was turned by regulators into a 298-page proposal that required affected firms to answer 383 questions. In Europe, regulators set up a bunch of bodies, including the European Banking Authority and the European Securities and Markets Authority.

The British authorities did revamp the regulatory system, but not, as might have been expected, by concentrating regulation under one roof. The Financial Services Authority was replaced by the Financial Conduct Authority, which will deal with consumer finance and those institutions that do not take deposits; responsibility for regulating the banks has gone back to the Bank of England, in the form of a new arm called the Prudential Regulatory Authority. The latter move makes some sense; in the end, it is the Bank of England that has the money available to bail out banks in times of crisis. But there is always the danger, with divided regulators, that issues will fall into the cracks.

THE BANKING ISSUE

What are the big issues that need attention? The first is the banks. We have always known that banks are risky; they borrow short (from depositors) and lend long (to companies). If depositors lose confidence, banks can be caught by 'runs' which lead them to fold.

Over the decades, authorities have taken different approaches to this problem.

After the crash of 1929, the US authorities separated commercial and investment banking activities; they did not want the risky activities of the latter to contaminate the former. They also guaranteed bank deposits to try to prevent the loss of depositor confidence. The quid pro quo was a fairly tight regime of bank regulation. In Britain, the Bank of England used its authority to keep rogue banks in line.

But the increasing sophistication of financial markets made it hard to enforce a distinction between commercial and investment banking activities. The use of complex derivative products made the risk exposures of banks hard for managers, let alone regulators, to understand.

Banks became more complex creatures; regulators tried mainly to control them through the use of capital ratios that, in retrospect, proved easy to get around.

There was also a view in the 1980s and 1990s that government regulations only introduce distortions into the market that prevent it from working efficiently. Those who worked for investment banks or hedge funds were wealth generators who knew what they were doing; after all, didn't they earn a lot of money? Interfere with them and they would move to a more friendly regime abroad. One need only gaze at those 'temples of Mammon' in Canary Wharf to see how the aura of success must have dazzled regulators and politicians.

But the 1980s and 1990s were uniquely favourable for the banking system. Interest rates were low or falling, asset markets were generally rising, recessions were short and mild. As a result, bad debts were small. As the late economist Hyman Minsky argued, these benign conditions encouraged banks (and almost everyone else) to take risks. If you are confident that the future will look roughly as it does today, you will be willing to lend (as a bank) and borrow (as a consumer or company). But the act of lending and borrowing increases your risk level and ensures that tomorrow will be less like today than you think. In the end, it means a small change in economic conditions can prove disastrous.

The regulators failed to recognize this. They thought that banks' risk models were sophisticated. But those models contained fatal flaws; they assumed that economic conditions would stay benign and they forgot that other banks were taking similar risks. For an example, take the Value at Risk approach. This was used by banks to control their trading risk. When markets were volatile, they committed less capital to trading; when markets were calm, they committed more. But what happens when calm markets turn volatile? Banks try to cut their positions. That means selling securities. But everyone else is doing the same. Such selling means more volatility and thus a further attempt to cut positions.

Repairing the system is not easy. Risk might be like the game of whack-a-mole; hammer it down in one place and it may turn up somewhere else. Governments have to balance different priorities. Banks had too little capital going into the crisis; when their assets fell in value, their balance sheets imploded. So the obvious answer was to make them hold more capital to make them safer. That could be achieved in two ways. One approach was to raise more capital from the stock market, but investors were not keen to buy those extra shares. The other answer was to shrink the balance sheet by lending less money. But we want banks to lend money to small businesses; that is one of their main economic functions.

Another example of divided authorities concerned the housing market. Banks had reacted to the housing crisis by tightening credit standards and insisting that buyers had bigger deposits. As a result, first-time buyers found it difficult to get their feet on the property ladder. So the 2010 coalition government created a scheme called help-to-buy which guaranteed buyers deposits (in effect, weakening credit standards). Then in 2014, the Bank of England suggested that banks be careful about making loans that were a big multiple of homebuyers' earnings – tightening credit standards, in effect. The left hand did not seem to know what the right hand was doing.

What about repeating the 1930s and separating the investment and commercial arms of banking? The government edged in that direction by accepting the Vickers report; it did not recommend that banks should be split up but did suggest that the different arms of the bank should have their own capital, so that a crisis in an investment bank did not take down the commercial bank. However, it is worth remembering that commercial banks can get into trouble on their own. Northern Rock was a commercial bank, taking deposits and making loans in the form of mortgages.

INCENTIVES

For much of the last twenty years, the best and the brightest from our universities have flocked to the financial sector. They believed that working for an investment bank or hedge fund was the fastest route to riches.

Bankers earned vast sums in the form of bonuses or share options in the companies they worked for. But there was a problem with this incentive structure. All too often the bonuses were based on short-term results. But such results could be achieved by bankers following a strategy that might lead to long-term ruin; by the time that ruin occurred, the bankers had already pocketed their money.

Take, for example, bonuses based on the amount of loans completed. A salesman motivated by such a scheme would have a natural incentive to lend to as many people as possible, regardless of their ability to repay the money. The inevitable default by the borrower would occur on someone else's watch.

Traders could follow strategies described as 'picking up nickels in front of steamrollers' – a long series of small profits culminating in a big loss. Time it right and you look like a genius, and you get a big bonus.

All this might not have mattered, were it not for the need for governments to bail out banks when they go wrong, either implicitly by cutting interest rates (which at least helps other borrowers) or explicitly, by outright injections of public money. This leads to an entirely unhealthy system where profits are privatized and losses are socialized. The anger of voters over the need for the government to fund Sir Fred Goodwin's pension, or, in America, the bonuses at failed insurance group AIG, was understandable. It did not seem to make much sense that bankers could be paid bonuses when the company was losing billions. The problem was that, under contract law, these bonuses had to be paid; they were usually tied to the performance of a particular division or department rather than to the fortunes of the whole bank.

Tackling incentives will be difficult. Some of the failed banks, like Bear Stearns and Lehman Brothers, gave bonuses in the form of deferred stock to try to get round the incentives issue; the employees lost a lot of their personal wealth when the banks collapsed. Clearly, the individuals concerned were blind to the risks they were taking. In 2014, the Bank of England introduced a scheme to allow banks to claw back bonuses paid at any time over the previous seven years if the bankers have exceeded their risk limits or broken conduct rules. That may be a tricky process if the bankers have already spent the money. In 2013, the EU passed rules that limited bankers' bonuses to 100 per cent of their pay or 200 per cent if shareholders approved; banks quickly strived to find ways round the rules. While these bonuses often seem obscene by ordinary standards, they do give the banks a lot of flexibility to cut their pay bill in bad times; if the cap were to be successfully enforced, the effect might simply be to drive up the basic salaries of top bankers.

SHADOW BANKS

The credit crunch has also shown that it is not just the banks that create problems. There is also a vast shadow banking system, consisting of hedge funds, private equity and structured investment vehicles or SIVs. These both invested in the mortgage debts that originated the problems and borrowed money from the banks to do so. When they collapsed, the banks were brought down with them; their disappearance also left a gap in the funding of the private sector.

Should they be regulated? The answer is clearly yes, if only because of the mess that they have left. But it will be very difficult. By their nature, hedge funds, for example, are vehicles designed to be as flexible as possible; regulate them too much and they might disappear altogether. Normal people might not weep at the prospect but the result might be less liquid markets and a higher cost of capital for businesses and home-buyers. It seems likely that the authorities will aim to increase the amount of information they hold about such funds, so they can see whether they pose a risk to the system.

One big hope for the future is macroprudential regulation. In the 1990s and 2000s, central banks seemed to have only one tool with which to curb financial excesses; interest rates. But pushing up rates affects a lot more than the banking sector; it hits consumers and companies too. Central banks were reluctant to cause a recession in order to pop a housing bubble. Instead, macroprudential regulation would use other levers; for example, telling banks to have tighter lending standards or hold more capital. The big question is whether this would work. Would central bankers be farsighted enough to change the rules in time? And would bankers find a way round the restrictions, especially in a world where capital can flow instantly across national borders?

No regulatory system will be perfect. Britain has spent much of the last thirty years tinkering with its system. The current set-up with the Financial Conduct Authority and the Prudential Regulatory Authority is the third system established since the mid-1980s. In the US, supervision has been hampered by the existence of a network of overlapping bodies.

It is, in any case, inevitable that the private sector will be able to pay more than the regulators and will attract people who will find ways around the rules. People like to speculate; even Sir Isaac Newton lost money in the South Sea Bubble. Without speculation, Britain would be a far less vibrant society. Fewer new businesses would be started and new products invented. Busts are a price worth paying, the creative destruction that allows an economy to start anew. But the 2007–2009 bust was a severe test of that thesis.

Glossary

ADR American Depositary Receipt – mechanism by which foreign shares are traded in the US

BEARS Investors who believe that share or bond prices are likely to fall

'BIG BANG' Strictly speaking the day when minimum commissions were abolished on the Stock Exchange. Also a term used to cover the whole range of changes taking place in the City in the 1980s

BILL A short-term (three months or so) instrument which pays interest to the holder and can be traded. Some bills do not pay interest but are issued at a discount to their face value

BOND A financial instrument which pays interest to the holder. Most bonds have a set date on which the borrower will repay the holder. Bonds are attractive to investors because they can usually be bought and sold easily

BROKERS Those who link buyers and sellers in return for a commission

BUILDING SOCIETIES Institutions whose primary function is to accept the savings of small depositors and channel them to house buyers in return for the security of a mortgage on the property

BULLS Investors who believe that share or bond prices are likely to rise

CASH RATIO The proportion of a bank's liabilities which it considers prudent to keep in the form of cash

CDO (COLLATERALIZED DEBT OBLIGATION) Complex security comprised of a portfolio of bonds or credit default swaps (see below). The CDO is divided into tranches, offering different combinations of risk and return

CERTIFICATE OF DEPOSIT Short-term interest-paying security

CHAPS Clearing House Automated Payment System – an electronic system for settling accounts between the major clearing banks

CHINESE WALL   A theoretical barrier within a securities firm which is designed to prevent fraud. One part of the firm may not pass on sensitive information to another if it is against a client's interest

CLEARING BANKS   Banks which are part of the clearing system, which significantly reduces the number of interbank payments

COMMERCIAL BANKS   Banks which receive a large proportion of their funds from small depositors

CONDUIT   Off balance sheet vehicle which banks used to house asset-backed securities

COUPON   The interest payment on a bond

CREDIT DEFAULT SWAP   Contract that allows one party to insure against default on a bond

DEBENTURE   A long-term bond issued by a UK company and secured on fixed assets

DEBT CONVERTIBLE   Bond which can be converted by an investor into another bond with a different interest rate or maturity

DEBT CRISIS   Any crisis that results from a failure of debtors to repay. It usually brings problems for the banks and an economic meltdown

DEFINED BENEFIT PENSION   Pension based on the employee's final salary (or career average salary). Being phased out from the private sector

DEFINED CONTRIBUTION PENSION SCHEME   Pot into which employers and employee put money over the course of the latter's career. On retirement, the worker gets a lump sum which he or she has to turn into an income. There are no guarantees; it all depends on investment performance

DEPRECIATION   An accounting term which allows for the run-down in value of a company's assets. Also used to describe a steady decline in the market value of a currency, as opposed to devaluation (see below)

DEVALUATION   Term, usually applied to currencies, which means simply a one-off loss in value (fall in price) of the currency concerned. Devaluations are normally announced by governments or central banks that previously tried to maintain a fixed rate for the currency

DISCOUNT BROKER   A broker who offers a no-frills, dealing-only service for a cheap price

DISCOUNT HOUSES   Financial institutions which specialize in discounting bills. For years the channel through which the Bank of England operated to influence the financial system

DISCOUNTING   The practice of issuing securities at less than their face value. Rather than receiving payment in the form of interest, the holder profits from the difference between the price of the discounted security and its face value

DISINTERMEDIATION Process whereby borrowers bypass banks and borrow directly from investment institutions

DIVIDEND A payment, representing a proportion of profits, that is made to company shareholders

ECGD Export Credit Guarantee Department – government agency which provides trade insurance for exporters

ENDOWMENT MORTGAGE Mortgage linked to a life-assurance scheme. Only interest is paid during the scheme's life; when the scheme matures, it repays the capital

EQUITY The part of a company owned by its shareholders. Also used as a synonym for share

EQUITY CONVERTIBLE Bond which can be converted into the shares of the issuing company

EURIBOR Rate at which banks in the Eurozone borrow from each other

EURO The European single currency

EUROBOND A bond issued in the Euromarket

EUROCURRENCY Currency traded in the Euromarket (e.g. Eurodollar, Eurosterling)

EUROMARKET The offshore international financial market

EURONOTE A short-term security (under a year) issued in the Euromarket. Under a Euronote facility, a bank agrees to buy or to underwrite a borrower's Euronote programme for a given period of years. The facilities come under various names, like NIFs and RUFs

EXCHANGE RATE The price at which one currency can be exchanged for another

EXCHANGE TRADED FUND Fund, listed on the Stock Exchange, that owns a basket of stocks usually tracking an index

FACTORING Factors provide both a credit-collection service and short-term finance

EXPECTATIONS THEORY The belief that long-term interest rates express investors' views on the likely level of future short-term interest rates. Thus if investors expect short-term interest rates to rise, they will demand a higher interest rate for investing long term

FEDERAL RESERVE The US central bank which plays a role similar to that of the Bank of England

FIXED COMMISSIONS Under the old Stock Exchange system, commission paid to brokers was set. This was seen as discouraging competition. Fixed commissions were abolished on 'Big Bang' day – 27 October 1986

FIXED EXCHANGE RATES Currencies with set values against each other which vary only in times of crisis when one or more currencies will revalue or devalue

FLOATING EXCHANGE RATES Currencies whose values against each other are set by market forces

FORFAITING Raising money by selling a company's invoices

FORWARD/FORWARD AGREEMENT Arrangement to lend or borrow a set sum at a date in the future for a set period at a set rate

FORWARD MARKET Market in which currencies are traded months or years ahead

FRA Forward-rate agreement – arrangement to fix a lender's or borrower's interest rate in advance: no capital is exchanged, only the amount by which the agreed rate differs from the eventual market rate

FRN Floating-rate note – a bond which pays an interest that varies in line with market rates

FTSE INDEX Index which tracks the share prices of 100 leading companies

FUTURES Instruments which give the buyer the right to purchase a commodity at a future date. In the financial markets they are used by those concerned about movements in interest rates, currencies and stock indices

GEARING The ratio between a company's debt and equity. See also leverage

GILTS Bonds issued by the UK government

GOLDEN HELLO Payment made to an employee of a rival firm to entice him or her to transfer. One of a whole range of City perks, including golden handcuffs and golden parachutes

GOODWILL An accounting term which describes the intangible assets of a company (e.g. brand names, the skill of the staff)

GOWER REPORT Produced in 1984, its recommendations were the basis of the new regulatory structure in the City

GROSS YIELD TO REDEMPTION The return which an investor will receive on a bond, allowing for both interest and capital growth, as a percentage of the bond's price

HEDGE FUNDS Private investment vehicles that use borrowed money and shorting (see below) in order to earn returns in both bull and bear markets

HEDGING The process whereby an institution buys or sells a financial instrument in order to offset the risk that the price of another financial instrument will rise or fall

IDB Inter-dealer broker. An official broker in the government securities (gilts and Treasury bills) market

IMF International Monetary Fund – supranational organization which plays an important role in troubled economies

INTEREST A payment made in return for the use of money

INVESTMENT TRUST Institution which invests in other firms' shares

ISSUE BY PROSPECTUS Method of selling shares in a company. The prospectus is distributed to potential investors, who are told the price at which shares will be sold

JOBBERS Under the old Stock Exchange system, those who bought and sold shares but could deal with outside investors only through the brokers

LEASING A kind of rental agreement whereby companies purchase land or equipment and pay for it by instalments

LETTER OF CREDIT A method of financing trade

LEVERAGE In speculative terms, the opportunity for a large profit at a small cost. Also a technical term for the ratio of a firm's debt to its equity

LIBID London Interbank Bid Rate – the rate at which a bank is prepared to borrow from another bank

LIBOR London Interbank Offered Rate – the rate at which a bank is prepared to lend to another bank

LIFE ASSURANCE A form of saving whereby individuals invest a small monthly premium in return for a much larger sum later on. If the saver dies during the scheme, his or her dependants receive a large sum. If the saver does not die, the sum will be paid out at the end of the policy

LIFE COMPANIES Institutions which market life assurance and insurance policies. As a group they are significant investors in British industry

LIFE INSURANCE A scheme whereby individuals pay a premium to a company which guarantees to pay their dependants a lump sum in the event of death. Differs from life assurance in that money is paid only on the death of the saver

LIFFE London International Financial Futures Exchange – exchange for trading futures and options. Now owned by the New York Stock Exchange

LIQUIDITY   The ease with which a financial asset can be exchanged for goods without the holder incurring financial loss. Thus cash is very liquid, whereas a life assurance policy is not

LIQUIDITY THEORY   The principle that investors will demand a greater reward for investing their money for a longer period

LLOYD'S OF LONDON   The insurance market

LOAN   An agreement whereby one party gives another use of money for a set period in return for the regular payment of interest. Unlike bonds, loans cannot be traded

MAKING A MARKET   Buying or selling a financial instrument, no matter what market conditions are like

MARKET SEGMENTATION THEORY   The belief that different parts of the debt market are separate and that therefore the yield curve will reflect the different levels of supply and demand for funds within each segment of the market

MATURITY   The length of time before a loan or bond will be repaid

MEMBERS' AGENTS   People who introduce names to Lloyd's

MERCHANT BANKS   Banks that specialize in putting together complicated financial deals. In origin they were closely connected with the financing of trade

MINIMUM LENDING RATE   Interest rate which the Bank of England will charge in its role as lender of last resort. Used by the Bank to influence the level of interest rates in the economy

MONEY-AT-CALL   Money lent overnight. It can be recalled each morning

MONEY MARKET   The market where short-term loans are made and short-term securities traded. 'Short-term' normally means under one year

MUTUAL FUND   Collective vehicle that gives small investors access to a diversified portfolio. See also unit trust

NAMES   Wealthy individuals who provide funds which back Lloyd's insurance policies. If they act as underwriters, they are known as 'working names'

NEW ISSUE   The placing of a company's shares on the Stock Exchange

OEIC (OPEN-ENDED INVESTMENT COMPANY)   New format for unit trusts. Investors buy and sell units at a single price and pay front-end charges separately

OFFER FOR SALE   Method of making a new issue. A bank offers shares in a company to investors at a set price

OPEC Organization of Petroleum Exporting Countries – which attempts to control the price and production of oil. Had most success in the 1970s

OPTIONS Instruments which give the buyer the right, but not the obligation, to buy or sell a commodity at a certain price. In return the buyer pays a premium. Under this heading are included traded options, currency options and interest-rate options

ORDINARY SHARE The most common and also the riskiest type of share. Holders have the right to receive a dividend if one is paid but do not know how much that dividend will be

OVER-THE-COUNTER MARKET Market where securities are traded outside a regular exchange

PENSION FUNDS The groups that administer pension schemes. They are significant investors in British industry

P/E RATIO Price/earnings ratio – the relationship between a company's share price and its after-tax profit divided by the number of shares

PREFERENCE SHARE Share which guarantees holders a prior claim on dividends. However, the dividend paid will normally be less than that paid to ordinary shareholders

PRINCIPAL The lump sum lent under a loan or bond

PRIVATE EQUITY Investment in unquoted companies by funds that use large amounts of borrowed money

PRIVATE PLACEMENT Method of selling securities by distributing them to a few key investors

PSBR Public-sector borrowing requirement – the gap between the government's revenue and expenditure

PURCHASING-POWER PARITY The belief that inflationary differentials between countries are the long-run determinants of currency movements

REAL INTEREST RATE The return on an investment once the effect of inflation is taken into account

REPAYMENT MORTGAGE Mortgage on which capital and interest are gradually repaid

REPURCHASE AGREEMENT A deal in which one financial institution sells another a security and agrees to buy it back at a future date

RETAINED EARNINGS Past profits which the company has not distributed to shareholders

RIGHTS ISSUE   Sale of additional shares by an existing company

SALE BY TENDER   Method of making a new issue in which the price is not set and investors bid for the shares

SAVINGS RATIO   The proportion of income which is saved

SCRIP ISSUE   The creation of more shares in a company, which are given free to existing shareholders. Also known as a bonus issue

SECURITIES   A generic form for tradable financial assets (bonds, bills, shares)

SECURITIZATION   The process whereby untradable assets become tradable

SHORTING   A bet that a share price will fall. The investor borrows shares, sells them and hopes to buy them back at a lower price

SINGLE-CAPACITY SYSTEM   The old way of dealing on the Stock Exchange. One group (jobbers) bought and sold shares; the other (brokers) linked jobbers with outside investors

SPOT RATE   Rate at which currencies or commodities are bought and sold today

SPREAD   The difference between the price at which a financial institution will buy a security and the price at which it will sell it

STAGS   Investors who seek to profit from new issues

STOCK EXCHANGE   A market where shares and government bonds are exchanged

SUBPRIME MORTGAGE   Loan made to borrower with low income or poor credit history

SWAP   An agreement whereby two borrowers agree to pay interest on each other's debt. Under a currency swap they may also repay the capital. (See also credit default swap)

SYNDICATED LOAN   A loan which several banks have clubbed together to make

TECHNICAL ANALYSTS   Those who believe that future price movements can be predicted by studying the pattern of past movements

UNDERWRITE   To agree, for a fee, to buy securities if they cannot be sold to other investors. In insurance, to agree to accept a risk in return for a premium

UNIT TRUST   Institution which invests in shares. Investors buy units whose price falls and rises with the value of the trust's investments

VENTURE CAPITAL   Investment in small start-up companies

WARRANTS   Instruments which give the buyer the right to purchase a bond or share at a given price. Similar, in principle, to options

WHOLESALE MARKET   Another name for the money markets, so called because of the large amounts which are lent and borrowed

YIELD   The return on a security expressed as a proportion of its price

YIELD CURVE   A diagram which shows the relationship of short-term rates to long-term ones. If long-term rates are above short-term, the curve is said to be positive or upward-sloping; if they are lower, the curve is said to be negative or inverted

ZERO-COUPON BOND   Bond which pays no interest but is issued at a discount to its face value

Bibliography

Margaret Allen, *A Guide to Insurance* (Pan, 1982)

Al Alletzhauser, *The House of Nomura* (Bloomsbury, 1990)

A. D. Bain, *The Control of the Money Supply*, 3rd edn (Penguin, 1980)

Lloyd Banksen and Michael Lee, *Euronotes* (Euromoney, 1985)

George G. Blakey, *The Post-War History of the London Stock Market* (Management Books 2000, 1993)

Rowan Bosworth-Davies, *Fraud in the City: Too Good to be True* (Penguin, 1988)

Bryan Burrough and John Helyar, *Barbarians at the Gate: The Fall of RJR Nabisco* (Jonathan Cape, 1990)

H. Carter and I. Partington, *Applied Economics in Banking and Finance*, 3rd edn (Oxford University Press, 1984)

William Clarke, *Inside the City*, rev. edn (Allen & Unwin, 1983)

C. J. J. Clay and B. S. Wheble, *Modern Merchant Banking*, 2nd edn, rev. by the Hon. L. H. L. Cohen (Woodhead-Faulkner, 1983)

Jerry Coakley and Laurence Harris, *The City of Capital* (Basil Blackwell, 1985)

Brinley Davies, *Business Finance and the City of London*, 2nd edn (Heinemann, 1979)

Peter Donaldson, *Guide to the British Economy*, 4th edn (Penguin, 1976)

——, *10 × Economics* (Penguin, 1982)

Paul Erdman, *Paul Erdman's Money Guide* (Sphere, 1985)

Paul Ferris, *Gentlemen of Fortune* (Weidenfeld & Nicolson, 1984)

Frederick G. Fisher III, *The Eurodollar Bond Market* (Euromoney, 1979)

——, *International Bonds* (Euromoney, 1981)

J. K. Galbraith, *Money: Whence it Came, Where it Went* (Penguin, 1976)

Bernard Gray, *Investors Chronicle Beginners Guide to Investment*, 2nd edn (Century, 1993)

Tim Handle, *The Pocket Banker* (Basil Blackwell/Economist, 1985)

Godfrey Hodgson, *Lloyd's of London: A Reputation at Risk* (Penguin, 1986)

R. B. Johnston, *The Economics of the Euromarket* (Macmillan, 1983)

William Keegan, *Mr Lawson's Gamble* (Hodder & Stoughton, 1989)

Charles P. Kindleberger, *Manias, Panics and Crashes: A History of Financial Crises*, 2nd edn (Macmillan, 1989)

Geoffrey Knott, *Understanding Financial Management* (Pan, 1985)

Anne O. Krueger, *Exchange-Rate Determination* (Cambridge University Press, 1983)

Paul Krugman, *Peddling Prosperity* (W. W. Norton, 1994)

Nigel Lawson, *The View from No. 11: Memoirs of a Tory Radical* (Corgi Books, 1993)

Harold Lever and Christopher Huhne, *Debt and Danger* (Penguin, 1985)

Peter Lynch (with John Rothschild), *Beating the Street* (Simon & Schuster, 1993)

Robert P. McDonald, *International Syndicated Loans* (Euromoney, 1982)

Charles Mackay, *Extraordinary Popular Delusions and the Madness of Crowds* (John Wiley, 1996)

Hamish McRae and Frances Cairncross, *Capital City* (Methuen, 1985)

J. Maratko and D. Stratford, *Key Developments in Personal Finance* (Basil Blackwell, 1985)

Martin Mayer, *Markets* (Simon & Schuster, 1989)

Alison Mitchell, *The New Penguin Guide to Personal Finance*, 1993/4 edn (Penguin, 1993)

Alex Murray, *101 Ways of Investing and Saving Money*, 3rd edn (Telegraph Publications, 1985)

R. H. Parker, *Understanding Company Financial Statements*, 2nd edn (Penguin, 1982)

K. V. Peasnall and C. W. R. Ward, *British Financial Markets and Institutions* (Prentice-Hall, 1985)

F. E. Perry, *The Elements of Banking*, 4th edn (Methuen, 1984)

John Plender and Paul Wallace, *The Square Mile* (Century, 1985)

Martin J. Pring, *Investment Psychology Explained* (John Wiley, 1995)

Anthony Sampson, *The Money Lenders* (Coronet, 1981)

Georges Ugeux, *Floating Rate Notes* (Euromoney, 1981)

Rudi Weisweiller, *Introduction to Foreign Exchange* (Woodhead-Faulkner, 1983)

Index